Library of
Davidson College

Memory and Fire

Twentieth Century American Jewish Writers

Daniel Walden
General Editor

Vol. 1

PETER LANG
New York • Bern • Frankfurt am Main • Paris

Gary Pacernick

MEMORY AND FIRE

TEN AMERICAN JEWISH POETS

PETER LANG
New York • Bern • Frankfurt am Main • Paris

Library of Congress Cataloging-in-Publication Data

Pacernick, Gary.
  Memory and fire : ten American Jewish poets / Gary Pacernick.
  p. cm. — (Twentieth Century American Jewish writers ; vol. 1)
  Bibliography: p.
  Includes index.
  1. American poetry—Jewish authors—History and criticism. 2. American poetry—20th century—History and criticism. 3. Jewish religious poetry, American—History and criticism. 4. Judaism in literature. 5. Jews in literature. 6. Jews—United States—Intellectual life.
I. Title. II. Series.
PS153.J4P34   1989   811'.5'098924—dc19   88-26658
ISBN 0-8204-0419-5   CIP
ISSN 0897-7844

CIP-Titelaufnahme der Deutschen Bibliothek

Pacernick, Gary:
Memory and fire : the American Jewish poets / Gary Pacernick. — New York ; Bern ; Frankfurt am Main ; Paris: Lang, 1989.
  (Twentieth Century American Jewish Writers; Vol. 1)
  ISBN 0-8204-0419-5

NE: GT

© Peter Lang Publishing, Inc., New York 1989

All rights reserved.
Reprint or reproduction, even partially, in all forms such as microfilm, xerography, microfiche, microcard, offset strictly prohibited.

Printed by Weihert-Druck GmbH, Darmstadt, West Germany

I am indebted to Wright State University, which granted me a timely sabbatical leave; to my colleagues at Wright State who read portions of the book and especially to David Garrison and Martin Maner; to Dan Walden, Stanley Chyet, Louise Kertesz, Guy Davenport, Marie Syrkin, Robert Alter, Jerome Rothenberg, Louis Simpson, David Ignatow, Philip Levine, and Howard Nemerov for their advice and encouragement; to Jill Donnina and Kim Willardson for their inspired typing; to my daughters Jennifer and Eden and especially my wife Dorothea for their love and understanding.

For Dotti, Jenny, and Eden

By the rivers of Babylon,
There we sat down, yea, we wept,
When we remembered Zion.
. . . .
How shall we sing the Lord's song
In a foreign land?
              Psalm 137

Jew by conviction or Jew in spite of himself, the Jewish writer *cannot be* anything else. What is most ironic is that even his rejection of his Jewishness identifies him.
            Elie Wiesel

And the imagination moves, the spirit opens, one knows again what it is to be Jewish; and what it will always be at its best in one's life and one's writing: memory and fire and poetry and the wandering spirit that never changes in its love of man.
            Muriel Rukeyser

Contents

	Acknowledgements	xi
1	Introduction	1
2	Charles Reznikoff: Personal and Documentary Memory	11
3	Jerome Rothenberg: Mythic Memory	31
4	Karl Shapiro: Memory Loss and Marginality	59
5	Louis Simpson: Narrative Memory	79
6	Louis Zukofsky: Patriarchal Memory	99
7	Allen Ginsberg: Prophet of Apocalypse	119
8	David Ignatow: Prophet of Darkness and Nothingness	143
9	Philip Levine: Prophet of Oneness	165
10	Howard Nemerov: Prophet of Divine Signatures	187
11	Muriel Rukeyser: Prophet of Social and Political Justice	209
12	Conclusion	225
	Biographies	231
	Notes	245
	Bibliography	253
	Index	261

Acknowledgements

Allen Ginsberg: "Howl," "Supermarket in California" copyright © 1955 by Allen Ginsberg; "America" copyright © 1956, 1959 by Allen Ginsberg; "To Aunt Rose," "Death to Van Gogh's Ear" copyright © 1958 by Allen Ginsberg; "Kaddish" copyright © 1959 by Allen Ginsberg; "Magic Psalm," "The Reply" copyright © 1960 by Allen Ginsberg; "Wichita Vortex Sutra," "A Vow" copyright © 1966 by Allen Ginsberg; "Ecologue," "Don't Grow Old" copyright © 1977 by Allen Ginsberg from *Collected Poems 1947–1980* by Allen Ginsberg. Reprinted by permission of Harper & Row, Publishers, Inc.

David Ignatow: From *Poems 1934–1969*, copyright © 1970 by David Ignatow; from *Facing the Tree: New Poems*, copyright © 1975 by David Ignatow; from *Tread the Dark*, copyright © 1978 by David Ignatow; from *Whisper to the Earth*, copyright © 1981 by David Ignatow. Reprinted by permission of Wesleyan University Press.

Philip Levine: From *Not This Pig*, copyright © 1968 by Philip Levine. Reprinted by permission of Wesleyan University Press. "Cry for Nothing," "Coming Home," "Detroit Grease Shop Poem," "The Angels of Detroit," "The Feed They Lion," "Angel Butcher," from *They Feed They Lion*, copyright © 1972 by Philip Levine; "Zaydee," "Goodbye," "Uncle," "1933," "Hold Me," from *1933*, copyright © 1974 by Philip Levine; "Ashes," "On a Drawing by Flavio," "The Red Shirt," from *Ashes*, copyright © 1979 by Philip Levine; "7 Years from Somewhere", from *7 Years from Somewhere*, copyright © 1979 by Philip Levine. Reprinted by permission of Atheneum Publishers.

Howard Nemerov: From *The Collected Poems of Howard Nemerov*, copyright © 1977 by Howard Nemerov and published by University of Chicago Press. Reprinted by permission of the author.

Charles Reznikoff: "Five Groups of Verse-14," "Uriel Accosta-28, 50," "Editing and Glosses-II," copyright © 1976 by Charles Reznikoff and published in *Poems 1918–1936*, published by Black Sparrow Press. "By the Well Living and Seeing-I," "Autobiography: New York-XII," Early History of a Writer-8, 10, 15," "Meditations on the Fall and Winter Holidays," "Kaddish," "In Memoriam: 1933," copyright © 1977 by Charles Reznikoff and published in *Poems 1937–1975*, published by Black Sparrow Press. "Gas Chambers and Gas Trucks," "Escapes," copyright © 1975 by Charles Reznikoff and published in *Holocaust*, published by Black Sparrow Press. Copyright © 1977 by Milton Hindus and published in *Charles Reznikoff: A Critical Essay*, published by Black Sparrow Press. Reprinted by permission of Black Sparrow Press.

Jerome Rothenberg: From *Poland/1931*, copyright © 1974 by Jerome Rothenberg; from *A Seneca Journal*, copyright © 1978 by Jerome Rothenberg; from *Vienna Blood*, copyright © 1980 by Jerome Rothenberg. Reprinted by permission of New Directions Publishing Corp.

Muriel Rukeyser: From *The Collected Poems*, copyright © 1979 by Muriel Rukeyser. Reprinted by permission of International Creative Management, Inc.

Karl Shapiro: "Poet," "My Grandmother," "Travelogue for Exiles," copyright © 1942 by Karl Shapiro; "Jew," "The Synagogue," copyright © 1944 by Karl Shapiro; "Recapitulations," "Israel," copyright © 1947 by Karl Shapiro; "Adam and Eve," copyright © 1953 by Karl Shapiro; "The First Time," "Messias," "The Alphabet," "The 151st Psalm," "The Murder of Moses," copyright © 1958 by Karl Shapiro; "I Am an Atheist Who Says His Prayers," "Privately Printed Poems," copyright © 1964 by Karl Shapiro; "Bath-Sheba," copyright © 1976 by Karl Shapiro; "My Father's Funeral," copyright © 1976 by Karl Shapiro. Reprinted from *Collected Poems 1940–1978* by permission of Random House, Inc. From *The Poetry Wreck*, copyright © 1975 by Karl Shapiro. Reprinted by permission of Random House, Inc.

Louis Simpson: From *A Dream of Governors*, copyright © 1959 by Louis Simpson; from *At the End of the Open Road*, copyright © 1963 by Louis Simpson. Reprinted by permission of Wesleyan University Press. From *Adventures of the Letter I*, copyright © 1972 by Louis Simpson. Reprinted by permission of the author. From "Baruch" in *Searching for the Ox* (1976) by Louis Simpson. Copyright © 1974 by Louis Simpson. By permission of William Morrow & Company. From *Caviare at the Funeral* by Louis Simpson. Copyright © 1980 by Louis Simpson. Used by permission of Franklin Watts, Inc.

Louis Zukofsky: From "A," copyright © 1978 by Louis Zukofsky. Reprinted by permission of University of California Press. From *All: The Collected Short Poems 1923–1964*, copyright © 1971 by Louis Zukofsky. Reprinted by permission of Norton & Co., Inc.

Chapter 1

Introduction

The phenomenon of a Jewish literature in America has elicited vigorous critical opinions. Such prominent critics as Harold Bloom and Robert Alter doubt there can be authentic American Jewish poets or writers, because they believe there is not an authentic Jewish culture in this country. Bloom goes so far as to expunge American Jewish poets from his version of the Western canon, because he thinks they lack a distinct tradition; however, he also dismisses them for failing to devote themselves to a great "Gentile precursor." One of his recent proclamations indicates that Jewish poets are all but doomed by an inextricably beleaguered and belated history.[1]

This catastrophic evaluation implies that Jewish poets should become fully assimilated Americans. For those few who wish to express their Jewishness, it might still be possible to live in Israel or, at the very least, to dedicate themselves to traditional law and lore. Such alternatives leave the American Jewish poets holding the horns of a dilemma. Other experts believe that, although Judaism and Jewish culture have evolved and changed, there are still writers who have created bona fide literary works about the Jewish experience in this country. But even these critics tend to overlook the poets and bask in the glory of the contemporary Jewish novelists, who have enjoyed considerable popular and literary success, culminating in Nobel Prizes for Saul Bellow and Isaac Bashevis Singer.

I believe there are significant American Jewish fiction writers and poets and that they complement each other. The poet's world is more solitary than that of most novelists, but it is often closer to those transforming moments when the poet confronts fundamental religious and universal questions. Who am I? What is my place in this world? Is there a God? What is the meaning of my being here?[2]

I do not want to suggest that the art of Jewish novelists and story writers lacks religious content. Many characters in stories and novels by Philip Roth, Bernard Malamud, Saul Bellow, I.B. Singer, and others undergo experiences involving religious concerns. I think of Roth's tormented lawyer Eli Peck, torn between loyalties to his comfortable suburban community and the Orthodox order of the Yeshivah and its unyielding master. Ozzie Freedman, another Roth creation, threatens to leap from the synagogue roof unless he can ask his overwhelming questions about God and Jesus so inimical to Rabbi Binder. I think of Malamud's brooding stories of Jewish life, such as "The Jew Bird" and "The Magic Barrel" and his portrayal of Jewish courage and suffering in *The Fixer*.

Although Saul Bellow's fiction is less ostensibly Jewish than that of his famous contemporaries, who can forget his story of the demise of Tommy Wilhelm, that schlimazel with the changed name, who experiences a moment of tragic suffering and grandeur as he wanders into the chapel at the conclusion of *Seize the Day*. Isaac Bashevis Singer's novel *The Slave* and the story "Gimpel the Fool," translated into English by Saul Bellow, have similar Jewish themes. In these Yiddish parables, Singer addresses the problems of good versus evil and the relationship between God and man from the latter's viewpoint. Although the list of American Jewish fiction with religio-universal subjects and themes could go on (for example, Chaim Potok and Cynthia Ozick), it has been my experience that while the fiction writers tend to dramatize conflicts between Jews and other people, including other Jews, that often center around sex, money, power, and other temporal concerns, the poets are free to use the music, imagery, figurative language, and other means of their art to explore the spiritual ramifications of one life, one self.

Most forms of secular Jewish letters have had a late arrival. Until the nineteenth century European Emancipation or Haskalah, during which many Jews began to question Halakic Judaism after centuries of acceptance, the literary concerns of the

Jewish people were limited mostly to the Hebrew Bible and some liturgical writing. Since the Emancipation, there has been a series of challenges to the Orthodox hegemony by Zionism, socialism, anarchism, and communism and by the Reform, Conservative, Reconstructionist, and secularist movements within Judaism.

Only after this questioning of the Orthodox tradition did secular Jewish writers begin to emerge and even in America they faced enormous challenges. It is true that American Jewish poetry had a conspicuous beginning when Emma Lazarus' sonnet "The New Colossus" was inscribed on the Statue of Liberty, proclaiming that majestic lady's magnanimity toward "huddled masses" of immigrants. A descendant of wealthy Sephardic Jews and a personal friend of Emerson, Lazarus wrote a number of poems with strong Jewish concerns that were collected in *Songs of a Semite*, published in 1882. Nevertheless, Emma Lazarus was the only Jewish poet to receive literary acclaim in nineteenth century America. Ada Isaacs Menken and others were barely noted.

A number of modern American Jewish poets and writers have attested to the bigotry that confronted them in their own country. Ludwig Lewisohn was told flat out early in the century that his "race" would preclude an appointment in an English department. Karl Shapiro recalls that when he was a young poet "it was impossible to get a poem published if you did not have an 'Anglo Saxon' name, but I decided to stick to my name; that decision made me 'Jewish.'" He decided to write about his Jewishness to discover why his name was such a "curse."[3] After winning a major poetry prize and graduating summa cum laude from Harvard, Stanley Kunitz was shocked and angered by his alma mater when he was "denied a post as teaching assistant on the ground that 'Anglo Saxons would resent being instructed in English by a Jew.'"[4] In Saul Bellow's *Humboldt's Gift*, the eccentric Jewish poet, modelled after Delmore Schwartz, does not fit in well at Princeton and is paranoid about his status as a Jew among the American Brahmins.

After World War II, more tolerance toward Jewish writers and poets became evident, and by 1960 a definite shift of perspective had occurred. This was intensified by a greater interest in Jewishness on the part of the writers caused at least in part by such social and political currents as the Holocaust, the civil-rights movement, 1960s radicalism in general, and the founding, struggles, and triumphs of the modern state of Israel. Perhaps because of the large Jewish audience for fiction, success for the popular novelists preceded recognition for the poets. In the more highbrow literary and academic realms of poetry, the authority of T. S. Eliot and such New Critics as John Crowe Ransom, Allen Tate, Robert Penn Warren, and Cleaneth Brooks was not easy to challenge, even though the emergence of a vigorous avant-garde with an open and experimental approach to poetry brought crucial changes with it.

Beginning in the 1950s and continuing into the sixties, William Carlos Williams, Charles Olson, Allen Ginsberg, and poets associated with such groups as the Beats, the Black Mountain poets, and the New York poets turned away from Eliot's tradition based on Dante, the French Symbolists, the Jacobean dramatists, and the Metaphysical poets toward the more radical Romantic influences of Blake, Shelley, and Whitman. Paradoxically, they looked to Eliot's old mentor, the openly anti-Semitic Ezra Pound, for bold advice about poetic craft and how to make poetry new.

When Ginsberg's *Howl*, was published in 1956, followed by *Kaddish* in 1961, a transformation began to take place in American poetry. No longer would it be possible to read a poem primarily as a genteel casebook of complex, erudite, and ironic uses of metaphor, symbol, and allusion, an artifact totally separate from the poet and based on the traditional English approach to poetic form, structure, and style. Under the guidance of Williams and Pound as well as Blake, Shelley, and Whitman, Ginsberg and other poets began to emphasize the image, consisting of concrete sensory details and the strange suggestions of dreams along with various approaches to the language and rhythms of speech. Poems were to embody personal visions, which would sanctify the poet's life and hopefully the reader's as well. Along with these Romantic tendencies, came more open and tolerant attitudes towards poets who had been struggling in near-oblivion under the old dispensation, including such notable Jewish poets as

Charles Reznikoff, Carl Rakosi, George Oppen, Louis Zukofsky, David Ignatow, and Muriel Rukeyser, among others. In 1958 Karl Shapiro published an entire volume of poems on the Jewish theme called *Poems of a Jew*, and in 1961, Allen Ginsberg's *Kaddish*, including the monumental title poem, was published by Lawrence Ferlinghetti's City Lights Books.

Since the 60s a number of Jewish poets have earned national recognition in American letters. I believe it is time to give them their due consideration, and I want to begin with several premises. American Jewish poets have made an important contribution to the literature of this country, and many of them have been inspired by the great tradition of prophets and psalmists they bear witness to as they grapple with the meaning of their lives in this country. Although most do not write from an Orthodox standpoint, they both maintain and challenge the tradition of their ancestors.

In order to develop and substantiate these premises, I have decided to study the works of ten poets. I have chosen these poets because I believe they are among the most outstanding twentieth century American poets, but also because they have written many poems of depth and power that reflect their bond of remembrance with the Jewish people and/or reaffirm the prophetic vision through an art of memory and fire.

The poets I will consider in this book are mainly descendents of the Eastern European immigration of 1881 to 1920, the third and largest Jewish exodus to this country after the Sephardic crossing (1654 to 1825) and the nineteenth century German immigration (1824 to 1894). Although they are not part of a self-conscious or programmatic school of Jewish poets, they express in their Jewish poems varying degrees of what I have chosen to call "memory" and "fire," suggested to me by Muriel Rukeyser's stirring words, which are noted in the title of this book. "Memory" refers to the imaginative remembrance (history) of a tradition beginning with the covenant between God and Israel and extending through the long Diaspora of the Jewish people to the present day. "Fire" suggests the prophetic viewpoint that concentrates on harsh criticism of existing social, political, economic, or religious conditions, strong advocacy of freedom and justice, and application to a secular context of the divine voice and will. While the poets of memory re-create the past to celebrate a meaningful cultural and religious heritage, which they often find lacking in their own time, the poets of fire attempt to transform the present by means of a messianic vision that is often sparked by Jewish memory.

In so far as American Jewish poets continue to experience the Diaspora, they identify with Jewish suffering, faith, and glory through generations of exile as a cultural, religious, and psychological heritage transmitted to them by their parents, grandparents, and other relatives, many of whom were victims of European atrocities. Although these poets do not often depict traditional Jewish rituals and practices, they do express in their poems a longing for what Will Herberg refers to as an "existential identification" with Israel's past, or what one could call a psychological Israel.[5] Five of the poets I discuss delineate the Jewish past through an art of imaginative memory. Using both his personal memory and a documentary memory based on the testimony of witnesses, Charles Reznikoff commemorates the miraculous saga of his people from antiquity to the present. In passages resembling rabbinic sayings, psalms, prophecies, and proverbs, Louis Zukofsky emulates the voices of the sages and the prophets. Calling upon the remarkable range and energy of his mythic memory, Jerome Rothenberg imagines a Poland of Jewish "mystics, thieves, and madmen" in *Poland/1931*. Louis Simpson preserves the memories of his mother and grandmother's Russia in moving and lyric story poems. Depicting the conflict and tension he feels toward generations of exile and suffering, Karl Shapiro dramatizes the marginality and alienation resulting from his loss of Jewish memory.

While the poets of memory identify with generations of wanderers who sustained Israel, Jewish memory is also essential to the prophetic poets, who often confront the world from a radical political standpoint and try to envision a righteous future that will sanctify both the living and the dead. For example, Allen Ginsberg's two rhapsodic poems "Howl" and "Kaddish" were both influenced by memory of his mother Naomi. To commemorate his mother, Ginsberg condemned materialistic, technological society and affirmed her mystical and mad vision in his apocalyptic poems. Memory of the prophetic tradition and especially the life of Akiba inspired Muriel Rukeyser to denounce injustice and oppression and to imagine a world of freedom, equality, and spiritual fulfillment.

Memory of his father, grandfather, and other family members is paramount to Philip Levine, who, along with his poems which express rage at injustice and tyranny, has invoked powerful visions of lamentation and praise. While he is best known for his images of city life, David Ignatow has long been engaged in a prophetic search for meaning in a world dominated by tragic suffering. Howard Nemerov is a most unusual prophet, yet I see in his biblical poems and in "Runes" and other poems a profound reading of God's influence in both nature and human society. All these poets of fire have depicted terrifying and ecstatic moments, as in Ginsberg's "Howl," "Kaddish," and "Wichita Vortex Sutra," Levine's "They Feed They Lion" and "1933," Rukeyser's "Akiba" and "The Book of the Dead," Ignatow's "I Felt," "God Said," and the three "Rituals," and Nemerov's "Runes" and his poetic plays *Endor* and *Cain*.

Much of the religious dynamism and energy of contemporary Judaism is maintained by poets who act as voices and exemplars of Jewish moral and spiritual rectitude and justice. While some impetus for this advocacy may come from such secular movements as socialism, communism, and anarchism, the essential poetic source is the strong ethical and moral cry of the Hebrew prophets for a people in the image of God, committed as Mordecai Kaplan says, to "the intellectual, moral, and spiritual progress of mankind."[6] No less a theologian than Abraham Joshua Heschel sees prophecy as poetry:

> What the poets know as poetic inspiration, the prophets call divine revelation.... What makes the difference between the prophet and the ordinary person is the possession of a heightened and unified awareness of certain aspects of life. Like a poet, he is endowed with sensibility, enthusiasm, and tenderness, and, above all, with a way of thinking imaginatively. Prophecy is the product of poetic imagination. *Prophecy is poetry*, and in poetry everything is possible, e.g., for the trees to celebrate a birthday, and for God to speak to man.[7]

Heschel also makes the profound point that the prophets wrote of "single moments in their lives beyond which lay the encounter with good and evil, light and darkness, life and death, love and hatred—issues which are as real today as they were three thousand years ago."[8]

A number of leading Jewish thinkers have stressed the closeness of man and God and the shift toward an ideal conception of man as "divinely human" along with the ideal creation of "a social order based on freedom, justice, peace and love."[9] According to Mordecai Kaplan, the new definition of God "will have to mean to the modern intellectual Jew that aspect of nature as a whole which makes for the maximum fulfillment of man's highest ethical and creative potentialities."[10] Inspired by Hasidic writings and practices, Martin Buber, who posits an I-Thou relationship between man and God, believes man can best approach God by "becoming human."[11]

Underlying the spiritual and imaginative dimension of memory and fire in the art of these poets is the historical and psychological experience of Jewish exile and the poets' dissociation from institutional Judaism and from much of mainstream American culture. Like Jewish novelists, Jewish poets portray the conflict and paradox of the American Jewish life of marginality and exile. Jewish poets also identify with past and present suffering, manifested most horrifyingly in the Holocaust, but everywhere in evidence. These ten American Jewish poets I have selected share in the complex interrelationship of memory and fire, exile and suffering.

Although sharing various Jewish tendencies, each of these poets is unique and I want to study each of them in a close and individual way to discover not only what he or she shares with other Jewish poets but what is the poet's own vision of his or her Jewishness. These are stiff-necked, stubbornly independent Jewish poets devoted to their imaginative perceptions of the world, but much of the Jewish past and present remains meaningful and inspiring to them. By identifying with their heritage, the poets extend the range of their experience beyond the personal to a bond with a great people and its tradition. For too long there has been an assumption by too many readers that twentieth century poetry can be neither enjoyable nor significant. Yet these poets write with passionate insight about the most basic human questions and concerns. It is with the hope that more readers will find these poets and their contemporaries an indispensable part of their reading lives that I undertake this study.

Chapter 2

Charles Reznikoff

Personal and Documentary Memory

When Charles Reznikoff was a boy his mother told him an unforgettable story. It was about her father, a salesman who wrote poems in Hebrew when he travelled alone in the Russian countryside. One day while he was a long way from home he died of influenza and among his belongings was a collection of verse written over thirty years time. Because she was afraid this writing might be construed as treasonous by the czar's government and, therefore, dangerous to her children, his wife burned all the poems.

Charles Reznikoff remembered his grandfather's unfortunate fate:

> My grandfather, dead long before I was born,
> died among strangers; and all the verse he wrote
> was lost—
> except for what
> still speaks through me
> as mine.[1]

As a poet, Charles Reznikoff honored and preserved his grandfather's heritage through the power of imaginative memory.

Reznikoff is often identified with the other Objectivist poets: Louis Zukofsky, George Oppen, and Carl Rakosi. These poets adopted Ezra Pound's Imagist pronouncements of 1913 and 1918 as the basis for a new poetics. Pound cautioned against unnecessary adjectives, abstractions, symbols, and description, especially of the flowery Romantic and Victorian variety, and extolled the lucidity of the image, the language of speech, and organic rhythms.

The Objectivists also admired the poetry of William Carlos Williams, and they organized To Publishers and later the Objectivist Press to print books by Pound, Williams, and others. In the now famous February 1931 issue of *Poetry*, Louis Zukofsky, acting as guest editor, selected poems that met his Objectivist standards. In his editorial essay, Zukofsky praised what he called Reznikoff's "sincerity," for presenting in his poems the correct details along with the proper rhythm and tone.

That Reznikoff, Oppen, Rakosi, and Zukofsky were Jews sometimes seems a silent undercurrent, an unacknowledged fact. Even in a 1975 interview with Martin Rosenblum, Rakosi understates the Jewishness that the poets shared: "Well, I was trying to discover why Reznikoff and I had some things in common and I thought maybe it's because both of us have strong Jewish identifications . . . . I haven't written many poems that have Jewish subject matter, so I don't know."[2] Oppen and Rakosi rarely wrote about Jewish subjects and most of Zukofsky's Jewish poetry is found not in his short poems but in his personal epic "A," which was published in installments beginning in 1959 and not in its entirety until 1978, the year of the poet's death. Among the Jewish Objectivist poets and, indeed, the other Jewish poets of his generation, such as Stanley Kunitz and Kenneth Fearing, only Reznikoff wrote continuously and openly about his heritage.

The key to Reznikoff's art is memory: personal memory of his family's immigrant experience and documentary memory of the Jewish people's suffering, exile, survival, and faith through the ages. Reznikoff always remembered that his roots were not only American but also Russian and Jewish and reached toward Israel. Even in his brief imagist poems, remembrance of the Jewish tradition serves as a counterpoint to perceptions of the immediate moment.

By comparing and contrasting the sacred past and the secular present, Reznikoff can impart a fine sense of historical nuance and irony to his urban images. The ancient tradition can make the present seem shallow by comparison:

> There is nobody in the street
> of those who crowded about David
> to watch me
> as I dance before the Lord:
> alone in my unimportance
> to do as I like.
>   (CP II, pp. 29–30)

Past generations worshipped together but this Jewish poet of twentieth century America is alone. Sometimes the Reznikoff protagonist, walker of the New York streets, seems devoid of religious faith, an updated version of Kafka's K. or Doestoevsky's Underground Man, conscious of his estrangement from the generations of those who lived such religious lives that God knew their very words and deeds.

Determined not to be "private as an animal," the poet identifies with traditional rituals, but the way is hard. Language, too, separates the poet from his heritage:

> How difficult for me is Hebrew:
> even the Hebrew for *mother*, for *bread*, for *sun*
> is foreign. How far have I been exiled, Zion.
>   (CP I, p. 72)

Certainly there are grounds for Robert Alter's assessment that Reznikoff "is supremely a poet of exile because he frequently senses in his own loving attachment to his chosen medium, the American language, an irreversible abandonment of his Hebrew forebears."[3]

Alter believes that Reznikoff's personal voice is more convincing than his public or historical voice: "The need to break out of that privacy into a large historical realm of collective experience moved him to anomalous poetic strategies, at times seemed to encourage the expression of a second self cruder in sensibility, less resistant to the temptations of the obvious gesture."[4] Alter does not see Reznikoff as an isolated case but rather as part of an international trend, even in Hebrew poetry, "toward the cultivation of a nuanced personal voice" and "the affirmation of selfhood, not peoplehood, as the proper sphere of literary expression."[5] Since

Alter criticizes modern Jewish writers for their lack of historical consciousness, it is surprising that he does not recognize at least some of Reznikoff's poems, such as "In Memoriam: 1933," "Inscriptions I," and "Meditations on the Fall and Winter Holidays," as valid expressions of the poet's identification with the roots of Jewish experience, a fervent imaginative remembrance of the tradition.

In his poems of personal memory, Reznikoff looks back at his own experiences and those of his family, friends, and acquaintances to create an account of Jewish immigrant life in the United States. In *Five Groups of Verse* (1927), which is filled with brief vignettes and stories, the poet writes at the border between poetry and fiction, combining the clear language and vivid details of his imagistic poems with an emphasis on action, conflict and characterization that most modern poets have relinquished to fiction writers.

While Pound's pronouncements that poetry should embrace the best of prose and that the language of poetry should approximate speech may have been important, it is doubtful that Pound's poetry would have served as a model for Reznikoff's narrative and dramatic poems, because, contrary to his own principles, Pound's language was often highly literary and idiosyncratic, and he relied more on discontinuous and fragmentary images, allusions, and associational devices than on action, dialogue, and other narrative techniques. If Reznikoff was influenced, his models might well have been, besides the short fiction of Babel, Chekhov, and Joyce, the stories in the Hebrew Bible and the Yiddish tales he might have heard when he was growing up, or that he could have read by such famous Yiddish writers as Sholom Aleichem, Isaac Peretz, and Mendele Mokher Sforim, the kind of stories that are still being written by Isaac Bashevis Singer, among others.

Many of Reznikoff's narrative and dramatic poems of personal memory in *Five Groups of Verse* describe events in a young Jewish boy's life. Reznikoff can convey a great deal about a character in a few words. For example, he describes how the sensitive young narrator is threatened by his fellow students and by strangers because he is a Jew:

> "Are you a Jew? I knock the block off every Jew I meet."
> "No," he answered.
> "I think you're a Jew. What's your name?" He told him,
> glad that his name was not markedly Jewish and yet foreign
> enough to answer for his looks.
> (CP I, p. 50)

Anyone who reads this, but especially any Jew who has been subjected to anti-Semitic assaults can feel the third person narrator's cold sweat and rapidly beating heart, his conflicting emotions of fear, shame, guilt, and relief.

Using his ability to narrate through realistic details and dialogue, Reznikoff can reveal the essence of an experience in a concentrated scene. For example, the narrator makes friends with a young man named Kore, who seems better equipped than him, at least physically, to endure the dangers of the streets and who instills confidence in the narrator, so that he is not afraid to walk about despite past troubles. The poet describes how the boys go to Coney Island, and late at night Kore decides to swim near the iron pier where steamboats dock:

> Kore boasted that he would swim around the pier and slid
> away into the black water.
> At last the people were gone. The booths were darkened.
> He waited for Kore at the other side of the pier, watching the
> empty waves come in.
> (CP I, p.51)

Reznikoff tells this story succinctly and honestly, with no attempt to make it poetic, and yet he evokes poignance and depth because he has wasted no words and subtly presented the relationship of the two boys from the third person narrator's point of view, so that at the poem's conclusion the reader feels the young Jewish boy's sense of desolation and wonder as the waves continue to pound in the dark.

The poems in *Early History of a Writer* are based on the poet's personal memories of three generations of his Russian Jewish immigrant family. While this series of poems has a slow, unmannered pace, it is highly immediate and dramatic. The first person narrator, who represents the poet as a youth, is particularly drawn to his paternal grandparents. He describes his grandmother as extremely tall and his grandfather as so diminutive that his fellow Jews called him "Simon the Flea." As the story unfolds, the reader discovers that despite their physical differences the poet's grandparents were married because the grandmother's father decided that the short, timid, scholarly Simon would make a respectable husband for his daughter. Sure enough, Simon became rich and successful and his wife became infamous for her bad temper. Years later, Simon became ill, and he and his wife travelled to America to be with their children.

The rest of this family history is told in a series of scenes, such as the arrival of the grandparents in America. As his father brings his grandparents home from the pier, the young boy looks down from his window, and then he and his brother run downstairs to meet them:

> My grandfather looked at us with his bleary eyes,
> whose rims were red,
> and turning to my father murmured in Hebrew
> what the patriarch Jacob had said to his son Joseph:
> "I did not think to see your face
> And God has shown me your sons also,"
> and, putting his swollen hands slowly on my head,
> began to bless me.
>
> (CP II, p. 146)

Through such details as the grandfather's "bleary eyes" and "swollen hands" and his repetition of ancient words and gestures, the poet has captured a highly dramatic meeting of the generations.

After the petulant grandmother admonishes her husband to hasten his blessing, the latter brings out a gold coin and puts it in the youthful narrator's hand, but the boy refuses to take it. Tradition forbids children to accept money from their elders. Because of this special occasion, his father relents and allows the boy to keep the coin. When he looks at the coin, the boy sees a "monstrous eagle . . . with two open beaks," symbolizing the czarist Russia his family has escaped. In this encounter of three generations of Jews, the poet shows how these people are involved in a shared way of life, expressed in simple words and gestures, as well as the almost frightening coin, which symbolizes the fear and oppression Jews have endured for so long.

The poet also demonstrates that the suffering and exile of the European Diaspora continue in twentieth century America. In one passage the boy describes how as he walks his grandfather home through a park, two young men who are flirting with a girl suddenly turn on the old man:

> They saw my grandfather—
> a little sick Jew with a short greyish brown beard
> ruffled by the cold wind.
> He knew that their merry glances
> boded him no good, and hurried ahead of me
> to get past them. Hands deep in his coat pockets,
> head drawn into his coat, the narrow shoulders hunched,
> he seemed to be even smaller than he was.
> (CP II, p. 150)

Although this verse might appear simple and straightforward on the surface, only the poet's skillful use of descriptive words, subtle inflections of pitch and tone, the parallel syntax of the subordinate clauses in the sixth and seventh lines, and the effective use of pauses and line endings to facilitate the rhythmic flow of the language can begin to account for the depth of this presentation.

After the young men knock him down, the grandfather rolls on the ground until an iron railing stops him. Helping his grandfather to get up and then running to get his hat, the boy comes back to see the old man supported by the railing, "holding the icy iron bar in his bare hands" (CP II, p. 151) only to be greeted by his grandfather's silence. Reznikoff often uses highly expressive details, gestures, or speech to create this kind of scenic revelation of a moment in time, which resembles the epiphanies in stories by

Joyce, Chekhov, and Babel.

One of the most moving passages in this sequence occurs when the boy, who is about to leave home to attend school in the West, comes to say goodbye to his grandfather. Rising with difficulty, the grandfather loudly blesses his grandson in Hebrew and then begins to weep. The boy promises to return in June; however, by June the grandfather has passed away. Although his grandfather cannot address him again, the boy thinks about the loss of the tradition his grandfather had lived and loved:

> Perhaps my grandfather was in tears for other reasons:
> Perhaps, because, in spite of all the learning I had acquired in high school,
> I knew not a word of the sacred text of the Torah
> and was going out into the world
> with none of the accumulated wisdom of my people to guide me,
> with no prayers with which to talk to the God of my people,
> a soul—
> for it is not easy to be a Jew or, perhaps, a man—
> doomed by his ignorance to stumble and blunder.
> (CP II, p. 167)

Remembering his grandfather, the boy shows a high regard for the very heritage he has almost forgotten. As in many passages in *Early History*, the poet presents the interaction of the generations in a manner that is universally human but also Jewish, not only in its religious and cultural references but also in mood and tone. The family portraits show how Reznikoff can combine the techniques of fiction and poetry to create an unassuming but effective art of personal Jewish memory with purity of language and vision.

In this same series of poems, Reznikoff describes his legal education and his first years as a poet. He tells how he was satisfied with neither traditional metrics nor straight prose. Above all, he wants to create "a Doric music." After considering various definitions of "Doric," Milton Hindus emphasizes "an austere beauty" in Reznikoff's verse.[6] Hindus also quotes Reznikoff on his own art: "I have read somewhere that among the ancient Greeks there was an intermediary between song and straight prose—I suppose that is chanted. A good deal of the Bible is read like that in the Orthodox service in Synagogue."[7]

Just as his father had his Ukranian village and his grandfather his city and synagogue, Reznikoff's home was New York City, and over the years he created a portrait gallery of New Yorkers, such as the Chinese girl in a railway station whose words in a pad resemble tiny flowers. In this instance, the poet was struck by the grace and loveliness of his oriental subject, but more often he wrote about seamier subjects: the disturbed Negro in the dark subway station who curses his mother for bringing him into the world and who wonders how whites must feel; a young man preaching Father Coughlin's pro-fascist propaganda on another subway involved in angry exchanges with passengers; the young Jewish boy who walks dangerously alone at night holding a tray of candy and gum. There is also the pathos of the Puerto Rican janitor who is struck by a Winslow Homer print of a palm tree in the Bahamas because it reminds him of home, and the humor of the Jewish laundryman, who, when the poet asks about a missing shirt, says that there are four ways to lose a shirt and to return later to see what happened. Reznikoff often wrote of minority and ethnic Americans, who, despite being poor and estranged from their primary cultures and homelands, struggled to survive in the giant city.

Besides personal memory, Reznikoff utilized documentary evidence and the testimony of witnesses or what I shall call documentary memory to preserve the past. Because his moral vision, his dedication to justice, extended to Americans of all descriptions touched by rootlessness, suffering, and injustice, Reznikoff spent many years compiling *Testimony*, a multi-volume work based on U.S. court records covering the years from 1885 to 1915:

> A few years ago, I was working for a publisher of law books, reading cases from every state and every year (since the country had become a nation). Once in a while I could see in the facts of a case details of the time and place, and it seemed to me that out of such material the century and a half during which the United States has been a nation could be written up, not from the standpoint of an individual, as in diaries, nor merely from the angle of the unusual, as in newspapers, but from every standpoint—as many standpoints as were provided by the witnesses themselves.[8]

He divided the material he had culled from the cases into geographical sections—"The South," "The North," "The West"—and subdivided those sections into topical headings: "Social Life," "Domestic Scenes," "Negroes," "Property," etc.

In *Testimony*, Reznikoff probed the relationship between poetry and law, art and documentation. Although he never became a practicing attorney, he was fascinated with legal documents. Study of the law taught the poet to look through words for "the hard essentials," the facts of the case, and the judge's reasoning. According to Milton Hindus, the poet contemplated the connection between history and law, which he called *Testimony*, and he created a verse form for this, which he called "recitative."[9]

Even when he described his approach to writing, Reznikoff the poet used legal terms:

> By the term *objectivist* I suppose a writer may be meant who does not write directly about his feelings but about what he sees and hears; who is restricted almost to the testimony of a witness in a court of law; and who expresses his feelings indirectly by the selection of subject matter and, if he writes in verse, by its music.[10]

Although this Objectivist aesthetic is germane to almost all of his work, it was in his creation of *Testimony* and *Holocaust* that Reznikoff applied his poetics most directly by editing and transcribing the recorded testimony of actual witnesses.

While the witnesses' voices in *Testimony* may lack the lyric, visual, and tonal richness and acuteness of Reznikoff's poems in his own voice, the sheer weight of evidence results in a memorable record of an arbitrary, merciless, and violent society. Along with fragmented and foreshortened incidents, some of the longer episodes have a raw power and reveal through dramatic conflict and lifelike details of setting and plot the horrible injustice and desperation that many unfortunate Americans experienced. The poet must be praised for preserving the stories of these lives. Behind this important social and poetic document, there is a moral commitment to law and justice which Reznikoff shares with the prophets and poets of fire.

Testimony and *Holocaust* are Reznikoff's most ambitious documentary works and have elicited praise from Shirley Kaufman, one of his most positive and enthusiastic critics: "In both these works a transformation has occurred. The Word, as presented in legal testimony, has taken the place of the Object. The word becomes, finally, the Thing." She believes that the *Testimony* poems are the culmination of the poet's career, because he "was arriving at a newly energized relationship of the Word as testimony (out of his legal and prophetic background) and the Object as visual image (out of his Imagist beginnings in poetry)."[11]

In *Holocaust*, the second of his crucial works of documentary memory, the poet employed virtually the same method as in *Testimony*. The poems are based on court records from the Nuremberg military tribunal and the Eichmann trial in Jerusalem. The categories which the poet used to classify the testimony tell their own frightening story: Deportation; Invasion; Research; Ghettos; Massacres; Gas Chambers and Gas Trucks; Work Camps; Children; Entertainment; Mass Graves; Marches; and Escapes.

Reznikoff's witnesses document the experience of twentieth century inferno:

> In the gas chambers
> the police wedged the people closely together
> until men and women were standing on the feet of each other—
> and the doors were closed.
> But the engine to furnish the gas.
> could not start.
> An hour and two and almost three went by,
> and in the gas chambers cries were heard
> and many were praying.
> The Professor who had been holding his ear against one of the wooden doors
> turned away, smiled and said, "Just like a synagogue."
> And then the engine started working:
> in about half an hour
> all inside the gas chamber were dead.
>
> (H, p. 46)

This kind of horrifying factual surface is more that an undeniable testament, because there is also a drama of gestures, details, words, and silences crying out with tragic force the unbearable suffering of people in the midst of genocide.

Driven by moral outrage, Reznikoff has the unidentified witnesses speak of the unnamed victims and their murderers and brings the reader as close to hell as art (or the reader) can bear. Although the reader may feel terror, rage, and revulsion, *Holocaust* is neither absurd nor nihilistic. David Lehman believes that Reznikoff's method of presentation "is arguably the only literary strategy that can avoid being overwhelmed by this knowledge" and that "the absence of editorial comment, the utter bareness of expression, ensures that these blows will not easily be cushioned."[12]

As the Jews defended their lives and their honor in the Warsaw ghetto, there was heroism at the end:

> But this handful who were to fight the thousands of Germans
> were elated—
> smiled at each other, even joked and shook hands
> Because they knew the Germans would pay a price for their lives.
>
> (H, p. 109)

Even after the Nazis brought in planes to bomb the ghetto and then resorted to systematically killing those Jews who hid in sewers, they could not complete their slaughter. Some Jews survived in the Warsaw ghetto to fight the Nazis:

> But a few Jews went into the sewers
> to make their way out of the ghetto,
> stooping in the narrow sewers
> with the cold dirty water reaching their knees
> and even to their lips,
> and, if they could get through the Aryan part of the city,
> reach the forest
> where Jewish guerrillas were still fighting the Germans.
>
> (H, p. 111)

Holocaust documents genocide, but it also shows that some Jews escaped and, however diminished, the tradition that began with the covenant between God and Abraham endured. Darkness and the devil did not completely win. *Holocaust* is Reznikoff's ultimate record of the unyielding Jewish affirmation of life, his documentary remembrance of unbearable suffering and miraculous survival.

Although *Holocaust* is haunting, even such a sympathetic critic of Reznikoff's work as Milton Hindus knows that its method raises serious questions. Should *Holocaust* even be considered a work of art? How does the poet's account differ from the material it is based upon? To these and other questions Hindus responds that only through "*selection, style,* and *understatement*" could *Holocaust* be created.[13] He then shows through careful study of the poet's manuscript pages his "tireless struggle to simplify, to clarify, and to objectify":

> The first person singular is consistently replaced by the third person (singular or plural) or by proper nouns. Lines are rearranged or broken up into different lengths in search of sound more appropriate to the sense. Words not absolutely necessary are eliminated, occasionally at some risk of obscuring the meaning . . . . "Strong" expressions are shaded toward understatement . . . . What seems like emphatic editorial comment—however legitimate—is toned down or dropped from the final version.[14]

This expert testimony helps to substantiate the premise that *Holocaust* is an authentic work of art by a poet with a relentless moral vision.

Early History of a Writer and *Holocaust* are examples of Reznikoff's two uses of memory in poetry: the art of personal memory in the former and the art of impersonal or documentary memory in the latter. As an extension of his use of documentary memory, he edited and adapted biblical texts with mixed results. "Editing and Glosses" from *By the Waters of Manhattan: An Annual* (1929) consists of incidents from Genesis, I Samuel, and so on in essentially the same language as the English translation of the original text. For example, in Genesis 45, Joseph asks Benjamin to bring Israel to Egypt:

> And ye shall tell my father of all my glory in Egypt, and of all that ye
> have seen; and ye shall hasten and bring down my father hither.

In his version, Reznikoff repeats almost the same language:

> You shall tell my father of all my glory in Egypt;
> You shall take wagons out of Egypt for your little ones and
> your wives, and bring our father and come . . .
> (CP I, p. 81)

The same is true for Reznikoff's description of Goliath and the battle between David and Goliath. The problem is that the biblical texts do not lend themselves to the poet's documentary method. As Howard Nemerov, Karl Shapiro, and others have shown, Hebrew Scripture can serve as the basis for successful twentieth century poetry, but there has to be more significant imaginative transformation of the original than is evident in "Editing and Glosses."

In the first of "Inscriptions: 1944–1956," the poet selectively and subtly narrates key elements in the Jewish history of suffering, faith, and survival. Each of the poem's seven stanzas is a catalogue of detailed references to Jewish history unified by the poet's theme of Israel's survival and God's compassion, concluding with a refrain blessing God for sustaining Israel. The poem ends with a tribute to the spirit of a great people: "and out of those who met only with hate,/a people of love, a compassionate people" (CP II, p. 61).

Reznikoff also wrote a series of religious poems, "Meditations on the Fall and Winter Holidays." These poems are notable because in a cautious voice blending awe and veneration with conflict and doubt the poet speaks of the God of his ancestors:

> The work of our hearts is dust
> to be blown about in the winds
> by the God of our dead in the dust
> but our Lord delighting in life
> (let the wild goat's horn
> and the silver trumpet sound!)—
> our God who imprisons in coffin and grave
> and unbinds the bound.
>
> (CP II, p. 65)

While describing the sacred celebrations of Jewish life, the poet acts as a witness to religious faith:

> Out of nothing I became a being,
> and from a being I shall be
> nothing—but until then
> I rejoice, a mote in Your world,
> a spark in Your seeing.
>
> (CP II, p. 67)

Reznikoff may be a poet of exile and suffering, but he is able to sing of Israel and God in a lucid, psalm-like voice, which echoes the sacred words and images of the past in "a new song."

The poet also adapted and edited translations of liturgical texts, such as R. Travers Herford's translation of "Kaddish de Rabbanan." In his version of "Kaddish," Reznikoff extended and developed the meaning of the original by adding images dramatizing the worldly violence Israel must endure ("whom the hundred hands of a mob strike") and similes showing Israel's vulnerability among strangers:

> upon Israel and upon all who live
> as the sparrows of the streets
> under the cornices of the houses of others,
> and as rabbits
> in the fields of strangers
> on the grace of the seasons
> and what the gleaners leave in the corners ...
>
> (CP I, p. 186)

Besides organizing the prose translation into poetic lines and stanzas, the poet has added an ironic and tragic dimension to the Herford translation.

I want to conclude my discussion of Reznikoff's poetry with "In Memoriam: 1933." In this significant work of imaginative memory, the poet composed seven scenes of Jewish suffering, exile, faith, and survival, beginning with the fall of Samaria in 722 B.C.E. and continuing through the Babylonian and Roman conquests to Jewish life in Russia around 1905. Each of these scenes is dramatized by voices speaking some of Reznikoff's finest poetry, combining his "Doric music," his gift for convincing details, his knowledge of Jewish history, his skill at scenic structure, and his religious vision.

In "The Academy at Jamnia: Anno 70," a rabbi speaks of his harrowing experience as a captive aboard a Roman vessel:

> When I was a boy, sent a captive to Rome,
> the ship was dashed, stern foremost, upon a rock,
> and other rocks, smooth with weeds, across which the waves
>   were sliding,
> stretched beyond, as far as we could see;
> when I heard the crash
> and saw the steep deck sloping
> to the dark water, into which Romans and slaves were spilled,
> their hands and feet
> finding no hold or step,
> and no cry from all those mouths
> sound
> in the howling wind,
> Yet there was no such terror in my heart
> as now.
>   (CP I, p. 142)

These lines are controlled by subtle modulation of stressed and unstressed syllables, pauses within the lines, the sustained movement of the rhythm, and the parallel structure of phrases and clauses right through to the end of the rabbi's speech. While the first line is anapestic, the second line begins with two iambs and then the stress of the second iamb on "dashed" is continued right through to "stern foremost" to accentuate the harsh effect of the crash. Three pauses add to the tension and force of the line. The alliteration of s, r, and w in line three produces sounds similar to the sense of the action. The trochees in line four and the feminine ending of line six are other instances of onomatopoeia. In addition to these and other fine touches, the flow of imagery is harnessed to the passionate speech rhythms of the speaker, resulting in descriptive verse of the highest order.

In the fifth section, "Spain: Anno 1492," Abrabanel, a dignified Jewish philosopher, debates the hostile voices of the Spanish Inquisition and defends the right and necessity of his people to retain their ancient faith:

> Would you have our religion
> like our clothes—for comfort and the eyes of men,
> put off at night,
> and we left lying naked in the darkness?
> The body is like roots stretching down into the earth—
> . . . .
> but the spirit—
> twigs and leaves
> spreading
> through sunshine
> or the luminous darkness
> of twilight, evening, night, and dawn,
> moving
> in every wind of heaven
> and turning
> to whatever corner of the sky is brightest,
> compelled by nothing stronger than the light . . .
> (CP I, pp. 154–55)

The same poet who renders images of sensory experience and the testimony of witnesses here distinguishes brilliantly between body and soul and creates metaphors of inner, spiritual experience in a lyric succession of short lines. Through the dramatic voice of the venerable Abrabanel, Reznikoff pictures "the spirit," growing like a tree in darkness and light, which has sustained his people through the ages.

Another intensely religious passage occurs in the long monologue of a young Jew, which comprises all of the seventh and final section: "Russia: Anno 1905." After describing life in the United States as one alternative to the harsh existence of the Russian Jew, the young man dreams of a return to the Promised Land. One can overhear in this voice the poet's deepest expression of exile and suffering blended with his affirmation of faith:

> how much better to live in the tip of the flame,
> the blue blaze of sunshine
> than creep about in corners,
> safe in cracks—
> dribble away your days in pennies.
> In that air
> salty with the deeds of heroes and the speech of prophets,
> as when one has left the streets and come to the
> plunging and orderly sea, the green water
> tumbling into yellow sand and rushing foam,
> and rising in incessant waves—
> upon your hills, Judah,
> in your streets and narrow places
> upon your cobblestones, Jerusalem!
> (CP I, p. 162)

The lines of the second half of this passage build through strong participles to a crescendo, concluding with the exclamation extolling Judah, the ancient kingdom, and Jerusalem, the capital of ancient and modern Israel, the holy land and the holy city. The poet's rhythmic and colorful description of the sea is particularly memorable.

In the sixth section, "Poland: Anno 1700," a young Jew, tired of stories about Jewish suffering, offers his own testimony as a witness to God:

> I see God only and my spirit brightens
> like a mirror;
> I touch Him touching all I touch;
> on earth I am as close to Him as those in Heaven.
> Could I teach myself to want nothing,
> nothing could be taken from me;
> I should be unafraid of today or tomorrow,
> and live in eternity like God.
> (CP I, p. 159)

Never has Reznikoff been so far from objective evidence and so close to divine vision. The youth's faith in God transforms his perception of the world around him until

> tasting God in the salt water
> and the sweet rain,
> I sink and my feet have nothing to rest on,
> I rise and my hands find nothing to hold,
> and am carried slowly,
> now swiftly,
> towards night and towards noon.
> (CP I, p. 160)

In this lyric verse with parallel structure of phrases and clauses and chanting rhythms, Reznikoff's dramatic voice sings a psalm to God, as he is "carried" by divine force. The Word and the image have become one.

There is something inspiring about this humble poet who said he had no triumphs and sat "at the common table." The voice of the grandfather whose verse was lost speaks through Reznikoff's voice. Determined never to forget Jewish exile, suffering, or glory, the poet called upon his personal memory of the past and the documentary memory of witnesses' testimony to preserve the tradition of his people, and he sang praises to God and Israel in poetry of tender beauty and loving sanctity.

# Chapter 3

Jerome Rothenberg

Mythic Memory

Jerome Rothenberg combines memory and fire in his dynamic art. Instead of preserving the normative tradition of Judaism, he explores his ancestral past and discovers a primal community of "mystics, thieves, and madmen," along with "a poetics of liberation & anger."[1] Inspired by the often overlooked sources of Jewish mysticism and the occult, Rothenberg assembles "details from the cultural organism that are vividly embodied in memory, and that subsequently spring to life again in the image."[2]

The "deep image" as an extension of visionary consciousness was crucial to Rothenberg's early poetics. Utilizing Martin Buber's terminology, he speaks of "deep image" as a unifying force, which is both "husk and kernel, perception and vision, and the poem is the movement between them" (PF, p. 57). In *Poland/1931*, the poet draws upon collage and other sources of remembrance to create a complex vision of his ancestral heritage consisting of a primitive creation myth of America; an awakening of sexual, psychic, and spiritual powers as part of a unified consciousness based on man's reintegration with nature; and reunification of Shekinah and God, signifying an end to divine and human exile. Since the Poland he writes about is beyond the range of his personal memory, the poet reconstructs the past from scraps and fragments of phrases, images, readings, interviews, and so on. The poet utilizes the resources of his imaginative memory to create a mythic connection between past, present, and future.

Rothenberg says he is not interested in confessional poetry, because he finds it limiting. Nevertheless, he has written the spiritual autobiography of his Jewish past in *Poland/1931*:

> The 1931 of the title is the year of my birth. Poland isn't where I was born—I was born in Brooklyn—but Poland is where my parents came from ten years before that. So, in other words, the date and place mark that part of my autobiography that precedes my own birth... So what I've been trying to do in various ways is to create through those poems an analogue, a presentation of the Eastern European Jewish world from which I had been cut off by birth, place and circumstance, and to which I no longer have any way of returning, because it doesn't exist in that place any longer.[3]

By concentrating on Eastern European Jewish life only until 1931 as well as a prophetic vision of America, Rothenberg largely circumvents both the attempted annihilation of European Jewry during the Holocaust and the ongoing story of mainstream American Jewish culture as well as the establishment of the modern state of Israel. Thus he portrays a way of life that survives almost solely in his imaginative memory.

The poet conceives of *Poland/1931* as a collage involving both literary and nonliterary sources, "a theatre piece, a mixed media piece, using slides and tapes, musical collage and song."[4] His structural method for bringing the Jewish past to life resembles that of his anthologies, especially *A Big Jewish Book*: "a large composition operating by assemblage or collage: my own voice emerging sometimes as translator, sometimes as commentator, but still obedient to other voices, whether 'out there' or 'in here'" (PF, p. 143). Also operative in *Poland/1931* is the poet-anthologist's fascination with "a specific set of language plays, feats of word magic & language-centeredness... that come to a visible point within the illusion of the ethnically specific" (PF, p. 143). Through such means, the poet ironically questions the power of memory while he, in fact, preserves the past through his art.

Rothenberg has also spoken of political motivations behind the writing of his Poland poems. Partly because of his hatred of America's involvement in the Vietnam War, he decided to posit his ancestral past as a moral and spiritual criticism of "the American present" and to augment his vision of this country as "a meeting place of nations," including his own Jewish tribe. Rothenberg's Jewish poetry is an integral part of his attempt "to rediscover the tribal and, on the other hand, to create the great universal powwow, the gathering of the tribes."[5]

There are many participants in *Poland/1931* but perhaps the most significant is the Shekinah. Rothenberg relies not on the traditional definition of Shekinah as God's presence in the world but on the Kabbalistic concept of the feminine element of divinity, who is in exile from God. Redemption can only be achieved by the reunification of God and Shekinah. Gershom Scholem explains that "in purely mythical terms, the masculine and feminine are carried back to their original unity, and in this uninterrupted union of the two the powers of generation will once again flow unimpeded through all the worlds."[6] The quest for divine reunification is a major motif in Rothenberg's Jewish poems.

In "The Bride," Rothenberg tells his own carnal version of the legend of the Shekinah as the mystical Sabbath Bride of God. Rothenberg's Shekinah is a victim who is triumphant in her very defeat. While strangers assault her in her exile, and Galician Jews dream of her return to God's tents, she serves as the poet's incarnation of sexual and spiritual oneness, who will someday be reunited with God:

> under thy tongue shall eat in Paradise thy fat buns
> & know no separation male & female
> shall be one in thee
> in thee the fingers of God shall come together
> shall know themselves in thee o Hole o Holy Mother
> (P, p. 26)

The Shekinah combines divine and human attributes, but she is oppressed and tormented because of both divine and human exile and discord.

No exponent of formal metrics or poetic diction, Rothenberg presents torrents of sexual images—often comic and obscene—which contribute to the poem's incantatory power. The poet wants to engender a constant oral sense of unfolding and changing in his verse. His approach to poetic form and structure resembles the exploratory art of composition by field and projective verse practiced by the Black Mountain poets. Dedicated to

Charles Olson, the chief aesthetician of the Black Mountain school, Rothenberg's poem "The Art of Poetry" proposes to emulate Olson's mythic quest in *The Maximus Poems* by telling of "a crazed rabbi" who becomes a "sea-bound/victim" and a "Seneca/at low tide," who peers out "across/the lake" (SJ, p. 90).

In "The Bride," the poet seems determined to burst through all sexual inhibitions in order to discover and render the mystical oneness which his Shekinah personifies. Although Rothenberg's rhythms are breathless and highly accelerated, most of the lines are end-stopped, and this constant pause and enunciation of long frenzied lines induces the magic spell he desires. The speaking voice sounding out the chant-like rhythms contributes to the "deep image" the poem conveys.

Another important personage not only in *Poland/1931* but also in *Seneca Journal* and *Vienna Blood* is the Baal Shem, the Master of the Divine Name, who, according to Kabbalistic and Hasidic texts, knew the secret lore of the Tetragrammaton and could perform miracles by the power of holy names. The Tetragrammaton consists of the four Hebrew letters YHWH or JHVH, which are used to symbolize the ineffable name of God. Those called Baal Shem were often Kabbalists, who performed healing and curing rites. In a more special sense of the term, the Baal Shem Tov is associated with Eliezer Baal Shem Tov or BeShT, the founder of modern Hasidism in eighteenth century Poland.[7] Rothenberg's Baal Shem is the holyman and mystic who symbolizes the male generative principle in the poet's primitive creation myth. In the two "Cokboy" poems, the Baal Shem undergoes an incredible sexual transformation and becomes part of the natural cycle of creation.

Analogous to the Shekinah and Baal Shem are Esther K. and Leo Levy, the main characters of two narrative sections entitled "Galician Nights, or a Novel in Progress" and "Esther K. Comes to America." In these two verse narratives, Rothenberg recasts his Kabbalistic legend of spiritual and sexual exile and reunification by dramatizing the suffering, exile, dreams, and ecstasy of twentieth century Jews, many of whom left Poland to become immigrants to America. Organized like one of Rothenberg's ingenious anthologies, *Poland/1931* begins with a series of lyric commemorations of the poet's ancestors, followed by "A Book of Testimony," narrative and dramatic poems which are Chaucerian in their earthy simplicity, "A Book of Writings," containing various scenes, anecdotes, amulets, events, etc., "A Book of Histories," and the sections I have cited.

For all his wild abandon and his concentration on sex, violence, and madness, Rothenberg's view of his ancestral Poland is closer to comedy than tragedy. While other Jewish poets, such as Ignatow, Ginsberg, Shapiro, and Nemerov, are quite capable of creating humor in their poems, they emphasize the darker, tragic side of life, which Jews have known only too well. Rothenberg affirms the triumph of the Orphic Jewish spirit, beginning with his individual and group portraits of Jewish life in the first two sections of *Poland/1931*.

It is significant that *Poland* begins with a marriage. Also, in the concluding legend of Cokboy, the Baal Shem dreams of being reborn as a beaver and later weds the mysterious "daughter of the mountain" in a mad mingling of Jewish and Indian mythology. The first poem in the "Poland/1931" section describes wildly animated celebrants at a black Polish wedding:

> a naked bridegroom hovering above
> his naked bride   mad Poland
> how terrible thy jews at weddings
> thy synagogues with camphor smells & almonds
> ....
> thy underwear alive with roots o poland
> poland poland poland poland poland
>
> (P, p. 3)

A wedding often serves as the happy ending of a comedy and signifies the victory of the comic spirit. Rothenberg mainly uses the wedding celebration to affirm the total expression of sexuality in his imaginary Poland where even underwear is "alive with roots." In the poet's vision, sexuality is the unifying force that brings together man and woman, flesh and spirit, God and Shekinah.

Rothenberg energizes the lines quoted above with the constant repetition of "thy" at the outset of each line, the naming of many objects, and the chanting of "poland" five times in the last line. In *Technicians of the Sacred*, he comments on the use of repetition and naming to extend time and call things into being. The poet's fondness for nouns and naming might well have been influenced by his reading of Gertrude Stein. Rothenberg chooses Stein, along with Whitman and Pound, as one of the three chief radical innovators of American poetry, and he laments the neglect of her poetry. He has written a group of poems entitled *A Steinbook & More*, which includes "A Valentine, No A Valedictory for Gertrude Stein." Because of her daring experiments with language, structure, and form, Stein has been a source of inspiration and a technical resource to Rothenberg.

Stein's influence can be seen in Rothenberg's constant search for new poetic possibilities. In "Satan in Goray," subtitled "A Homage to Isaac Bashevis Singer," the poet refers obliquely to Singer's early novel in twelve brief verbal vignettes, consisting of key words and phrases repeated in short lines:

> Crutches.
> Crutches cockcrow.
> Crutches cockcrow Jews.
> Crutches impure.
> Crutches impure cockcrow.
> Crutches Jews.
>
> (P, p. 7)

Rothenberg's method is to set Singer's "vocabulary to the exact structure of a Gertrude Stein poem called 'Dates.'" The eleventh section, in which the poet puns on the Jewish holiday of Passover, is verbatim Stein except for the last line:[8]

> Pass over.
> Pass over.
> Pass.
> Pass.
> Pass.
> Pass.
> Pass pass.   (G. Stein)
>
> Pass water.
>
> (P, p. 9)

Using words in Stein's cubistic manner, the poet creates unusual sound patterns through repetition, and he experiments with chance combinations of words juxtaposed almost randomly on the page.

While Stein's playful and innovative approach to language is evident in "The Connoisseur of Jews," the very incongruity of the poem's form, structure and syntax contributes to the dramatization of the miracle of Jewish survival and the creation of the Jewish poem:

> if there were locomotives to ride home on
> & no jews
> there would still be jews & locomotives
> just as there are jews & oranges
> & jews & jars
> there would still be someone to write the jewish poem
> (P, p. 12)

There is more than incongruity here. There is irreverence in the way the poet juxtaposes Jews and other things. But beneath his nonsensical surface, he makes a serious point. No matter how crazy the world may be, the Jews survive and someone writes the Jewish poem. And so this Jewish poem unfolds in its strange way as "the first Jew" tells of Jewish alphabets, fingers, hair, and so on. At the end, the poet repeats his thesis: there will always be Jews and Jewish poems.

In "The Fish," Rothenberg becomes more ostensibly serious and personal as he reveals why he writes Jewish poems:

> the dead fish has no eyes
> says my son, poland
> has no eyes
> & so we live without associations
> in the past we live
> nourishing incredible polands
> (P, p. 15)

The poet suggests that only through imaginative memory can he establish roots in the past and bring Poland back to life for himself and for his son. Along with other American Jewish poets, Rothenberg, the radical innovator, believes that memory of the heritage is essential but also very elusive. After some playful iconoclasm in which he denies that his poem is Jewish, Polish, or even human, the poet speaks of creating through memory "a tender treasure an illusion" in order to breathe life into his ancestral past.

In the initial section of the book, the poet dramatizes the lives of mothers, grandmothers, fathers, brothers, among others. Instead of using the monologue form, Rothenberg tells the stories of these people from a point of view that shifts between the third and first person, and he creates a unique mixture of racy narrative details, nonstop rhythms, and elusive syntax. The one thing that distinguishes these characters, besides the fact that they are Jewish, is that they are not boring. If anything, they are so energetic, so reeking with sensuality, they seem bigger than life. Even the grandmothers dance on tables and are obsessed with their bodies. Like Ginsberg, Rothenberg often mixes the sacrilegious with the religious. Inspired by his knowledge of primitive art and culture and the Jewish mystical and occult tradition, the poet presents an alternative to the stereotype of the stoic, scholarly, mercantile Diaspora Jew. Although his Jewish characters can be demented and blasphemous, they are also comic, inspired, and heroic.

Harris Lenowitz stresses the importance of fluids, especially blood, in all of *Poland/1931*. In "The Grandmothers" the emphasis is on blood:

> "have respect for the body of a grandmother
> "have respect for the vessel of blood
> "emptied   bearer of offspring from her damp nostrils"
>
> (P, p. 17)

Concerning part six of "from The Code of Jewish Law," Lenowitz notes, "Here the connection between woman and chaos is asserted in the relationship of the two female fluids, milk and blood, which must be kept separate, totally, since any proportion of blood totally assimilates the milk, force of continuing generation." Lenowitz believes, "The overall thrust in *Poland/1931* is towards acceptance of fluidity, sex, violence, etc., with all its felt dangers."[9]

Besides concentrating on myth and symbolism, Rothenberg can also depict a meaningful and dynamic scene in a few deft lines:

> some were in love & grew
> beautifully in the half darkness of the home
> for which they lit candles
> & waited still confident of business
> hot for betrayals & clarity
>
> (P, p. 20)

In this description of the "fathers," the poet paints an archetypal portrait of Jewish existence in Poland and in America by combining references to different facets of the fathers' lives in vivid and suggestive language and imagery. The "brothers" are also eccentric. One still masturbates at the age of fifty; one is obsessed with "telling time." Like Isaac Bashevis Singer's Polish characters, these people are sometimes possessed by demons and they are no strangers to the dark forces of evil, but the poet does not condemn them, because he believes these Jews know something that more prudent people often do not. They exemplify Rothenberg's mythic remembrance of Jewish sexual and mystical freedom and prowess.

In "A Book of Testimony," the poet commemorates individual lives: the beadle, the steward, the rabbi, the slaughterer, and the student. "The Beadle's Testimony" is noteworthy because of its buoyant rhythms. Not primarily a lyric poet, Rothenberg uses his narrative and dramatic gifts to tell strange and wonderful stories; however, there is a lyric precision throughout this poem:

> The boy who throws the ball
> A jewel of a boy
> His coat down to his feet
> Earlocks flying
>
> (P, p. 31)

The metrical regularity of the first three iambic lines of this stanza accentuates the highly stressed irregular last line. It may well be that the most important thing about the boy is that he is not exceptional. He is a boy, a human being, later an adult with no earth-shaking ambitions except to sell candles, eat hotdogs (or even a real dog in Shanghai), and smoke cigars. Maybe that is the point. Jews are people too. This Jew is a boy, "a jewel of a boy," who continues to "bless his mother" while growing up into a mercantile, secular, and erotic existence in such places as Kansas City.

The rest of the characters who offer testimony to primal Jewish consciousness are no longer innocent. The steward tells of a fat old man, the timber merchant, who is obsessed with sex and will stop at nothing to satisfy his appetites, yet is sickened by the sight of his own penis. Despite the shifting point of view and elusive syntax, there is a narrative continuity to the poem. The main action concerns a young bride who joins the timber merchant in a magical and mystical sexual romp. In the beginning, after looting the holy relics of the bride's father, the couple engages in a strange occult ritual complete with herbs, wolves' teeth, and devil's fingers.

The steward imagines he sees the couple butcher a calf, cover themselves with its blood, stick chicken feathers on their thighs, and scream like cows. Tormented and mad, driven by black magic, the merchant drops sausages in Sabbath pots, steals the foreskins of circumsized infants from the synagogue, coats his phylacteries with "goatshit," washes his beard with kvass, a fermented Russian beverage, and hears Turkish voices. Returning home, he finds the housemaid sitting, holding the young bride's head in her lap in a strange sexual liaison. As if there are no limits to this mad story, the steward describes how the timber merchant loses his skullcap in the soup, imagines that strange teeth are biting him, learns to fly and becomes an owl. Bandits and martyrs claim him as their kind, but he responds by defiling his own flesh and while visiting "wooded shrines" makes up a series of Egyptian "god names," such as the merchant transformed into a god of the woods "to suit himself."

The slaughterer is as demented and as inspired as the timber merchant. In the first half of the poem, a genuine tour de force, Rothenberg re-creates the slaughterer's milieu through an outpouring of images. Suddenly, as brides depart from the bathhouse, their blood sticks to the slaughterer's eyelids, blinding him, and tables and walls turn red. A host of animals offer themselves to him. A second slaughterer prays in a synagogue basement. Urinating blindly, he puts his own penis on the chopping block. In this chaotic dream-narrative, the slaughterer receives his knives from the last empress of the Gentiles. He reciprocates by sticking his fingers up her hole and blowing two trumpets.

The slaughterer's saga has the frightening surreal logic of dreams. One slaughterer becomes a strange "meat god." Another cuts open his skull and hangs himself from a hook as "a martyr to kashrut," the Jewish dietary laws. A visionary angel helps the slaughterer blasphemously feed blood to merchants and artisans, who mumble the holy name in Hebrew and other holy tongues. Their words turn to gold and gleam like fat. Even the pious drink angels' blood to keep "a universe alive." Seeing blood as Rothenberg's principle symbol of the relationship "of desire and control," Harris Lenowitz perceives the Jews of *Poland/1931* as "God's army in the chaos war," who constantly "engage the fluids, again and again, with heroism, especially in the bloody desires of their lives; lust for sex, for food, for taste, for blood itself."[10] According to Rothenberg, "There's also a memory of the blood-lie used against the Jews and intensifying a withdrawal from blood, flesh, body, etc."

In his own first person voice, the student tells of his demon with whom he sipped the Gentiles' beer and shot paperclips against the rabbi's clothes in the synagogue's back room. In a Kabbalistic vision, the student sees letters dance off their pages and fall on him, scribbling a double "yod" upon his penis. Rothenberg has depicted yod elsewhere as a "small letter, is itself a point, an opening through which creation, as another letter (number) in the shape of yod, can enter" (BJB, p. 80). Yod is also significant because it is the first letter of God's name: Yahveh.

Sharing various escapades with his demon, the student engages in the same kind of dream experience as the steward and the slaughterer. When the demon meets with the tsaddik, the righteous holy man, they find very different ways to love two women, who turn out to be sacred and profane versions of the Sabbath Bride.

In addition to telling stories of past lives, Rothenberg uses a number of experimental and traditional techniques to render his imaginative Jewish memory. In "A Book of Writings," he includes brief anecdotes, which he calls "Ancestral Scenes," amulets, dreams, and poems based on Jewish law, consisting of fragments from an English translation of the "Shulhan 'arukh" by Joseph Karo.[11] Rothenberg also includes various "events," resembling primitive rituals: "Repeat the 221 alphabets while walking in a circle./Repeat the event 442 times" (P, p. 72).

The poet also writes poems based on the systematic usage of letters and numbers known as *gematria*, whereby he imagines "correspondences between words or series of words based on the numerical equivalence of the sums of their letters or on the interchange of letters according to a set system" (PF, p. 158). Rothenberg is fascinated by the similarity of *gematria* "to a poetry of correspondences in our own time . . . based on (more or less) mechanical formulas for the generation of both simple and extended series of permutations & combinations" (PF, p. 158). In a similar vein, "A Book of Histories" is a collection of excerpts varying from several words to a long prose paragraph in length from the writings of Buber, Singer, Babel, Kafka, Opatoshu, and other Jewish authors. Taken as a whole, these fragments work like a collage to create a deep and varied impression of Jewish life.

"Galician Nights, or a Novel in Progress" tells the story of Esther K. and Leo Levy. Because Esther K. in all her glorious sexuality is a latter-day reincarnation of the Shekinah, the section ends with the poet's version of "Hymn to Shekinah by Isaac Luria." At first Leo Levy is not on the scene. Esther K. becomes the mistress of a Gentile governor, whom she calls her "little goy," and bears him a child. "Galician Nights" is filled with the comic and erotic details of Esther K.'s sensuous life and loves. Esther subsequently gets a letter from China. Ironically, while trying to entice Esther to visit China and meet a wonderful man whose initials are L.L., the monotonous and naive voice of the letter writer provides its own criticism of a community that specializes in the "Ashkenazic variation" of Mah Jong.

The next poem in this brief novel in verse is entitled "A Morning in the Life of Mister Leo Levy." Leo's entry into the action of the story is not auspicious. Waking up in Jewishtown, discovering that demon and bench are gone, he fiddles with his socks and boots. Concerned about his illness, he undergoes surgery and thinks of Esther K.'s breasts. Then he composes "An Angry Song" against Esther K., ending with the lament, "OY OY OY IT'S HARD TO BE A JEW! (P, p. 94).

Rothenberg's conception of "Galician Nights" is both highly ambitious and personal. As he explains in a letter to me, the story of Esther K. and Leo Levy parallels the myth of Shekinah and Messiah. "The 'story' is the myth of their exile & search proposed as poem, song & 'novel' (or fragments thereof)." Esther's name alone has many tantalizing associations for the poet: the queen who rescues her people from the evil Haman; the poet's mother, whose name is Esther and whose pictures on pages eighty-two and 100 of the New Directions text represent Esther K.; the Jewish Hadassah's Persian name, which the poet "connects with the goddess Ishtar (& also Astarte or even the Germanic Auster from which comes Easter, etc.—therefore 'thou my Easter excellence' in the 'novel')":

> The "K." is modelled on Kafka's Joseph K., but I discovered later ... that the bride of the first Polish Emperor Casimir was a Jewess named Esther or in the diminutive "Estherke"=Esther K. Leo Levy I first used because the name sounded both Jewish & funny, & because it played twice on the word "lion" (in Latin & Hebrew); only later on I realized that the initials L.L.=El El were a play on the name of God.

According to Rothenberg's own testimony, the story of Esther K. and Leo Levy concerns universal exile, which is a central myth in the entire volume.[12]

In Kevin Power's ingenious reading, Esther K.'s story parallels Israel's destiny:

> As a manifestation of the Shekinah, Esther K.'s story is clearly joined to that of the fate of Israel: her *novel in progress* is that of a nation's history, and given the fact of her additional male identity her novel truly becomes his/tory. She suffers the vicissitudes of her people and accompanies them into exile, whether the exile be in China or in New York. She experiences their hopes and despairs. She becomes, in fact, the Knesseth Yisrael, the personified female community of Israel.

Power believes that Leo Levy "might be both the Lion of Judea and the Moses to whom the Shekinah, according to the Zohar, is married." He views Leo Levy and Esther K. as "one person, the male and female presences of the Shekinah."[13]

"The Seven Melodies of Esther K." is a fragmentary rendition of the Esther K. and Leo Levy story in seven parts. The first part begins with Steinian frivolity:

> The pink head of her father
> under a black skullcap.
> Radishes.
> (P, p. 94)

Through a series of elusive tones and voices, the poet shows how Esther K. and Leo Levy meet and fall in love. In the fourth part, Esther K. decides to marry the Jewish king Leo Levy on a Chinese holiday. He asks her to ride on his white leopard. After she replies that you can't enter Jerusalem on a leopard, she and Leo debate about the proper means of entry. Then she recites a carnal love poem, which is slightly changed in "Variation on a Jewish Love Song (The Sixth Melody of Esther K.)":

> In love with a gypsy
> how beautiful
> my days are   my feet
> begin in Vilna
> & carry me to Havana
> He rubs my pudenda
> & stuffs it with his frankfurter.
> I will follow his motorcycle
> up the Great wall of China.
> (P, p. 96)

The poem contains the blend of comic and erotic elements that characterize "Galician Nights or a Novel in Progress," except for the final poem.

Rothenberg concludes his "Novel in Progress" with his rendition or setting of Isaac Luria's "Hymn" to Shekinah. Luria was the great sixteenth century mystic of the new Safed Kabbalah. This poem parallels "The Bride," Rothenberg's ode to Shekinah concluding the "Poland/1931" section. Except for the final line, the entire poem is in couplets of one to four words per line. Rothenberg often writes in long, intense, highly accelerated and concentrated lines, which, like Ginsberg's sometimes interminable breath units, occasionally lack fine lyric tuning. In "Hymn," Rothenberg is in complete control of his craft.

The Kabbalistic conception of the Sabbath Bride or Queen serves as the basis of Luria's "Hymn." Because Kabbalists viewed the Sabbath as a queen or bride, who was to be greeted each week with great joy, they loved to sing poems like the famous "L'chah Dodee," "Come, my friend, to meet the bride," composed by Rabbi Solomon Halevy in Alkabetz around 1540. In "Hymn," the thirty two paths, three branches, seventy crowns, and other designations are part of a Kabbalistic system of magical names for mystical powers. For example, while the thirty two paths represent the "thirty two secret paths of wisdom," the thirty two paths and twenty two elemental letters of the Hebrew alphabet are considered the pillars of creation.[14]

In this "Hymn" for the Friday evening meal describing the preparation of the Sabbath Bride for the mystical marriage with God, the poet refers to such ritual Sabbath items as bread, wine, and candles. At the poem's conclusion, the heavenly forces triumph over the demons. "Hymn" complements "The Bride," Rothenberg's rendition of the Shekinah's tormented exile among strangers on earth. In "Hymn," the poet brings his Shekinah home to God.

The "Esther K. Comes to America" subsection is a series of portraits of immigrant Jews, who, according to Eric Mottram, interact with other cultures to create "a prophetic 'America.'"[15] Now that his ancestors have left their religious and cultural roots, the poet introduces economic and political concerns. The immigrant hero of the picaresque adventures depicted in "The Immigrants" (dedicated to Charles Chaplin) becomes a laborer and must endure hardship while he lusts after women. Assuming the role of a union organizer, he leads striking workers in a march to heaven. As in many of Rothenberg's narrative poems, the action unfolds in surreal flashes. (Some of the images are from such Chaplin films as "The Immigrant" and "Gold Rush.") The immigrant eventually goes to Alaska and becomes obsessed with gold. Sometimes it seems all of the realistic and earthy imagery and action of Rothenberg's story poems becomes enveloped in dreams. In this instance, the immigrant becomes infatuated with Midas' dream of gold.

Esther K. and Leo Levy are also dreamers. In "Esther K. Comes to America: 1931," Esther K. and Leo Levy meet in a cafeteria named The Wilderness and remember their fantastic adventures of exile and search as fleshly Shekinah and Messiah. Everything in this country is new to them. Undaunted, Leo still lusts for money and power. After trying various commercial ventures, he decides to go into the movies by remaking "1931" as a talkie. Although his quest for money and power inspires Leo Levy to become romantic about Esther K. and about Jerusalem, he is not able to prevent the end of their lives together from being hard. Although his name is now Ben Messiah and her name is now his, they are an old couple somewhere in The Wilderness, sipping tea and sucking bitter almonds, jelly, and a lemon, which symbolizes the Succoth celebration of the harvest season and is also a slang expression for failure.

In "Poland/1931-'The Paradise of Labor,'" the fourth poem in the "Esther K." subsection, there is no punctuation, no capital letters at the beginnings of lines, and few pauses as Rothenberg sings his explosive litany to the new religion of communism. The poem is centered around a young unnamed Jew, who joins the revolutionaries and lives in a world of comrades, pamphleteers, and orators. However, his Orthodox Jewish heritage is in direct conflict with his radical politics. Rothenberg describes him sitting most bizarrely "in the dust of" a synagogue:

> a shoebox on his head
> pendant of garlic cloves down to his waist
> & a dead goose
> he held a herring-head in one hand
> an almsbox in the other
> grandfathers walked over him & spat in his face
> (P, p. 112)

Once again, the real and the surreal merge in the young man's strange sacrilegious dream—based in part on the old excommunication ritual—which signifies the shame, guilt, and degradation he must overcome in order to reject the tradition of his people. In the grandfathers' eyes, the young communist is a sinner.

Without transition, the dream ends and the narrative switches immediately to Karl Marx, the Jewish intellectual who promises a new red paradise. Walking through the snow, the young man is a true believer:

> as a straggler he comes down the center
> of the road   on either side
> rows of hooded men saintly processions
> of workers to whom he speaks
> in Yiddish
> like an oriental Christ
> (P, p. 113)

Not only does Rothenberg capture the spirit of communism, which became a dynamic secular creed for so many Jews of Europe and America, but, like Sholom Aleichem, he dramatizes the conflict between the old religion and the new politics.

In "Murder Inc. Sutra," Rothenberg writes of Jewish bandits and murderers. Mixing the criminals of Isaac Babel's Odessa with those of Warsaw, Brooklyn, and the Catskills, the poet shows how these men drive incredible winged Cadillacs, drink, eat, and smoke like fiends, sniff cocaine, chase black girls, dream of sex and old Poland, steal and murder, while searching for freedom and money. Like their counterparts Esther K. and Leo Levy, these Jews dream big dreams and refuse to be defeated by the circumstances of their lives. Although they flirt with demons, they act out

Rothenberg's seminal Jewish myth of a mad, powerful, inspired people.

In "Portrait of a Jew Old Country Style," the poet becomes personal and speaks of his own family but denies autobiography at the end. He begins by portraying an old man who offers his penis for girls to suck, sings of the passage of time, blows his nose, pins money to his caftan, speaks simply and wisely of Jews and love:

> This is a portrait of a jew old country style
> the gentile will fail to understand
> the jew come on better days will run from it
> how real
> the grandfathers become
>
> (P, p. 117)

Rothenberg would seem to find this old Jew and other Jews of *Poland/1931* compelling, because in their earthy simplicity, their free expression of sexuality, their mad dreams and visions, they embody the seminal energy of creation.

The poet speaks of his grandfather, who was a hasid in Rizhyn, journeyed to the United States in 1913, and worked in the shoe business, as did his brother-in-law, who was called *The Uncle*. The poet recalls the last time he saw his feeble old uncle sleeping behind a curtain in an East Bronx tenement. Seeing the poet, the uncle mistakes him for the poet's brother. The poet's grandfather had died in 1920, and on the same night his parents went to Warsaw, got married, and the next day his father left for the United States without knowing of his own father's death. Rothenberg's father never became a talmudic scholar. Instead, he went from working in a shoe factory to selling insurance, then back to shoes, and ended as an unsuccessful businessman. No beards for the poet's father. No dirt, no bizarre sexual exploits, no Kabbalah, no magic spells or visions. A Jew in America must be clean-shaven and polite. He must not be different from his Gentile neighbors. He must assimilate in order to survive. The poet's religious grandmother becomes angry when she sees him with his first beard, because Jews are not supposed to have beards in the land of gold.

The poet's grandfather returned to Poland around 1915 in order to escape a silent life in an alien America. Although he has spoken of his feelings of exile and alienation in interviews and on other occasions, the poet's presence is only implied in *Poland/ 1931*, which is mostly about Jews whom he has never actually met in the flesh. Rothenberg wants to write a poem not about himself and not just about Jews but about the oneness, the humanity, that all men and women share:

> for which reason I deny autobiography
> or that the life of a man
> matters more or less
>   "We are all one man"
> Cezanne said
> I count the failures of these jews
> as proof of their election
> they are divine because they all die
>   screaming
>   like the first
> universal jew
>   the gentiles
>   will tell you had some special deal
>   (P, p. 119)

Inspired by visionary fire as well as memory of his tradition, the poet indicates that all Jews and all men and women are mortal and share in the one worldly kingdom.

Now that the poet has brought his Polish Jews to America, he concludes *Poland/1931* with a primitive creation myth of America. Rothenberg imagines certain traditional and "saintly" Jewish figures in direct contact with nature. Learning the language of the animals and other "deep tongues," they will come to know the "universal speech," which will lead to oneness. The poet's main character is the Baal Shem, the "Master of the Divine Name," the mystical holy man, who participates in the birth of America and becomes known as Cokboy.

The tone and tenor of the two "Cokboy" poems is comic. In both poems, the narrator, who has multiple identities, speaks in the voice of an old Jewish cowboy:

> saddlesore I came
> a jew among
> the indians
> vot em I doink in dis strange place
> met deez pipple mit strange eyes
>
> (P, p. 143)

Rothenberg's America is a creation filled with Indians and Jews, who intuitively know and express the earth's divine energy. (The poet spent two years on the Allegheny Seneca reservation in Salamanca, New York and has translated American Indian poetry extensively, as evidenced in his *Shaking the Pumpkin, the 17 Horse Songs of Frank Mitchell*, etc.) In this constantly shifting saga, the narrator suddenly thinks of Barry Goldwater. The senator from Arizona—descended from converted Jews—implicitly "hates" both Jews and Indians and yet dresses alternately as Jew and Indian while remaining "a little Christian shmuck" and "the champion of their Law."

When the Baal Shem first sets foot in America, he cannot read the signboards, because the letters seem backward. The locals think he is a cowboy. But no, he is a Cokboy. No stoicism for the poet's mythic, primitive, orgiastic Jew. Searching for his brother Esau, the Baal Shem vows to put his sacred penis to work to create divinely inspired children in this new Eden. While on his odyssey through America, the Baal Shem discovers a glass city. Inside of buildings there are immobile statues with brown-skinned faces symbolizing materialistic white man's conquest of the Indians. According to the poet, the image is from "the vision of a Cuna shaman (Nele), including the glass city and the elevators—traveling into the 'other world.'" Then the Baal Shem has a vision of all slaves whose eyes "opened into stars" despite their often terrible circumstances.

On a mountain the Baal Shem's spirit meets an iggle (or eagle) who lifts him over the sunrise and gives him a song: the famous

Hasidic melody ("yuh-buh-buh") which has been sung without words for centuries and is here associated with the wordless Indian song ("hey heya heya"). Into his peddler's bundle and also Indian medicine bundle the Ball Shem puts his beaverskin cover, showing his status as an Indian beaver, the prayershawl bag and the esrog fruit of Succoth to represent his religious faith, and garlic from his native Poland. Then an old Indian comes forward and the Baal Shem shares visions with him. Smoking a pipe, these two unlikely prophets participate in an ancient and magic ritual. The Baal Shem cracks a walnut in his handkerchief, and they eat, play wolves and lambs—"a threatening game from both sides"—and then the creation myth of America begins.

A believer in completely opening up the mind and imagination to all their original creative energy, in Part Two of "Cokboy," Rothenberg brings forth a stunning and original poem combining Jewish and American Indian myth. The poem begins with continental birth pains:

>   comes a brown
>   wind curling from
>   tense tissues sphincter
>   opened over the whole continental
>   divide & shot the people up
>   (P, p. 147)

Out of this primordial setting comes a little girl, later referred to as "the Cacique's daughter," with beaver breasts, furry nose, and "eyes of the Redman's/Sabbath." From her womb the doctor pulls a little Moses and in Blakean fashion America is born.

In "Seneca Journal 1," the poet meditates on the meaning of beavers, because, as his note to the poem informs us, in 1968 the Seneca Indians adopted him into the Beaver clan, and while living on the Allegheny reservation in Salamanca, New York he became interested in what it meant to be a "beaver." In the midst of his meditation, the poet thinks of the poem about the Baal Shem in which the beaver is born as "the generative part of man" (SJ, p. 4). In the poet's imagination, his Baal Shem is part of the very bowels of the earth. He is as much beast as man and is totally integrated with nature.

Whether he is being humorous, ironic, deadly serious, or some combination of the three, Rothenberg is definitely writing his American creation myth, starring an Indian-Jewish-beaver, who is a totally animated sexual creature, a primal Cokboy. By an incredible metamorphosis, as described in "Seneca Journal 1," the Baal Shem turned beaver enters a fluid stream of the mind and "of sex transformed" where

> the Baal Shem leaves the light of Torah
> & becomes
> any old animal inside
> the sacred wood
>
> (SJ, pp. 4–5)

Animal, man, spirit are joined in the pun of "wood": the shittimwood of the Holy Ark and the beaver's wood. Part of the poet's grand scheme is to go beyond written Scripture, the Law, and the wooden confines of the Ark to create a Jewish myth of the primordial wood where man is at one with nature and the mysteries of creation.

Shouting at the sun and moon, the exhibitionistic Cokboy, who is synonymous with the Baal Shem, goes to the old Indian mother's hut, and like a traditional Indian trickster, drops a stone on her brains, and dreams of making love with her daughters. After this frenzied passage, there is another sexual sequence filled with kaleidoscopic imagery. It appears that while bathing Cokboy makes love with an Indian princess. This motif is from the famous trickster story in Paul Radin's book The *Trickster*, sending his gigantic penis through the water to lodge in a bathing princess. Then, after getting to Topeka and entering the bridegroom's quarters, he sees, as in a dream, a new moon like a sliver growing in the bride's abdomen or like a silver dollar over Barstow. In this "Marriage of America," Cokboy calls his Indian bride "the daughter/of the mountain" and taking her to his father's Jewish tribe does a snake dance to God.

This creation story is the finale of the book. America has been born in the person of Moses-Baal Shem-Cokboy, who has become an Indian and beaver involved in primitive rites that put him in touch with primal sexuality. Rothenberg has created a multidimensional mythic hero. Unfortunately, Cokboy now has nothing to do but continue his journey across America, an America the poet castigates because of what he considers its various sins. Four times near the poem's conclusion he repeats "America disaster" to signal his discontent and a primary reason for staking out a new country of mythic Jewish memory. Finally, after invoking the ghost of Ishi, whose name means man in his own language and in Hebrew, the poet refuses to even conclude the poem, as an expression of his own conflicts and doubts about America but also about his ancestral past, which he finds terrifying and absurd, as well as exalting.

In *Vienna Blood and Other Poems* Rothenberg deepens the course of his mythic Jewish memory. Unlike *Poland/1931*, which ends before the Holocaust, in this volume the poet remembers the Nazis' crimes of genocide. In "Vienna Blood," the title poem, he describes a visit to Vienna where his talks with a Jewish survivor "raised further phantoms & horrors that colored the rest of Vienna visit" (VB, p. 23). "Vienna Blood" is about the ghosts of European Jewry haunting a European culture tainted by Nazi crimes.

In a discontinuous, frenetic, and surreal style, the poet describes Hitler's dream of meeting the devil in the guise of the poet's grandfather. The fuehrer becomes so scared he runs to Linz and buries his face in whipped linzer torts. However contorted the poet's syntax, he says exactly what he means in the lines following the dream sequence:

```
—o triumph of the will-
—disasters of the modern state—
   the gentile's mind
   is dumb & cruel
   the song says
   proven right
              (VB, p. 19)
```

Suddenly, almost shockingly, Rothenberg speaks directly of European disaster in a straightforward style.

In the second part the scene switches briefly to Chicago, referring back to "The Chicago Poem" (VB, p. 27–28). The poet indicates that the Windy City's architecture can't compare with that of the old empire city, but Chicago is not haunted by ghosts of dead Jews.

>   so old   like Jews
>   forever gone
>   we walk too among ghosts
>   the sounds of poetry
>   —ka ka—
>   the only music left us
>   (VB, p. 20)

Rothenberg has now made his ghost-ridden memory of Hitler's victims part of his poetic music. In short, spare, solemn lines, he deepens his art and brings it close to his reader's own mournful memories.

Surrounded by memories of the Holocaust, the poet watches frenzied dancers and artists with crosses carved in their skin leaving a punk rock concert. He finds himself in a crowded bar where a German boy sings a Yiddish song about "Rayzeleh my pretty one." Jealous of the suffering of the Nazis' victims, these young people are driven to hurt themselves. In the fourth part, at the threshold or "place between," the narrator sees terror everywhere. He meditates about the eye within his eye and, looking back, wonders at what dark city's edge he will stop and what phantom will stop him. The terror is outside. The sacred is within the self, but so is terror. Terror is everywhere in Europe where the poet-narrator reads his poems. All he can do is aspire, like Artaud, "'to break through language/'" in order to touch life'" (VB, p. 22). Rothenberg wants to live in sacred time, to bring all his senses into full being, to improvise and name everything, to go beyond space, time and rationality in order, like a prophet, to burn with visionary fire.

Included in "From 'The Notebooks,'" "a letter to Paul Celan in memory" is about a German-Jewish poet who survived the Holocaust, wrote brilliantly, and in 1970 committed suicide. The poem is based on an actual meeting in 1967 between the German poet and his American translator and fellow poet Jerome Rothenberg at the Ecole Normale where Celan was teaching. Speaking beyond the language barrier that threatens to separate them, the two poets discuss their Jewishness and eventually stumble upon the Yiddish language, which they share but have failed to use.

The empathy goes on. One says, "image," and they both respond "sound," but then they turn to silence and the inner language of mythic symbols in their own poems. They drink "wine's words" until there is a scream and then a vision of a tree growing out of shadow, which Rothenberg equates with the roots of poetic discourse residing in silence and in what he might call meaningless animal sounds. There is also the silence of Celan's death. Although there is no menorah, no seven-branched candelabrum symbolizing the seven days of creation, there is a table set for the Sabbath, perhaps to welcome the Shekinah, the Sabbath Bride; however, the chairs are empty, suggesting Celan's suicide. An old man next to a woman raises his arms. The poet remembers the words of Celan, who could transform the world's mysteries into poetry, including a final Yiddish word. As an indication of his admiration for his fellow poet, Rothenberg dedicated his selection of *Poland* poems in *Poems for the Game of Silence* to Celan.

One of Rothenberg's most ambitious poems to date is a sequence called "Abulafia's Circles," included in *Vienna Blood*. It concerns what the poet calls "afterimages of largely unresolved messianic figures" from his *Poland/1931* and *A Big Jewish Book*. Being the historian and commentator that he is, Rothenberg provides brief biographies of his three subjects in his note to the poem. All are mystics and madmen, if not thieves. Abulafia (1240–c. 1291) was a mystic and poet who created two hundred mandalic circles composed of letters and words. He also named himself the angel Raziel and, as a self-proclaimed messiah, questioned the pope and was almost executed but escaped after the pope died. Jacob Frank (1726–1791) was another self-acknowledged messiah and a follower of Sabbatai Zvi, who left Judaism for Islam and later Catholicism. Tristan Tzara, born Sammy Rosenstock in Rumania, was the poet of Dada, a believer in holy madness and banditry. Unlike the other two, he did not claim to be messiah.

In these biographical poems, Rothenberg has indeed tapped a rich vein of Jewish memory. Again, Hitler and Nazi atrocities beset the poet's imaginative memory of Europe. In the first of the "Circles," concerning Abulafia, the narrator, who assumes many masks and voices, dreams of Hitler, who tells the narrator and other Jews they are dirty and need soap. Abulafia, the Jewish prophet, challenges Hitler but admits they are both of this world. While Hitler destroys life, Abulafia sustains it. This is a classic confrontation between good and evil and a manifestation of "G-d's double nature" as creator and destroyer, tyrant and messiah.

In life, the poet seems to say, there is not the oneness and wholeness of myth. Each person is incomplete and impotent. Nevertheless, Abulafia experiences a messianic vision:

> thus the prophecy: messiah
> giving birth
> dance of the colored winds
> & lights
>
> (VB, p. 77)

As magical letters sing to Abulafia and flowers are spun from glowing alphabet colors, he sees circles of letters dancing and exploding into "the mystical poetry of our time/on loops of tape" (VB, p. 77). Rothenberg thinks of Abulafia's art of permutations and *gematria* as comparable to contemporary oral and mixed-media art: "an improvisatory meditation on a fixed base (torah, names of God, etc.) whose true meanings are not 'literal' but the occasion for an ongoing process of reconstruction (revelation) & sounding" (PF, p. 161.) The poet concludes the poem but not the poem series, with a magic spell of fragmented statements and a final tribute to the primitive nature singing through Abulafia's inspired letters.

Rothenberg's motives may in many ways be the same as those of the other poets of Jewish memory. He wants to preserve his ancestral heritage for himself and the next generation. Even this mercurial maker of myth, this devotee of esoteric and mystical texts, can write a nostalgic poem, voluminously entitled "B'R'M'Tz'V'H: A poem from memory for Matthew Rothenberg's 13th birthday celebrated as a 'bar mitzvah event' one month after the date three decades three years past my own." In this autobiographical poem, the poet addresses his son, who is about to become a man according to Jewish law. This is presumably the son who in "The Fish," from *Poland/1931*, says that the dead fish is without eyes and thus prompts his father to revivify the Poland of his ancestors.

Recalling his own thirteenth year, the poet remembers reports of cousins killed during the war. Only their photos remain. When his son asks who someone is, the father can only say it is a child; however, he knows the child has been killed. The poet muses that despite hopes of a decent world, one awakens to "stifled flesh." The only way he can give life to the dead so that his son might know them is through poetry, and so he alludes to the creation of his imaginary *Poland*.

> I began around
> their deaths your life
> fathers mothers grandmothers
> set there as titles
> ancestors the imagination made
>
> (VB, p. 33)

The poet suggests that recollection of the past, revitalization of tradition, is fundamental to poetry and to life, and thus he creates his imaginary Polish community and sings of King David, the great Jewish king and poet.

Alluding to the loss of the Orphic Jewish spirit, the poet remembers his immigrant mother and father's frustrations and disappointments in this country. Knowing there is nothing but the mystery of life and death and the faces one meets along the way, the poet sings of this bar mitzvah celebration of his son's manhood on the Sabbath, which divides the day Jesus died from the day he was reborn. Thinking of his mother's name, Esther, he concludes by praising his son's life, by remembering the dead, and by quoting the pygmy poem that opens *Technicians of the Sacred*:

> when all the dead arise
> in mind they sing
> song that first ushered in your birth
> a man child   son
> grown old & beautiful
> at last
> "joy   joy
> "praise   praise
>   (VB, p. 43)

Surely the dead have sung in Rothenberg's poems. In *Poland/1931* and in his other Jewish poems, the poet remembers his ancestors and imagines a primal Jewish people of mystics and messiahs. By rendering the "deep tongues" of many ancient tribes, including his own Jewish tribe, Jerome Rothenberg endeavors to create his own vision of the one kingdom that all peoples share.

Chapter 4

Karl Shapiro

Memory Loss and Marginality

Karl Shapiro believes the modern American Jewish writer has become a victim of cultural amnesia:

> The Jew is the mythic wanderer, but the American Jew is the one who has forgotten where he wandered from. The American Jew has no longing for Israel and possibly only an intellectual sympathy with it. He has little or no cultural memory of the religion or of the tradition.[1]

Even in his "Introduction" to *Poems of a Jew*, a book devoted to what he calls "the theme of the Jew," the poet tends to be iconoclastic. Having said he is repulsed by religion in art and literature, he posits that Jewishness cannot be defined; however, "Jewish consciousness" is "inescapable" for the Jew. He goes on to claim that Judaism is the "minimum religion" and the Jew "represents the primitive ego of the human race" (PJ, p. ix–xi). Given the nature of the poet's beliefs, it should not be shocking that, unlike Reznikoff, Rothenberg, Simpson, and Zukofsky, he does not try to preserve the Jewish tradition through imaginative memory; nor does he attempt to reaffirm the prophetic vision, as Ginsberg, Rukeyser, Levine, Ignatow, and Nemerov have in their diverse ways. Torn by conflict and doubt, Shapiro is a Jewish poet of memory loss and marginality, describing the Jew's crisis of identity and the subsequent threat of assimilation.

In "Poet," Shapiro's rootlessness and despair as an American Jew who feels estranged from his tradition is integral to his personal conception of the maker of verse:

> Towards exile and towards shame he lures himself,
> Tongue winding on his arm, and thinks like Eve
> By biting apple will become most wise.
> (CP, p. 42)

Not only does the poet, like the Jew, experience feelings of exile and shame, but he emulates Eve, because he, too, follows the dictates of his passion. Then the analogy shifts from Eve to the Jewish businessman:

> He is the businessman, on beauty trades,
> Dealer in arts and thoughts who, like the Jew,
> Shall rise from slums and hated dialects
> A tower of bitterness.
> (CP, p.42)

According to Shapiro's analogy, the poet, like the immigrant Jew, has so much adversity to overcome he never loses his bitterness. Finally, the poet drowns and his name is forgotten. The conclusion indicates that, though the poet is a wanderer who must try to find his way in the world and rise above his precarious circumstances, it is doubtful that this pariah, who resembles the Jew in Shapiro's imagination, can overcome the harshness of his fate.

The feelings of bitterness, exile, and shame experienced by Shapiro's poet are evident in his poems about Jews. In "My Grandmother," an unrhymed sonnet divided into a sestet and an octave, Shapiro eulogizes his grandmother and mourns her fate as a Jew:

> I pity her life of deaths, the agony of her own,
> But most that history moved her through
> Stranger lands and many houses,
> Taking her exile for granted, confusing
> The tongues and tasks of her children's children.
> (CP, p. 18)

As Shapiro's poet is a victim of exile and must fight to overcome his legacy of "slums and hated dialects," his grandmother is trapped by the Diaspora of her landless people.

Shapiro agonizes over the Jewish destiny of always being a stranger in a strange land. In "Travelogue for Exiles," everywhere the poet looks he confirms his exile: *"The earth is taken: this is not your home"* (CP, p. 45). In this early poem each of the three six line stanzas has a refrain in the first and last lines. The tone and the formal structure, rhythm, and diction of this lyric lament for the landless show the strong influence of W.H. Auden: "The waves arise; sea wind and sea agree/*The waters are taken: this is not your home*" (CP, p. 45). Auden's art served as a model for Shapiro during his formative years as a poet.

In the first section of "Recapitulations," Shapiro shows how the rootless Jew is assaulted by Christian influences literally from the moment of birth. In four rhyming stanzas with a staccato iambic tetrameter beat, the poet describes how he was born in a Catholic hospital, surrounded by nuns and crucifixes. Even in his own house, he cannot avoid Christian icons: "A virgin in bronze and marble/Leered from the balustrade" (CP, p. 109). Shapiro strikingly reveals the absurd contradictions and conflicts in the life of the American Jew, who must maintain his or her Jewish identity while living in a predominantly Christian society.

In "The First Time," Shapiro depicts a young Jewish boy's first encounter with a prostitute and presumably with the sexual act. The poem consists of five sestets rhyming a b c a b c, d e f d e f, etc. in iambic pentameter. Few modern story poets could prevail against such challenging strictures. Even Frost, the master storyteller among American poets, often used blank verse and did not contend with rhyme when spinning his poetic yarns. Because he has honed his traditional skills so well, Shapiro is able to achieve formal symmetry and still clearly and convincingly describe every nuance of the young man's embarrassing initiation.

Through key details of setting, dramatic nuances, and suspense the poet steadily builds the action toward the surprise ending. At the outset the boy must anticipate his appointment in a "shadowy" waiting room. Then, as if preparing to see the doctor, he removes his clothes and staggering into the whore's chambers, he observes the young stranger who is about to engage him in love. The prostitute studies her visitor:

> Transfixing him in space like some grotesque,
> Far, far from her where he is still alone
> And being here is more and more untrue.
> Then she turns round, as one turns at a desk,
> And looks at him, too naked and too soon,
> And almost gently asks: *Are you a Jew?*
>
> (CP, p. 148)

Having seen the boy's circumsized penis, the prostitute asks a stupid question. This question not only exacerbates the boy's painful and embarrassing experience but in a comic and pathetic way heightens the more inclusive drama: the Jew's agonizing vulnerability among the Christians.

In "The Confirmation," where there is no explicit conflict between Jews and Christians, because the poem is told from a Christian standpoint complete with Sunday morning churchgoers, the young narrator who serves as Shapiro's persona is overwhelmed by the sexual appeal of an actress with whom he can consummate a relationship only in his imagination:

> And to confirm his sex, breathless and white
> With benediction self-bestowed he knelt
> Oh tightly married to his childish grip,
> > And unction smooth as holy-oil
> > Fell from the vessel's level lip
> > Upon the altar-cloth . . .
>
> (CP, p. 145)

Shapiro presents the boy's act of masturbation through metaphors of Catholic ritual. In "The First Time," the young Jewish protagonist's sexual identity is threatened by his feelings of inferiority and shame. The boy's Jewishness is never mentioned in "The Confirmation." Shapiro's youthful protagonist in "The Confirmation" must turn to both symbolic Catholic ritual and the act of masturbation to temporarily "confirm his sex," albeit in fantasy.

If he is to be liberated from his feelings of inadequacy, the young Jewish narrator who speaks for the poet must at least implicitly try to forget his patriarchal heritage. "Messias" describes a boy's flight from an old Jewish man who comes to ask for charity. While reading poetry in his apartment, the boy goes to answer the doorbell and sees an old man who terrifies him. Overwhelmed by this bearded patriarch, who speaks a strange language and dresses in forbidding fashion, the boy runs away, as if to escape the past. The very act of reading poetry instead of studying Scripture or praying is at least an implicit act of rebellion. Once again Shapiro depicts his youthful protagonist's troubled consciousness. Rejecting the tradition of his ancestors, represented by the visitor, and feeling like "a dead thing," the boy tears the fabric of memory that has sustained the generations of his people. To the boy there is something frightening and repulsive about this old man, but the poem's title, which refers to the long anticipated deliverer and king of the Jews, adds an ironic and tragic dimension to the boy's fearful reaction to his visitor. The patriarch must wait alone to ask the young man's mother for a contribution to Israel.

Assailed by religious and psychological doubt and conflict, Shapiro's persona seeks the radical cure of conversion. Momentarily ignoring his own injunction in his "Introduction" to *Poems of a Jew* that even a Jew who converts to Catholicism or any other religion is still a Jew, Shapiro tries to imaginatively reject his Jewish past: "Upon his new-found knees/He treasures up the gold of never-ending day" (CP, p. 102). Such religious rhetoric seems to be an aberration for a poet who has so candidly stressed worldly uncertainty, conflict, and suffering. Instead of refuting the cynics and iconoclasts, he says he will pray for their souls and walk near the saints while he contemplates the loving signs of "many significant conversions." Whatever the personal circumstances of Shapiro's experience of conversion, "The Convert" shows the precarious position of a Jew who has almost forgotten his past and is not sure how to face the present and future.

Just as the crucifix burns from the wall of the Catholic hospital room where the poet was born, another crucifix glares from his filing cabinet drawer in "The Crucifix in the Filing Cabinet." Picking up the crucifix, the poet studies it, and then he finds a bag used by Jews to hold a prayer shawl and phylacteries. Then he drops the crucifix into the pouch, anticipating some distant time that will "Crumble the cross and bleed the leathery vein" (CP, p. 152). Although Shapiro might refer to the messianic vision of universal peace and oneness, it is more probable that he imagines some point in the future when the tragic conflict between Judaism and Christianity will cease along with the power of their rituals and symbols.

Even the poet's passionate Jewish memories are measured against the predominant Christian influence. Shapiro has described how he was incited to write Jewish poems because of the negative reactions to his name when he first tried to publish. In order to find out why his name was such a "curse," he decided to write about being a Jew (PW, pp. 210–11). In "Jew," one of his most memorable poems, Shapiro defines a Jew as one who bears the immortal name:

> But the name is a language itself that is whispered and hissed
> Through the houses of ages, and ever a language the same,
> And ever and ever a blow on our heart like a fist.
> (CP, p. 78)

Shapiro writes this poem in the extremely demanding Terza rima, the rhyme scheme of Dante's *The Divine Comedy* and Shelley's "Ode to the West Wind." The meter is also exceptional because, while it is not unusual to find anapests and dactyls as variations to the iambic line, it is unusual to find almost an entire metrical pattern based on them.

Being a Jew, says Shapiro, is a bitter and cruel fate, "our bondage of murder and shame!" The catastrophic event that brought the curse of the ages down upon the Jews was the crucifixion:

> And the word for the murder of God will cry out on the air
> Though the race is no more and the temples are closed of our will
> And the peace is made fast on the earth and the earth is made fair;
> Our name is impaled in the heart of the world on a hill
> Where we suffer to die by the hands of ourselves, and to kill.
> (CP, p. 78)

The three stresses on "will cry out" in the first line of the passage emphasize the powerful feelings the poet expresses. In these lines of resignation and agony, the poet indicates that there will never be a resolution to the crucifixion and its aftermath because it is so ingrained in the human psyche.

Shapiro's agonizing reaction to the crucifixion recurs in "The Alphabet," another of his virtuoso performances. While the first stanza is twelve lines long and rhymes a b c, a b c, d e f, d e f, the second is thirteen lines and is identical in rhyme to the first except for the last four lines: d e g f. In addition to this remarkable exhibition of rhyme, the poet continues to demonstrate his skill at the iambic pentameter line. Although "The Alphabet" is ostensibly about the Kabbalistic fascination with Hebrew letters and their occult meanings, the poem's emotional content concerns Jewish double jeopardy in a hostile world, because the Jews have rejected Christ and yet their Messiah has not yet come.

As in so many of his Jewish poems, Shapiro sees Judaism in a historical context dominated by Christianity and particularly the crucifixion:

> The letters of the Jews are black and clean
> And lie in chain-line over Christian pages.
> The chosen letters bristle like barbed wire
> That hedge the flesh of man,
> Twisting and tightening the book that warns.
> These words, this burning bush, this flickering pyre
> Unsacrifices the bled son of man
> Yet plaits his crown of thorns.
>
> (CP, p. 143)

The poet skillfully varies the iambic pentameter to accentuate the dual stress on "chain-line" in line two and "barbed wire" in line three of the passage above. Strong alliteration in lines three, five, six, and seven reinforces the meaning. Associating the Hebrew letters, which lie over "Christian pages," with irreparable human suffering, Shapiro refers to the concentration camps when he metaphorically depicts the letters as barbed wire. In the last two lines of the stanza, the poet implies that because it does not recognize Christ's mission to die in atonement for man's sins, Judaism accentuates the omnipresence of suffering and underscores Christ's mortal agony.

In the second stanza the poet recounts the history of the Jews among hostile European neighbors. He indicates that the Jews will be a beleaguered people until the coming of the messianic kingdom:

> These are the letters that all men refuse
> And will refuse until the king arrives
> And will refuse until the death of time
> And all is rolled back in the book of days.
>
> (CP, p. 143)

In "The Alphabet," Shapiro expresses his impassioned doubts and fears as a Jew living among Christians while the Jews' letters, symbolizing stubborn Jewish resistance to Christian doctrine, burn and tear into the flesh of the crucified Christ.

Even in "The Synagogue," one of his most impressive Jewish poems, Shapiro compares and contrasts Judaism and Christianity as he focuses on the synagogue, the Jewish house of worship. In the seventh stanza of this eleven stanza poem, the poet stresses the absence of an afterlife in Judaism. Then, in the eighth stanza, he depicts Israel's unwillingness to bestow "grace" upon some of its most venerable women:

> And Zion womanless refuses grace
> To the first woman as to Magdalene,
> But half-remembers Judith or Rahab,
> The shrewd good heart of Esther honors still,
> And weeps for almost sacred Ruth, but doubts
> Either full harlotry or the faultless birth.
>
> (CP, p. 81)

In the second line Shapiro refers to Eve and to Mary Magdalene. According to the account in Joshua, Rahab was a prostitute who lived on the wall of Jericho. Because she hid two of Joshua's spies from the enemy, the Hebrews spared her and her family when they attacked and burned the city. Judith, the beautiful widow, saved her people from siege by killing Holofernes, the brutal Assyrian general. Esther was the Jewish queen of King Ahasuerus who counteracted Haman's evil designs against the Jews. Following her Hebrew mother-in-law to Bethlehem, Ruth became the quintessential convert. The poet's point is that because Judaism values commitment to life in this world—"factual holiness"—above all else, none of these women was offered divine grace.

Just as the Jews, according to the poet, are denied grace, so Jewish rituals differ from those of the Christians: "Our wine is wine, our bread is harvest bread/That feeds the body and is not the body" (CP, p. 81). As in "Jew" and "Alphabet," Shapiro emphasizes the haunting agony of the crucifixion: "We were betrayed to sacrifice this man" (CP, p. 81). In the final stanza the poet tries to be philosophical about the fate of his people:

> We live by virtue of philosophy,
> Past love, and have our devious reward.
> For faith he gave us land and took the land,
> Thinking us exiles of all humankind.
> Our name is yet the identity of God
> That storms the falling altar of the world.
> (CP, p. 81)

These six lines contain several of Shapiro's basic Jewish themes: the painful Jewish exile in the world; an ambivalent God, who gives and takes away; and the name "Jew," which signifies God's presence in the broken world. The off-rhymes of this stanza as well as the iambic pentameter and the poetic discourse are all marks of Shapiro's propensity for traditional form. "The Synagogue" concerns the poet's heritage, a heritage he comes more and more to question because of what he considers to be the dire consequences it has brought to the Jews among the Christians.

Given Shapiro's preoccupation with Jewish rootlessness and exile, it is understandable that he would be inspired by the modern state of Israel, the Zionist dream come true of a Jewish homeland. In "Israel," a poem containing four sestets with irregular rhymes, the poet expresses his hope and pride in the Jewish state:

> When I see the name of Israel high in print
> The fences crumble in my flesh; I sink
> Deep in a Western chair and rest my soul.
> I look the stranger clear to the blue depths
> of his unclouded eye. I say my name
> Aloud for the first time unconsciously.
>   (CP, p. 125)

Shapiro uses roughly parallel lines to communicate his enthusiastic response to Israel. Now he can seemingly overcome his feelings of shame and inadequacy as a Jewish stranger among the blue-eyed Christians and proudly say his name, which he has viewed as a curse. Now he can hope the agonizing "myth" of the crucifixion and the terrifying reality of the camps have been replaced by the land of Israel, the living land of the Jews.

Despite the poet's stirring tribute to Israel, he, as well as most other American Jewish poets, has chosen to remain in the United States. Thus, he continues to have feelings of exile, despair, and doubt. In his "Introduction" to *Poems of a Jew*, Shapiro speaks of the intimate but tense relationship between the Jew and God. "The 151st Psalm" concerns this strained relationship in modern America. Whereas the biblical writer of the last and 150th psalm expresses sustained praise of God, Shapiro's persona is ambivalent and ironic:

> Are You looking for us? We are here.
> Have You been gathering flowers, Elohim?
> We are Your flowers, we have always been.
> When will You leave us alone?
>   (PJ, p. 6)

While he celebrates the establishment of the modern state of Israel because it offers all Jews a "living land," Shapiro still feels alienated in America, and the strong implication of "The 151st Psalm" and other poems is that he would just as soon throw off the harsh yoke of Jewish suffering, exile, and sacrifice: "And what new altar will You deck us with?" (PJ, p. 6).

Although the poem ends in praise to the Lord, the tone of the third stanza is ambivalent:

> Immigrant God, You follow me;
> You go with me, You are a distant tree;
> You are the beast that lows in my heart's gates;
> You are the dog that follows at my heel;
> You are the table on which I lean;
> You are the plate from which I eat.
>
> (PJ, p. 6)

Revealing part of the conflict that he feels as a Jew in twentieth century America, the poet expresses hostility toward the same divinity which he implies he cannot live without. In the first two lines, the poet indicates that God, too, has wandered from his home and shares the Jew's immigrant status. In the reference to "distant tree," the poet associates God with either the tree of life or the tree of knowledge in the Garden. The next four lines present Shapiro's contrasting perceptions of the Jewish God. Despite the disparaging implications of "beast" and "dog," the metaphors of the last two lines—"table" and "plate"—show that the poet, like the ancient psalmist, needs divine sustenance to survive in the world.

Although there is no deprecatory imagery or figurative language in "Lord, I Have Seen Too Much," the message is similar to that of "The 151st Psalm." In this Petrarchan sonnet the poet alludes to his shocking recognition of human evil while he was a youthful soldier serving in Europe during World War II. In the initial stanza, the octave, the poet's language is abstract and detached. The narrator speaks of himself as a young man who lives in his own mind and is out of touch with the world. All hell breaks loose in the second stanza, the sestet, as the narrator experiences a human inferno much worse than what Adam saw. The poem ends with an indictment against the agent of such horror: "The lust of godhead hideously exposed!" (CP, p. 73). Besides his painful response to Jewish exile, the poet questions and challenges the Jewish God, who can apparently tolerate evil and suffering in the world.

In "Adam and Eve," Shapiro compensates for his loss of personal Jewish memory and his religious turmoil and doubt by turning to the biblical story as the basis for this poem about primordial sexuality. Each of the seven sections shows Shapiro's virtuosity as a practitioner of formal verse. In the first section, "The Sickness of Adam," the poet uses ten quatrains in iambic pentameter which rhyme a b a b, c d c d, etc.

Shapiro begins by showing Adam's lonely existence before the creation of Eve. The poet adds sexual ramifications to the sparsely written biblical narrative. For example, after throwing his staff at copulating sheep and striking the ram, Adam laughs, and when God hears Adam, He makes the animal lame. Later God says He caused Adam's cruel gesture. Then Shapiro describes how God brought forth Eve from Adam's rib.

In the second part, "The Recognition of Eve," Shapiro imagines Adam's initial shock upon first seeing Eve. The poet divides this canto into five stanzas of seven lines each that rhyme irregularly and are in iambic pentameter. As if she knows what lies ahead, Eve struggles against birth, but she loses her fight, and the poet first presents Eve in a seductive pose:

> Whatever it was she had so fiercely fought
> Had fled back to the sky, but still she lay
> With arms outspread, awaiting its assault . . .
> (CP, p. 119)

After describing Adam's first painful perceptions of Eve, Shapiro pictures their initial touch. The second part ends with Adam's revelation that this strange new creature is indeed beautiful.

In the third part, "The Kiss," a Shakespearean sonnet, the poet describes the first human kiss in lush language and imagery. Even as they taste the inside of each other's mouths, Adam and Even hear a frightening sound and try to hide. The turning point in the drama occurs in "The Tree of Guilt," section four. Shapiro's sultry Eve bears a resemblance to the Eve of midrashic legend. In *The Religious Imagination*, Richard Rubenstein compares two versions of Eve: "In the Bible she offends by eating the forbidden fruit. In the Aggadah her sin is explicitly sexual. Eve was infused with lust when she copulated with the serpent."[2] While in Genesis 3 the serpent plays sophist in order to tempt Eve with divine power if she eats the forbidden fruit, in Shapiro's version Eve is tempted not by promises of power but by lust.

Holding her breasts, Eve kneels before the tree of knowledge praying that "the great power," the serpent, rise up from the tree. Like the erect penis of sexual intercourse, "the snake began to rise/And dropt its head at her loins" (CP, p. 121). Then Eve falls to the ground and covers her face until she sees the snake stand perfectly straight at the point of climax:

> And all the seed were serpents of the good.
> Again the snake was seized and from its lip
> It spat the venomous evil of the deed.
> (CP, p. 121)

The sexual act consummated, Eve lies back and feels the cold clammy effects of sin.

Section five, "The Confession," is another departure from Scripture. While the biblical Eve says nothing to Adam but merely offers him the apple, in "Adam and Eve" she does not explicitly give the forbidden fruit to Adam. Rather, she offers a false account of her encounter with the snake:

> "Under the tree I took the fruit of truth
> From an angel. I ate it with my other mouth."
> And saying so, she did not know she lied.
> (CP, p. 122)

Although metaphorically she refers to her womb when she says "other mouth," Eve deceives Adam, who feels free from uncertainty, and then the first man and woman taste the fruit of their bodies.

In part six, "Shame," rather than furthering the action Shapiro creates an ornate rhetorical account of the aftermath of sin. While in Genesis 3:7 Adam and Eve quickly show their guilt and shame by covering their bodies, Shapiro takes five stanzas, each with three successive couplet rhymes, to convey the same event, but the ending is powerful: "Like animals they bellowed terrible cries/And clutched each other, hiding each other's eyes" (CP, p. 123).

"Exile" is the poem's finale. At the end of Genesis 3, God expeditiously banishes Adam and Eve from Eden. As the sword whirls and flashes to protect the tree of life, Adam and Eve leave silently. Shapiro's Adam and Eve both give departing speeches. While Adam complains that God has taken back all He has given, he speaks proudly to Eve, saying he is happy to leave Eden, because now they will have what they wished for, a land of their own. The less enthusiastic Eve prays to be shown the way back to paradise. Turning back, Adam and Eve see Eden burning: "And it was autumn, and the present world" (CP, p. 124).

According to Richard Rubenstein, both Freud and Reik believed Adam was "the primal son in rebellion against God, the primal father, for the possession of the primal mother."[3] Although he has been influenced by the psychological theories of Freud and Reik, Shapiro's rendition of the Adam and Eve story is based largely on the biblical and rabbinic sources. Like Lilith, Adam's legendary first wife, Shapiro's Eve is driven by sexual desires. First, she seeks out the serpent as her "oracle of love," and then in a strangely occult and yet Freudian ritual she worships the forbidden sexual power of the "Tree of Guilt" and experiences a vision into the mystery of sexuality. Bringing his imagination to bear on the ancient text and its concomitant legends and interpretations, Shapiro has written a modern poem of virtuosity and power. While Adam and Eve are not even conscious of religion or culture, they initiate the history of exile, suffering, and sexual conflict that the poet sees as the essence not only of the Jewish experience but of all humanity.

In "Bath-Sheba," Shapiro follows the biblical narrative more faithfully than he does in "Adam and Eve." The poet retells this ancient story of sexual attraction, guilt, and atonement in a sequence of five parts. Although the poet uses traditional form, the stanza structure of "Bath-Sheba" is less rigidly formal than in many of the earlier poems and the meter is freer. For example, in the first part, the stanzas are uneven in length: five lines, eight lines, and four lines. While the rhymes are almost excessively regular, the iambic meter is often irregular.

Looking down from the roof of the palace, King David sees a beautiful woman at her bath: "The King gazed, gazed as the sun/ On a distant flower, imparting fire" (CP, p. 229). In both of these lines, Shapiro breaks the iambic pattern. In the first line, there is an iamb followed by a spondee and an anapest. The line could also be scanned as an iamb followed by a single stress, with the long pause substituting for the missing syllable, and then a trochee and an iamb. In the second line, an anapest is followed by a dactyl and two iambs. Shapiro varies the meter to show the stunning effect that Bathsheba's image has on David, who orders his servant to bring this woman to him.

The second part depicts an elaborate sexual encounter between the adulterous lovers:

> He with his cunning harp
> And golden hands that slew the bear
> Applies his love and beauty,
> Binds and unbinds her hair.
> The kiss of David savors
> Sweetly of myrrh and holiness,
> Before their God the lovers
> Dress and undress and dress.
> (CP, p. 230)

Although rhyme is still apparent in this stanza (a b c b d e d e), rhythmic variations often take precedence over the iambic meter, especially in the third, fourth, fifth, sixth, and seventh lines. Due to the feminine rhymes, most of these lines have an extra syllable at the end and the third and seventh lines begin with trochees. As in "Adam and Eve," sex is shown as the force that brings men and women in direct conflict with God. Having depicted David and Bathsheba's sexual ecstasy, Shapiro brings them to the brink of tragedy. First, Bathsheba's husband Uriah the Hittite refuses to be a ploy in David's attempt to legitimate Bathsheba's pregnancy. Instead of living with his wife, Uriah demands to go to battle. Although he dies at David's instigation, Uriah at least knows that he will "fall upon no couches in my death!" (CP, p. 231).

Shortly after David and Bathsheba marry, the latter bears a son, but God decides to punish David and the boy dies. When David shows he is a faithful servant of the Lord by accepting his son's death as God's will after seven days of fasting and prayer, God blesses David with another son, Solomon. In the last ten lines of the poem, which are all in couplet rhyme, Shapiro presents a litany of praise for Solomon resembling the rhythmic chant of a Negro spiritual. Then, after building up Solomon to colossal proportions, Shapiro ends the poem with a pithy couplet about Solomon's parents: "Bath-Sheba was his mother, beautiful to see,/And she lay with King David in adultery" (CP, p. 234).

In both "Adam and Eve" and "Bath-Sheba," the protagonists' illicit consummation of sexual desire leads to conflict with God, who punishes Adam and Eve with a life of exile and hardship and David and Bathsheba with the loss of their first child. What they have done is wrong in the eyes of God, and so they must suffer the consequences; however, in both of these biblical poems Shapiro indicates that their sexual passions are what make these characters human. They represent what Shapiro refers to in his "Introduction" to *Poems of a Jew* as "the primitive ego of the human race," the almost "suicidal" drive of the Jews "to accept the mission of the ego." At the center of this expression of ego is sexuality, the kiss of fire that is the driving force behind "Adam and Eve" and "Bath-Sheba."

"The Murder of Moses" tells the story of the great prophet from the point of view of his followers. The poem consists of ten stanzas of five lines each. Not only is there no rhyme but the lines are not scannable. This virtuoso technician of metrical form has decided to write without a regular meter:

> We watched where you overturned the calf on the fire,
> We hid when you broke the tablets on the rock,
> We wept when we drank the mixture of gold and water.
> We had hoped you were lost or had left us.
> This was the day of our greatest defilement.
>   (CP, p. 150)

The parallelism of these lines creates a strong rhythmic buildup, and Shapiro writes with power of the conflict and tension between Moses and the Israelites. Instead of rendering Moses' story by means of a concentrated dramatic action, the poet has Moses' anxious and hostile followers summarize the main points of the biblical narrative. The poem ends with an eloquent tribute to the great leader: "Converse with God made you a thinker,/Taught us all early justice, made us a race" (CP, p. 151).

Although Shapiro gives the prose poems of *The Bourgeois Poet* a prominent place in his *Selected Poems* and his *Collected Poems*, there is little evidence of passionate Jewish concerns. Echoing the style and tone of Ginsberg's "America," Shapiro becomes a comedian of one-liners in "I Am an Atheist Who Says His Prayers":

> Pitchpots flicker in the lemon groves. I gaze down on the plains of Hollywood. My fine tan and my arrogance, my gray hair and my sneakers, O Israel!
> (CP, p. 181)

Shapiro's long prose line is funny, but there is little emotional depth in his reference to Israel.

There are also incidents and references in these occasional poems that are not funny. For example, in a poem bearing her name as title, Caitlin Thomas, wife of Dylan Thomas, calls Shapiro "a Jewish pig." Seemingly undaunted by this insult, the poet-narrator quickly forgets the remark and hurriedly shepherds Dylan and his wife around Chicago. In "Jazz," after describing black night life, the poet ends the poem by depicting a black woman who empties a bottle of perfume between her breasts in the "Jew-store." Meanwhile, "Privately Printed Poems" contains references to the increasing anglicization of Jewish names:

> In gold I also use my middle initial but spelled out JAY. J is for Jacob. My father dropped his first name Israel. My son is named Jacob. Upper-class Jews call him Jack. My father-in-law's name was Jack, probably Jacob.
> (CP, p. 166)

The discussion of names is only an aside in this poem about publishing a book of poems. In "A Poor Relation," Shapiro describes the sad uncle who teaches him to play chess. Because of his sensitive and scholarly nature, the uncle was never happy in this country. The poem implies that he would have been more content in a place where religious devotion was more highly appreciated.

Although "The Mezuzah" has poetic line structure, including iambic tetrameter and irregular rhymes, it resembles the prose poems from *The Bourgeois Poet* because of the dispassionate way it describes an incident that touches upon the poet's Jewishness. When two Adventist or Mormon missionaries (the poet is evidently not sure) knock on the narrator's door, he points to the mezuzah on his doorpost and tells them they should pass by his house. Containing a piece of parchment inscribed with several biblical passages and "Shaddai," a name of the Lord, rolled up in a container and then secured to a door frame, the mezuzah is a sign that a Jewish family lives in the dwelling. Aside from the slight note of ironic humor, it is hard to know what the point of this incident is. The prose poem "Mozart's Jew" reads like a brief biographical sketch of a man who earns a reputation writing libretti for Mozart and other composers. Besides several references to the fact that the subject is Jewish, there is no development of the theme.

Shapiro's most vital Jewish poems came relatively early in his career. One of the few Jewish poems of genuine power he has published since those collected in *Poems of a Jew* is "My Father's Funeral." This elegy consists of five stanzas of eleven lines with a final ten line stanza. Although the poet does not use rhyme, he does utilize iambic pentameter with occasional variations. Concentrating on his father's funeral, Shapiro creates a scene filled with vivid details and dramatic nuances:

> Lurching from gloomy limousines we slip
> On the warm baby-blanket of Baltimore snow,
> Wet flakes smacking our faces like distraught
> Kisses on cheeks, and step upon the green
> Carpet of artificial grass which crunches
> Underfoot . . .
>
>   (CP, p. 302)

The onomatopoeia of the trochee "lurching" begins the poem with a strong sense of immediacy reinforced by the l, s, and b alliteration in the first and second lines. Through rich, sensuous sounds, such as the verbs, "smacking" and "crunches," and the descriptive details of the setting, such as the "gloomy limousines," snow, artificial turf, the canopy, and the "scrolly walnut coffin," Shapiro allows the reader to share in the experience of his father's funeral.

Perhaps because of the occasion of his father's death, the poet concentrates on the culture he has almost forgotten, but, unlike the earlier Jewish poems collected in *Poems of a Jew*, Shapiro's own passionate and precarious identity as a Jew in America is not central to the poem. No Hebrew letters burn his mind or tear his flesh. No Torah scroll unravelled and read from by the rabbi inspires his imagination. No thought of the land of Israel makes him stare back at blue-eyed strangers. Now it will suffice to gently praise the rabbi for his eulogy and for reciting the Kaddish prayer. The mourners seem so relaxed and indifferent that a child says the reception resembles a cocktail party. It is as if these people, who have just come from the funeral where the rabbi recited the ancient Kaddish, are not even conscious of their Jewishness. Having become assimilated into American society and culture, they concentrate on the latest pleasures and are insensitive to their ancient heritage.

After describing his father's burial in the first three stanzas, the poet introduces an intrusion in the fourth stanza. He begins by noting such famous modern literary works as Dylan Thomas' villanelle "Do Not Go Gentle Into that Good Night" and Sylvia Plath's "Daddy," and then he mentions his father's unpublished opus on the art of salesmanship and his devotion to books, which led him to build a huge home library. None of this contributes to the central action of the poem. The fifth stanza catalogues various images of the father's life, as if the poet is turning the pages of a photo album or recalling memories flashing through his mind.

Finally, in the last stanza, the poet reflects upon his father's death and the passing of time:

> In the old forgotten purlieus of the city
> A Jewish ghetto in its day, there lie
> My father's father, mother and the rest,
> Now only a ghetto lost to time,
> Ungreen, unwhite, unterraced like the new
> Cemetery to which my father goes.
> Abaddon, the old place of destruction;
> Sheol, a new-made garden of the dead
> Under the snow. Shalom be to his life,
> Shalom be to his death.
>
> (CP, p. 303)

There is little left to remember now except old and new cemeteries, which the poet compares to biblical abodes of the dead. The poet says hello and goodbye to his father, his last link to the tradition of his ancestors.

Chapter 5

Louis Simpson

Narrative Memory

In his autobiography *North of Jamaica*, Louis Simpson describes a strange conversation between himself and the famous Russian poet Andrei Voznesensky. While the two poets were travelling by plane from California to New York, as they flew over Salt Lake, the Russian poet spoke of an artificial lake that the Russians had built to conceal the grave of Jews killed during the Second World War. He said that when he went fishing in that strange Russian lake he felt the fish might be Jews. Responding to Voznesensky's story, Simpson speculated about the fate of his Russian Jewish relatives and his own fate as the son of a Russian Jewess. If his mother had not gone to America, he might have been one of those Jewish fish, or if he had escaped Stalin and Hitler, he might have been discussing poetry with Voznesensky somewhere in Russia. He wondered at the power of life to both disperse and bring together nations and people.[1] Louis Simpson's poetic identification with his Russian Jewish heritage, his attempt through narrative memory to tell stories about Russia and to establish roots in the past with a people he barely knew while growing up exemplifies his fascination with life's dual power to unite and tear asunder.

The poet's mother Rosalind, a Russian Jewess from Lutsk, came to the United States prior to World War I, worked in sweatshops, became an actress, and while filming a movie in Jamaica met and was courted by Aston Simpson, whom she subsequently married. Although the Simpsons lived in well-to-do colonial style, their marriage was troubled. It was bad enough that the poet's mother was an actress but in Jamaican high society it was unthinkable that she be Jewish. Responding to social pressures, she tried to affect the best English manners and to make sure her son became a proper English gentleman.

While she concealed from others that she was Jewish, the poet's mother told him unforgettable stories about Russia. In *North of Jamaica*, the poet describes his fascination with his mother's Russia of snow, freezing winds, wolves, bells, and Cossacks. He recalls how she almost froze to death on her way to school and how she almost died from typhus. He also retells her charming story about bringing home a basket of plums on the train from Odessa as a gift to her parents. When warm weather caused the plums to spoil, she ate them on the train to Lutsk, so that they would not be wasted, and cried because she would not have any to bring home to the family. When he went to bed after hearing these stories, the poet dreamed of a snowy plain, a white moon, howling wolves, and people wrapped in furs riding in sleighs, images that would later appear in his poems.

While he had no formal Jewish education, Simpson was required to read the Old Testament along with the Psalms at the school he attended in Jamaica and the Hebrew Bible became part of his thinking:

> To this day the imagery of desert and rocky places presents itself to my mind's eye as though it were my native ground. I do not need to be told how the Jews lived three thousand years ago—I understand the despair of the people in the Wilderness better than I understand their lives in the suburbs. My reading of the Old Testament, before I knew that I was a Jew, gave me a love of the solitudes in which the God of ancient tribes appeared and spoke.[2]

As a lonely child in Jamaica, Simpson's "longing for some power that would arrive from outside, do something spectacular and awe-inspiring" affected his vision of the Jews as wanderers in the mythic wilderness.

According to the autobiographical narrative of *North of Jamaica*, it was only after he had come to Brooklyn to visit Pearl Marantz, his maternal grandmother, that Simpson realized he was Jewish. Although he was a Jew according to religious law, because his mother was Jewish, the poet, who had been raised as a Christian, experienced feelings of alienation and hostility as he first encountered the Jews of Brooklyn:

> But to be a Jew! What did I know about Judaism? I didn't like what I had seen of the Jews on New Lots Avenue. The side-curls! The religious complexion, like the belly of a dead fish . . . . And the language they spoke! If turnips and cabbages had a voice, they would speak Yiddish.
> (NJ, p. 88)

Nevertheless, this young man from Jamaica, who perceived Jews in exotic and unkind terms, began to feel at home as his grandmother embraced him, and he smelled the Jewish delicacies she was cooking. He realized that since his mother's family was Jewish, he was indeed a Jew.

Besides the influence of his maternal Russian ancestry, the fact that millions died in Europe because of what racist fanatics considered "Jewish blood" also induced the poet to identify with his Jewishness. As he recuperated in the hospital after the war, Simpson thought about the meaning of the Holocaust. He felt the worst result of the camps was that man could never again see himself as basically good and kind. Man had lost his innocence forever in the ashes of Belsen and Buchenwald.

In an early poem entitled "The Bird" (DG, pp. 68–72), Simpson tells a story of the Holocaust from the third person point of view of a young German miner named Heinrich whose friend Hans is killed in the war. Skillfully building the narrative through key details and crisp dialogue, the poet show how Heinrich, who continually sings, "I wish I were a little bird," joins the Nazi Army and becomes an exterminator of the Jews. Finally, as the Russians draw near the camp, Heinrich flees. A Russian soldier who is writing a report sees a bird flying from tree to tree but no sign of Heinrich. Somewhere the latter still sings his song about his wish to fly like a bird, and his children weep.

"The Bird" is divided into six parts, each containing six quatrains rhyming a b a b, c d c d, and so on. While the second and fourth lines are in iambic trimeter, the first and third lines are in iambic trimeter with an extra unstressed syllable due to the feminine rhymes. Although he uses the means of traditional verse to tell an intriguing story of a young German's search for freedom from poverty and oppression that ends with his participation in genocide, Simpson never personally enters the poem. He describes the death camp experience from the Nazi's point of view and keeps a safe emotional and aesthetic distance from the Jewish victims.

In "A Story About Chicken Soup," Simpson presents a very different treatment of the Holocaust. As if to immerse the poem in his personal Jewish response, he begins in the first person point of view by referring to his grandmother's chicken soup and her talk of life in the Old Country. By describing his grandmother's house, he not only emphasizes the warm and pleasant associations of Jewish life, which contrast so drastically with what follows, but he refers to the very perceptions that made him feel Jewish for the first time. The reader can respond to this poem without knowledge of Simpson's life; however, the poet's feeling that part of his cherished past had been destroyed by the Nazis was undoubtedly crucial to his conception of the poem.

Simpson's grandmother had many Russian relatives whom she visited in the 1930s and then continued to help as best she could until time ran out for many of them. In the first section of "A Story About Chicken Soup," the poet tells of two Russian lovers whom his grandmother had sent a dowry. After they married, they were killed by the Nazis. In the second section, the poet describes seeing a young German girl near the ruins of Berchtesgaden. She laughs at the American soldiers, but they spare her because they have killed many young German soldiers. Because she is so thin, she does not have enough skin and bones to make chicken soup. Therefore, her life cannot be taken in retribution for the murdered Jewish lovers. In the final part, as Simpson thinks about the lovers, he believes they cry out for him to be more serious. They demand that he know the meaning of life and death in this tragic world.

In a long passage in *Riverside Drive,* Simpson writes about seeing a German girl as he eats his K-ration in a village during the war. Revealing the depth of his rage toward the perpetrators of mass genocide and their silent collaborators, the poet visualizes the girl's face as the prototypical mask of the German maiden, which has not been penetrated by all the evil and agony it has seen:

> That face would not understand such things even if it stared at them. It is framed in flowers, that face. Sometimes it emits snatches of *lieder*; sometimes it laughs, revealing pearly teeth. The eyes are cornflower blue. And the fact is, the creature to which that face belongs is burning in hell, while the eyelids et cetera are constrained to keep the gemütlich smirk of a valentine.
> (RD, p. 75)

One does not need to analyze every implication of these words to realize that the feelings and insights rendered in "A Story About Chicken Soup" result from the poet's own piercing reactions to the war and the Holocaust, his knowledge of the haunting victimization of his mother and grandmother's people, whose suffering and glory he now shared.

While Simpson tells "A Story About Chicken Soup" from an intimate first person point of view, as opposed to the detached third person narrator of "The Bird," the craft and style of the former also vary considerably from that of the latter. Gone are rhyme and meter and most other traditional marks of poetic form, which Simpson used with distinction in his early verse, and in their place is his meticulous version of the American experiment with open forms begun by Whitman. The poet has said that he began to feel constrained by traditional form and wanted instead to write a less willful poem in which he would communicate his feelings through images.

Although he began his poetic career at a time when tightly crafted lyric poems of wit, irony, and paradox were in vogue, Simpson has always been primarily a narrative poet who tells stories about everyday life. Along with his fascination for his mother and grandmother's Russian stories and the Jewish stories that "have illustrated virtues and vices by referring to the behavior of people down the street," the poet became interested in the narrative art of the great Russian writer Anton Chekhov: "I have tried to bring into poetry the sense of life, the gestures that

Chekhov got in prose." Simpson says he thinks of Chekhov as a Jewish writer, because he "has the pathos, the sense of dispersal, the desire to bring things back together, and the humor, that are found in the best Jewish writers." Other great Russian writers, such as Dostoyevsky and Gogol, have influenced Simpson because they describe "the Old Country that is so much a part of the history of my people."[3]

While he knows that humor is not unique to the Jews, Simpson believes the Jews have cultivated a certain kind of humor "that turns a sad situation around so that we can see the comical side." This special Jewish humor "can change an intolerable situation in the twinkling of an eye into a magical cave in which words flit about and the darkness gleams with hidden riches."[4] Simpson has come to see his poetry as an attempt to record the sights and sounds, the tears and laughter, the very bread of life itself.

It is obvious in many of Simpson's poems that he feels out of place in American society, especially in California:

> Here I am, troubling the dream coast
> With my New York face,
> Bearing among the realtors
> And tennis-players my dark preoccupation.
> (OR, p. 11)

Although he does not use rhyme or a regular meter, there is an epigrammatic concentration and wit and a deft sense of timing in Simpson's short free verse lines from "In California." His free approach to form enables him to open his poetic sensibility to fresh possibilities of language, image, and humor. Like Reznikoff, Zukofsky, and other Jewish poets of memory, Simpson's imaginative remembrance of the spiritual past often clashes with his perceptions of the secular present dominated by images of shallow materialism.

Another poem in which Simpson juxtaposes past and present is "In the Suburbs":

> There's no way out.
> You were born to waste your life.
> You were born to this middleclass life
>
> As others before you
> Were born to walk in procession
> To the temple, singing.
>   (OR, p. 12)

With wit and symmetry in this poem of two tercets, Simpson compares and contrasts lonely modern bourgeois existence in the first stanza with the communal religious spirit of the past in the second. Although he does not picture the ancient religious community in detail, he skillfully suggests the solitary exile of most modern lives from their roots of religious faith and community. In addition to the parallelism of the second and third lines, there is a strong trace of meter, especially in the first stanza: iambic dimeter in the first line; an anapest followed by two iambs in the second; and anapestic trimeter in the third.

In several of his most widely anthologized poems, Simpson laments the end of Whitman's rhapsodic prophecy of America and engages in his own brand of dour prognosis. "Walt Whitman at Bear Mountain" depicts an imaginary meeting between the poet and Whitman. Asking Walt pointed questions, the poet-narrator is not satisfied with Whitman's attempt at rapprochement, because the latter's vision of the Open Road has led "to the used-car lot." In this poem Simpson condemns the capitalistic hustlers who have denigrated Whitman's America:

> All that grave weight of America
> Cancelled! Like Greece and Rome.
> The future in ruins!
> The castles, the prisons, the cathedrals
> Unbuilding, and roses
> Blossoming from the stones that are not there....
>   (OR, p. 65)

Although he usually communicates his thoughts and feelings through subtle humor and pathos, Simpson can also issue strong prophetic condemnations, as he does here. Simpson's California poems reflect his Jewish belief that there must be "a justifying design in experience" and his "criticisms of society, especially where it fails to show a sense of community and purposive life."[5]

In the third part of "Lines Written Near San Francisco," the poet again speaks of Whitman:

> Whitman was wrong about the People,
> But right about himself. The land is within.
> At the end of the open road we come to ourselves.
>
> (OR, p.69)

Instead of "the great companions" whom Whitman met on his Open Road, Simpson's protagonist encounters the slick capitalists. Now that the limitless vistas of the American frontier have closed, we must turn inward to a new psychological frontier, which the poet associates with death. He refers to those who discover the inner or spiritual life as "the colonists of Death—" (OR, p. 70). Death is seen as an unknown, mysterious continent that remains to be explored.

Simpson's harsh criticism of this country reaches its climax in his poems satirically lamenting the end of Whitman's Open Road. Instead of continuing to engage in prophecy, he tries to re-create the past in order to establish imaginative and psychological roots in his mother's Russia. In "Why Do You Write About Russia?" the poet describes, as he has in his prose works, how as a child he loved to listen to his mother's Russian stories of wolves, Cossacks, courtly officers, and their ladies:

> These stories were told
> against a background of tropical night . . .
> a sea breeze stirring the flowers
> that open at dusk, smelling like perfume.
> The voice that spoke of freezing cold
> itself was warm and infinitely comforting.
>
> (CAF, p. 51)

At the heart of the poet's remembrance of Russia is his attachment to the warm maternal voice, which in the next stanza he associates with poetry that speaks of life with a spirit of love and awe. Like Ginsberg, Simpson comes to his Jewish heritage as a poet not through his father or the tradition of the fathers but through the maternal voice and vision. While Ginsberg shares his mother Naomi's penchant for visionary experience, Simpson's art shows the influence of the bittersweet Russian tales his mother and grandmother told him in a voice filled with love and wonder.

At his grandmother's Brooklyn apartment, the poet meets his other maternal relatives, and he discovers that they suffer from false American dreams. Instead of wolves and Cossacks, they encounter cars and power mowers, and they worship security:

> a life that shuns emotion
> and the violence that goes with it,
> the object being to live quietly
> and bring up children to be happy.
> (CAF, p. 52)

Unlike most contemporary poets, Simpson writes openly about suburbia, and he pokes fun at himself in the process, as he does in "In the Suburbs" and "Sacred Objects":

> I am taking part in a great experiment—
> Whether writers can live peacefully in the suburbs
> and not be bored to death.
> (ALI, p. 62)

When he speaks of the lack of emotion and purpose in most middle class lives, Simpson is not afraid to express his ideas and feelings explicitly. He warns that it is not enough to be happy; there must be emotional and spiritual fulfillment.

In "Why Do You Write About Russia?" as he sits listening to the noise of a power mower and a motorboat, the narrator sees a man who looks like an Orthodox Jew in his black hat and his long black coat. When the narrator tells his new acquaintance that he is reading about Chekhov, the latter praises the writer Leskov and then tells tales about "the same far place the soul comes from." Simpson's first person narrator says he writes not of the geographical Russia but of a very special Russian sound:

> It's a sound, such as you hear
> in a sea breaking along a shore.
>
> My people came from Russia,
> bringing with them nothing
> but that sound.
> (CAF, p. 54)

In his imaginative memory of his mother's Russia, the poet identifies with his people, the Jewish people, whom he associates with the emotional depth and grandeur of the sea rolling in upon the shore, making a sound antithetical to that of power mowers and saws. Rootless and alienated in an America he both loves and loathes, Simpson creates an imaginary family, a religious and cultural heritage in "the same far place the soul comes from" (CAF, p. 54).

When he watches his grandmother say the blessing over the Sabbath candles in "New Lots," the poet remembers his Russian Jewish relatives, whom he has seen only in photographs, and one face in particular:

> One pale rabbinical face . . .
> wearing an overcoat that is too long
> and yet too short in his sleeves,
> standing with his back to a wall.
> (CAF, p. 17)

This man, his wife, and children and their Russian village were destroyed by the horrible tyranny that swept over Europe. Only through imaginative memory can the poet know this man and others whose lives were once made meaningful by a shared religious and cultural community.

Gone are the poor religious Jews who lived close to the Russian soil and in their place are the poet's relatives, who having emigrated from Russia to the United States prefer wall-to-wall carpeting to muddy streets. Having left behind their simple Russian way of life, these relatives of the poet have lost their emotional and spiritual empathy with other people and with nature. In their apartments, they look down at traffic and listen to

Jack Benny on the radio. While they eat Pearl Wanateck's Jewish delicacies, perhaps the last reminder of their Russian past, the relatives speak of their jobs as hairdresser and druggist and the celebrities who were and are their customers. As in "New Lots," Simpson also deals with the subject of his Jewish family in "The Man She Loved" (CAF, p. 61–63).

After leaving his grandmother's apartment and taking the subway, the poet gets off the subway and walks the rest of the way home. He is struck by the items for sale in store windows. A travel agency liner makes him think of those who remain in the city, like his relative, Dave, the druggist whose life is vindicated because Al Jolson spoke to him and recommended a stellar chiropodist in Los Angeles. And there is the woman who caused a minor uproar in Dave's drugstore because she reacted repulsively when Dave asked her to stop sampling lipstick on her arm. Using his considerable gift for description, the poet pictures this woman in a bleak apartment near Times Square:

> seated next to a radiator
> in a bathrobe, drying her hair.
> Sections of newspaper strewn on the floor . . .
> Listening to her breathe . . .
> A faucet drips, the radiator hisses,
> there is a siren off somewhere.
> (CAF, p. 19)

Through significant details, Simpson creates what Eliot called an "objective correlative," a dramatic crystallization of the woman's existence. Using the techniques of Imagism, such as economy of language and concentration of visual detail, he provides the reader with a deep glimpse into this anonymous life salvaged from oblivion.

The earliest of Simpson's Russian poems, "The Troika," from *At the End of the Open Road*, is more abstract and symbolic than the later Volhynia Province poems. Instead of telling a story that renders the conflict between Russian Jews and their hostile and violent non-Jewish neighbors, the poet describes an imaginary carriage ride through the Russian countryside via a tapestry of dream images, which begins with the snow moon shining in the forest and includes bleak references to the destructive impact of the two world wars. There is a rich lyric quality to these descriptive lines, many of which are at least roughly iambic.

After the dream landscape of the first half of the poem, the narrator, who rides the troika drawn by his father's horses, sees a white bird in the forest. Although he momentarily holds the bird, he loses it and while watching it disappear sees a lovely girl:

> I held the bird—it vanished with a cry
> and on a branch a girl sat sideways, combing
> her long black hair. The dew
> shone on her lips; her breasts were white as roses.
>
> (OR, p. 27)

Aside from the girl's black hair, the narrator is surrounded by white. Even the white bird returns to fly over the sea:

> When morning breaks, the sea
> gleams through the branches,
> and the white bird, enchanted,
> is flying through the world, across the sea.
>
> (OR, p. 28)

Simpson says the white bird "is only an evocative image. It means what it looks like, something desirable that is vanishing and luring one."[6] Ronald Moran believes the white bird is a dove symbolizing the internal peace the speaker gains during the morning following his dream and also his hope for world peace at the poem's conclusion. Depicting "The Troika" as a "symbolic dream odyssey backward in time," Moran characterizes the poem's structure as "a leaping out beyond the boundaries of reality into fantasy, a series of epiphanies." He believes the poem "reveals the 'drama and narrative of the subconscious.'"[7]

Most of Simpson's Russian poems are included in the "Volhynia Province" section of *Adventures of the Letter I*. In "Dvonya," the first of these poems, the poet's persona declares his love for his cousin Dvonya, a young black-haired Russian woman from Odessa, though he has never seen her. Like the girl with long black hair in "The Troika," Dvonya is extremely sensuous:

> I love her black hair, and eyes
> as green as salad
> that you gather in August
> between the roots of alder,
> her skin with an odor of wildflowers.
>
> (ALI, p. 5)

After the imaginary lovers meet in several romantic settings, the dream suddenly ends, and neither the narrator nor the girl survives the ravages of time:

> We are only phantoms, bits of ash,
> like yesterday's newspaper
> or the smoke of chimneys.
> All that passed long ago
> on a summer night in Odessa.
>
> (ALI, p. 5)

While "The Troika" moves from nightmare to a vision of whiteness and peace, there is an antithetical movement in "Dvonya" from the dreamlike evocation of feminine beauty and romantic love to the ashes and chimneys of European devastation. This passage from light to dark creates a tone of disillusionment and pathos at the end of the poem.

While the narrator's lyric voice in "Dvonya" has subtle Jewish inflections, the voice of "A Son of the Romanovs" is more explicitly Jewish and echoes the comic intonations of Sholom Aleichem and other Jewish writers. The narrator's Yiddish voice may be comic, but he tells a tragic tale. In this highly episodic poem, Avram the cello-mender and the only Jewish sergeant in the czar's army was singled out by the czar while he was marching with his taller comrades and given a position at the imperial headquarters. After meeting and marrying a rich widow, the lucky Avram lived splendidly. He and his wife even hired a crazy beggar, who referred to himself as the natural son of the Grand Duke Nicholas, to be their doorman.

As in "Dvonya" violence shatters the dream. Avram's luck runs out when the Nazis come to Odessa. As they enter Avram's house and scrutinize the doorman, the latter responds with his habitual reply that he is the Grand Duke Nicholas' natural son and is taken to the gas chamber. Despite the tragic denouement, the narrator concludes the poem with his grandmother's sardonic observation that the doorman should have kept quiet, but he just couldn't because he was a crazy Romanov. Simpson ironically mixes the grandmother's comic reference to the doorman's belief that he was a son of the Russian royal family with the tragic dimension of the action.

In "Meyer," Simpson tells another lyric but gloomy story. The poet has developed a witty voice with strong Yiddish inflections to narrate his Old Country story about a Jewish student of Hebrew named Meyer, who was attracted by the communist red star and joined the party. Although the poet provides only brief fragments of action and concentrates on details of the romantic Russian past, the implication at the end is that the communists have killed Meyer, the idealistic young student of Hebrew who dreamed of joining Lermontov and Pushkin in the Russian pantheon. "Meyer" is in five line stanzas with a brisk, almost breathless cadence. The poet depicts Meyer's fate with the quick, unpredictable progression of dreams.

In "The Country House," Simpson spoofs the manner and style of popular Russian fiction by summarizing the plot of an imaginary novel by a writer named L.V. Kalinin. The story begins with a stranger at a railroad station and then moves to a country house where the leading characters are presented: a beautiful girl and a radical young man. After engaging in drawing room discussions and picnics in various settings, the young man is harassed by his father and leaves the house. There are tears. All this is supposed to be connected to the tenor of the times. In the last stanza, Simpson quotes from one of Kalinin's letters:

> 'The Polish girl I told you about, who is living with us,
> has a wart. Two days ago, the idiot
> tried to remove it with lye.
> For hours on end the house has been filled with howling,
> and I can't think or write.'
>
> (ALI, p. 9)

As the letter reveals, this writer of Russian romance must bear the vicissitudes of real life. In this and other poems inspired by his narrative memory of Russia and written in his mature and open style, Simpson has been able to capture the subtle Jewish blend of humor and pathos, which he was not able to articulate in his earlier poems written in traditional forms.

In another dream narrative entitled, "A Night in Odessa," Simpson describes the brutality always lurking near his Russian Jewish characters. Simpson has spoken of the surrealist poet's use of images to create a "drama and narrative of the subconscious." In this poem he probes deeply into the subconscious fears of his protagonist, the grandfather. Mixing elements of dream and reality, the poet describes the old man's experience of living through a pogrom. Simpson's depiction of the grandfather's nightmare resembles Isaac Babel's description of the boy who loses his dovecot and almost his life as he, too, encounters a pogrom in "The Story of My Dovecot." In both instances realistic description of violent events is transformed into a frightening surreal dream.

In "A Night in Odessa," while the grandfather walks through the streets past drunks and assorted villains, he clutches his umbrella, and when he encounters a wolf in the forest, he stabs it with the point of his umbrella. This incident suggests the protagonist's lonely terror as he confronts his brutal attackers. In the fourth stanza the narrator addresses the grandfather and encourages him to survive against evil and to keep holding his umbrella. Finally, when the old man gets home, his pretty young wife Ninotchka meets him and goes to make his dinner. As she sets the table, she presses her hand to her side and the grandfather can see blood dripping from her hand. She is the wolf. The revelation of Ninotchka's wound makes the conclusion uncanny and unforgettable.

The grandfather, Meyer, and Avram are victims of Russian and German cruelty. Isidor is a radical activist who wants to revolt against the regime. While he dreams of revolution, he and his family live in poverty. Then one day comes the ominous knock at the door, and the police enter the apartment. They are foiled, however, when Isidor's wife feigns labor pains while he hides under the mattress. Although the frenetic action is conveyed in a comic manner, the reader knows about the historical facts of mass murder that implicitly underlie the explicit surface action of the poem. When Isidor decides the oven would be the next logical place to hide, he alludes to the Nazi ovens and the millions of victims who could not hide from their murderers.

Whether or not Isidor did in fact die in a Nazi oven, in the poem's conclusion he is resurrected from the dead:

> The mourners are sitting around
> weeping and tearing their clothes
> The inspector comes. He looks in the oven . . .
> there's Isidor, with his eyes
> shut fast . . . his hands are folded.
> The inspector nods, and goes.
> Then a leg comes out, and the other.
> Isidor leaps, he dances . . .
>
> 'Praise God, may His Name be exalted!'
>
> (ALI, p. 11)

Here Simpson deftly accentuates the actual cruelty that he alludes to through the incongruous and distorted imagery of dream and fantasy. The reader knows that millions of Isidors were murdered in Europe and that realistically this Isidor probably would have been one of them. Only by some miracle of the imagination does he escape as he had before to continue his comic saga of the irrepressible Jewish spirit. There are several levels of irony at work here. While the reader would like to rejoice and praise the Lord because of Isidor's miraculous escape, he or she knows that this is a pyrrhic victory at best because millions died in the extermination camps. If Isidor dances, it is in a dream or a poem and, therefore, why should God's name be exalted? Yet haven't

Jews always rejoiced in the power and glory of life as a reflection of the Lord despite all evidence to the contrary?

In the first of the four parts of "Adam Yankev," each of which consists of three tercets, the poet's remembrance of the past slowly fades after he describes several brief Russian scenes: his mother's family talking like "the famous Russian theater" in the kitchen and his mother and her sisters returning from the river with armfuls of flowers. Then, while he observes Brooklyn Jews walking about before his eyes, the poet speaks not of the past but of the present. Until this point he has poignantly re-created the tragic Jewish past with a comic voice of love and wonder in the "Volhynia Province" poems. Now that he no longer speaks through his stylized Old Country persona, the poet is free to envision his fellow Jews with the same probing eye and subtle wit with which he sees through the salesmen and bankers in *At the End of the Open Road*.

The poet describes these American Jews through incisive images that in their very fragmentation show the incompleteness of the Jews at the Diaspora's end. Missing from the momentary glimpses of these transplanted lives are the violence, pathos, laughter, and beauty of the Russian story poems. Although some of these Jews wear beards and yarmulkes, they are in exile from their roots in Russia and elsewhere and can only talk about the Old Country:

> Talking about their lives in the Old Country . . . .
> The passing headlights hurl
> their shadows against the wall.
> (ALI, p. 12)

Both spiritually and physically, Russia and Israel are far away. As the image of the car headlights forming shadows of the old Jews against the wall suggests, there is little room for religious faith and community in the twentieth century American Diaspora.

In the third part of "Adam Yankev," Simpson expresses the incongruity he perceives between his remembrance of his ancestors' spiritual past and the materialistic mecca of the present in contemporary America. Although he feels that he is a Jew "with a head full of ancient life," the poet believes that his people have not found themselves in the United States where their lives are dominated by the proliferation of "phenomena": "Yet, these people—their faces are strangely familiar" (ALI, p. 13). Somehow, these Jews are part of an ancient lineage, just as this country is part of the same world as Volhynia Province. Everywhere in the world and during all times, there is desire, sorrow, and the quest for knowledge:

> and the moon, so softly gleaming
> in furs
> that put a hole through Pushkin.
> (ALI, p. 13)

After depicting the rootlessness and alienation that he feels as a Jew in America, the poet ends the poem, the last of the "Volhynia Province" poems, by referring to the romantic Russian moon shining luminously in his imaginative memory where past and present exist simultaneously.

Simpson also writes of Russia in "A Friend of the Family," a sequence in five parts. In the first part the poet criticizes those lost souls, the California dreamers. In the second he satirizes both Yevtushenko's glorification of Russian expansionism and progress and the American version of the conquering pioneer spirit. The third section is a burlesque of the Russian space program, starring Chichikov the astronaut, named after the hero of Gogol's *Dead Souls*. Looking back to the past in part four, the poet-narrator creates a story about his uncle, who lived in Lutsk but travelled to Moscow to see Chekhov at the latter's invitation only to find that the great Russian writer had died.

In the first line of the fourth section, when the narrator says, "Andrei, that fish you caught was my uncle" (ALI, p. 55), he refers to the story the Russian poet Andrei Voznesensky had told him about the Russian lake constructed to cover up the bodies of dead Jews. When Voznesensky wakes up, he thinks he has been fishing in that macabre lake. Thus, Simpson uses a personal reference, which most readers will not understand if they have not read *North of Jamaica*. There is another obscure allusion to one of

Simpson's "Volhynia Province" poems. When the Nazis come, the uncle tells them not to forget Isidor, who can be found at the pickle factory. Since Isidor is the name of the Russian escape artist of the poem bearing his name, Simpson must indeed refer to the same man. The reader still cannot determine whether Isidor has been killed by the Nazis or magically escaped the ovens, as he does at the end of "Isidor."

As in "Why Do You Write About Russia?" Simpson then speaks candidly of his narrative memory of Russia:

> Andrei, all my life I've been haunted
> by Russia—a plain,
> a cold wind from the *shtetl*.
>
> I can hear the wheels of the train.
> It is going to Radom,
> it is going to Jerusalem . . . .
>
> In the night where candles shine
> I have a luminous family . . .
> people with their arms round each other
>
> forever.
>   (ALI, p. 56)

Because he reveals his own deepest feeling about his heritage, this is one of the most significant moments in Louis Simpson's Jewish poetry. He indicates that he is looking for a community, a shared way of life, a dream of an imaginary family of love. Because the Russian Jewish life he envisions exists no more and he is not ready to join those who have journeyed to Israel, he continues to have an imaginative empathy with the Jewish people.

The closest that Simpson comes to touching upon the religious spirit of his heritage is "Baruch" from the collection *Searching for the Ox*. In this story poem the main character is Baruch, a manufacturer of dress hats whose first love is study of the Torah. When his factory burns down, Baruch, whose name suggests the great Jewish philosopher Baruch Spinoza, decides to devote his life to the Torah. And so he studies the Torah until he dies. The second part of the poem concerns Cousin Deborah, whose only connection to Baruch is that she is an avid reader. When her family arranges her marriage to a timber merchant from Kiev, she rebels so violently on her wedding night that the timber merchant races back to Kiev alone.

In the third part of this three part poem the poet, who is alone in a train, reflects about the Jewish devotion to words:

> We have been devoted to words.
> Even here in this rich country
> Scripture enters and sits down
> and lives with us like a relative.
>
> (SO, p. 62)

While most of Simpson's Jewish poems spring from the memory of his mother and grandmother's Russia and his attempt to imagine a mythic family, this passage from "Baruch" shows a new response to Judaism based not only on family and culture but also on Scripture. The poet goes on to imply that study of the Torah prompts the Jew to see the past everywhere.

Sitting on the train surrounded by card players, the narrator watches prairie lights through the window:

> Then I see a face, pale and unearthly,
> that is flitting along with the train,
> passing over the fields and rooftops,
> and I hear a voice out of the past:
> "He wishes to study the Torah."
>
> (SO, p. 63)

Perhaps this train "is going to Jerusalem" and the voice from the past and the "unearthly" face reflect the poet's deepening devotion to the sacred words of his Jewish heritage. Whatever the future may hold, Louis Simpson has been able to bring to life his ancestral Russian past through narrative memory as manifested in his extraordinary story poems.

Chapter 6

Louis Zukofsky

Patriarchal Memory

(I am, after all, of the people whose wisdom
May die with them)
Louis Zukofsky "Anew: 42"

When Louis Zukofsky, paraphrasing the prophet Zechariah, asks, "Where are your fathers?/And do the prophets live for ever?"[1] he touches upon those aspects of the Jewish legacy that remain crucial to the American Jewish poets of memory and fire. Drawing upon memories inspired by his father Reb Pinchos, Zukofsky renders the voices of the fathers in passages resembling rabbinic sayings, psalms, prophecies, and proverbs in "A," his masterpiece. By transmitting the wisdom of the past and the sanctity of the relationship between parents and children to his son and to the reader, as well, the poet upholds the heritage of the generations.

It is a curious twist of fate that while he stayed close to home and was largely ignored by the literary and academic communities in his own country, Louis Zukofsky's devoted advocate was the expatriate Ezra Pound, who helped launch the younger poet's career. Celia Zukofsky remembers that "it was Ezra Pound who was the first to print Louis Zukofsky at all. And the first to see any merit in his work. That, in itself, would have a great influence on a particular person."[2] Although he was later to be indicted for treason for broadcasting pro-fascist propaganda over Rome radio while the United States was at war with Italy, it was Pound who provided this son of an Orthodox Jew not only with praise, publication, and friendship, but with the basis for a poetics by way of his famous Imagist principles of 1913 and 1918: that the poet should concentrate on the image, use no unnecessary words, and listen for the organic flow of the rhythm of phrases.

With these guidelines Pound challenged the traditional poetics of the metrical poem. His efforts to make poetry new had a profound influence on the poets of this century. Zukofsky certainly took Pound to heart. He must have been intrigued by Pound's notion of "an 'absolute rhythm,' a rhythm, that is, in poetry which corresponds exactly to the emotion or shade of emotion to be expressed" and his belief that technique is "the test of a man's sincerity." As if more was needed from Pound, there was always the example of his meticulous craftsmanship in his individual poems and translations and his sustained efforts on *The Cantos*.

It was at Pound's insistence that Harriet Monroe asked Zukofsky to edit the February 1931 issue of *Poetry*. For this purpose he gathered a group of poets under the rubric of Objectivist and provided his own rather arcane definition. Much of Zukofsky's editorial commentary is contained in his essay on Reznikoff. Zukofsky explains that "Objectification" has to do with the overall musical structure of the poem. Almost forty years later, Zukofsky's definition of Objectivism was still evolving: "The objectivist, then, is one person, not a group, and as I define him he is interested in living with things as they exist, and as a 'wordsman,' he is a craftsman who puts words together into an object."[3]

Zukofsky's literary reputation has been based mostly on his association with the Objectivist poets. Even his fellow Objectivists, however, have found it hard to fathom his achievement and have commented at various times on his obscurity and complexity. Besides Pound and Williams, Zukofsky's most ardent admirers have been younger avant-garde poets, such as Allen Ginsberg, Robert Creeley, and Robert Duncan, moved by his dedication to poetic craft. Ginsberg offers insight into Zukofsky's very special influence.

> The very quality of mindfulness and sensitivity accompanied his relative social isolation. And a purity of personal manner, a purity of life. Contented, domestic, private. Attention always on, to me, at least to my young eyes, attention always on quality of language and quantity only in the sense of measurement of his own language—that served as a model for me in a period of great storm and publicity, served as a model of manners, humor, a kind of rectitude, and a courage in pursuing near scientific studies of the musical qualities of language and the measurement of sound and its placement on the page.[4]

Robert Creeley, Gilbert Sorrentino, and others have praised the magnitude of Zukofsky's art. Guy Davenport even compares him to Whitman: "Our greatest living poet is usually a man as unknown to the professariat as to the living corps of reviewers and the deaf custodians of the laurels. It was true of Whitman in 1873, and it is true of Zukofsky in 1973."[5]

It is an astonishing fact that this brilliant and original craftsman of the English language grew up in a house where no English was spoken and conversed in Yiddish with his Russian immigrant parents. Zukofsky tells of the formative influence of Yiddish in *Autobiography*:

> My first exposure to letters at the age of four was thru the Yiddish theaters, most memorably the Thalia on the Bowery. By the age of nine I had seen a good deal of Shakespeare, Ibsen, Strindberg and Tolstoy performed—all in Yiddish. Even Longfellow's *Hiawatha* was to begin with read by me in Yiddish, as was Aeschylus' *Prometheus Bound*. My first exposure to English was, to be exact, P.S. 7 on Chrystie and Hester Streets. By eleven I was writing poetry in English, as yet not "American English," tho I found Keats rather difficult as compared with Shelley's "Men of England" and Burns' "Scots, wha hae.."
>
> (AU, p. 33)

Like so many of his generation, Zukofsky learned English as a second language. Hugh Kenner accounts for Zukofsky's mastery of the English language, his phenomenal word play, because he came to English with "the passion of a rabbinical boy who learned it word by word, having first encountered 'Hiawatha' in Yiddish translation."[6]

Unlike Allen Ginsberg, whose legendary life is a matter of public record, Zukofsky kept his intimate affairs to himself:

> I too have been charged with obscurity, tho it's a case of listeners wanting to know too much about me, more than the words say.
>
> As a poet I have always felt that the work says all there needs to be said of one's life.
>   (AU, p. 7)

The reticent poet does, however, provide a brief survey of his movements about New York City:

> But the bare facts are: I was born in Manhattan, January 23, 1904, the year Henry James returned to the American scene to look at the Lower East Side. The contingency appeals to me as a forecast of the first-generation American infusion into twentieth-century literature. At one time or another I have lived in all of the boroughs of New York City—for over thirty years in Brooklyn Heights not far from the house on Cranberry Street where Whitman's *Leaves of Grass* was first printed.
>   (AU, p. 13)

As the son of immigrant parents, Zukofsky was well aware of the condescending attitudes of many prominent American men and women of letters toward emerging ethnic and minority writers. It was Whitman, of course, who encouraged all Americans to express their poetic genius, but he did not speak for the literary establishment.

The poet's love for his wife Celia and his son Paul and their shared family existence served as the cornerstone of his life as man and poet. In addition to providing him with the privacy and security he evidently craved, the poet's domestic life enabled him to preserve his particular version of the exalted family heritage, which has been so essential to Jewish survival and which is a constant theme in his verse:

> Blest
> Ardent good
> Celia, speak simply, rarely scarce, seldom—
> Happy, immeasurable love
>
> (CSP, p. 127)

In this acrostic Zukofsky spells out BACH, the name of his favorite composer, while expressing his love for his wife. Celia's efforts to set her husband's verse to music is a rare and important artistic endeavor.

Zukofsky writes poignantly of his Jewish heritage in "Poem beginning 'the,'" which L.S. Dembo characterizes as "semi-farcical piece that, like The Waste Land, presents a chaotic sensibility in quest of order."[7] The poem is preceded by an exhaustive list of footnote references. Although Zukofsky parodies the "Notes" to *The Waste Land*, he also makes serious use of his sources in order to show the tension between past and present. In this poem of six movements and 330 numbered lines, the poet describes the conflict in his own mind between the teachings and values of the Russian Jewish culture of his ancestors and the twentieth century America in which he lives.

Now, instead of stern rabbinic prohibitions against graven images, there are English professors who encourage the Jewish son to read Shakespeare and Donne. Forced to adapt to a new culture, the narrator feels the ambivalence of his marginal identity:

> If I am like them in the rest, I should
> resemble them in that, mother,
> Assimilation is not hard,
> And once the Faith's askew
> I might as well look Shagetz just as much as Jew
>
> (AU, p. 20)

Zukofsky's protagonist seems to want to forget he is a Jew. He reasons that he might as well look like a Gentile, if, in fact, he lives like one. Instead of the great Jewish texts, his literary tradition will be English. He will read Donne and Coleridge as if they were part of his own heritage and become like "Plato's Philo." Speaking for

Zukofsky, the narrator says he will learn to exceed his instructor's demands by mastering the language and literature of a culture he questions; however, he is also skeptical of his Jewish heritage. Although he is the son of an Orthodox Jew, he says rather abruptly that the rabbis don't care about him.

Zukofsky's narrator is confronted with the challenge of finding a way to live and write in the United States without losing his Jewish identity through assimilation. Apparently, he is not content to sever all ties with his past. In addition to questioning American capitalism, in line 197 he refers to Russia as "free," though it is not clear whether he means revolutionary Russia or the Russian Jewish society of his parents and grandparents. While he reads Donne and Coleridge with zeal, he knows his beloved mother will never be able to read Shakespeare, and he quotes a number of lines translated into English from Yehoash, the pen name of a Yiddish poet named Samuel Bloomgarden. Zukofsky also cites a Jewish folk song in which a son tells his mother that the words of his song, which are really the prophet's words, will save him from hell. He also alludes to the Shulamite of Song of Songs. At the poem's conclusion, he tells his mother he has not forgotten her, and he extols the art of his own small song, which he believes will sustain him against adversity.

While "A," Zukofsky's personal epic, is a complex verbal symphony of many subjects and themes, some of the most beautiful and accessible passages concern the poet's Jewishness, especially that portion of "A"-12 where he remembers his beloved father Reb Pinchos. This act of patriarchal memory must have motivated Zukofsky to recall various voices of the tradition in the form of sayings, psalms, prophecies, and proverbs. Thus, the poet revivifies the voices of the past in the most venerable modes of Jewish writing.

"A"-4 serves as a prelude to the poet's tribute to his father in "A"-12. After the first twelve imagistic lines, which describe a harbor at night, the poet refers to the fathers: bearded, heads covered by hats, always observant of the Law. Having differentiated between the fathers' exalted "Speech" and the "jargon" of the children,[8] Zukofsky invokes the psalmists:

> We prayed, Open, God, Gate of Psalmody,
> That our Psalms may reach but
> One shadow of Your light,
> That you may see a minute over our waywardness.
> Day You granted to Your seed, its promise, Its
>   Promise,
> Do not turn away Your sun.
>   (A, pp. 12–13)

Beginning with the piety of the opening line and its succession of pauses after almost every word, Zukofsky writes in the spirit of the ancient Hebrew poets calling upon the Lord's gift of light.

As the poet expresses hope for the granting of the divine "promise," he mixes memory of the tradition with the psalmist's praise to God. Then, almost without transition, Zukofsky turns from his psalm of hope and praise to a lament over the degeneration of a once great heritage:

> Fierce Ark!
> Gold lion stomach
> (Red hair in intaglio)
> Dead loves stones of our Temple walls,
> Ripped up pebble-stones of our tessellation,
>   Split cedar chest harboring our Law
> Even the Death has gone out of us—we are void.
>   (A, p. 13)

Zukofsky, like Pound, is a master of subtly modulated rhythms and vivid image clusters. For example, the first two lines, which consist of a series of spondees and caesuras, communicate the glory of ancient Israel. The poet's lament for the loss of the sacred heritage begins with the almost iambic fourth line and is rendered by means of alliteration, assonance, and counterpointing of stressed and unstressed syllables in the fifth and sixth lines.

The poet suggests that the sacred Hebrew tradition has been replaced by a "jargon" of the "void," a language and a way of life lacking God's holy presence as well as such mythic references as the Ark of the Covenant, which has become a fractured container where the Torah is kept. Both the dead stones of the ruined temple and the "Split cedar chest" indicate that the religious heritage of Israel has been desecrated by a hollow and abstract materialism. Because of such present dangers, the poet must look back for inspiration to the tradition of the fathers and the prophets.

Throughout "A," the poet creates lines resembling talmudic maxims: "Saying, it's a hard world anyway,/Not many of us will get out of it alive" (A, p. 22). Besides his love for musical techniques and structures, Zukofsky was most interested in what he calls "Condensed speech," language approaching the condition of both music and wisdom. Although a poetry of discourse seems incompatible with the principles of Imagism and Objectivism, Pound, Zukofsky, and even Williams, the great empirical poet, loved to engage in talk about various subjects, and their poems—especially their epic performances *The Cantos*, "A," and *Patterson*—are filled with discursive and abstract language. Because the University of California Press edition of the complete text of "A" includes an index of subjects supplied by Celia Zukofsky, "A" can be read, at least in part, as a Jewish book of wisdom and knowledge tuned by the poet's art to verbal music.

In a passage echoing his lament for the loss of the sacred heritage of Israel in both "Poem beginning 'the'" and "A"-4, the poet speaks again of the fathers, whose words and whose way of life have almost vanished:

> Fathers, wherever they put their hats,
> Spiralled with tessellation as sands of the sea,
> The speech no longer spoken and not even a Wall,
>   to worship,
> Holy, laundered into a blank and washed over
> Tradition's pebbles . . .
>   (A, p. 22)

In the second line, Zukofsky creates an exhilarating combination of sounds based on the alliteration of s and l, which adds a musical component to the metaphorical analogy of a venerable but embattled tradition. While "tessellation" literally refers to a mosaic pattern of small squares of stone or glass—perhaps, as Guy Davenport suggests, the mosaic synagogue floors of the Roman-

Hellenistic period—the poet puns on the similar sound of tassel to suggest the threads or cords that hang from Jewish prayer shawls. In place of the Hebraic religious tradition symbolized by prayer shawls, hats, sacred "speech," and temple walls, there is the barrenness of modern secular life "laundered into a blank."

The lines I have cited thus far serve as a prelude to Zukofsky's moving remembrance of his father in "A"-12. The poet's patriarchal memory induces him to recall the voices of the fathers and to emulate their words of wisdom and glory in his contemporary verse. Two lines at the beginning of "A"-12 might serve as an epigraph for Zukofsky's Jewish poetry: "Who had better sing and tell stories/Before all will be abstracted" (A, p. 126). For some Jewish poets, including Zukofsky, the tradition represents a way of life replete with religious and cultural depth that is largely missing from contemporary existence. The poets must preserve this full-blooded heritage in their verse. Thus, in Zukofsky's case, we have the seeming paradox of an avant-garde poet who devotes much of his art to remembrance of things past.

The tradition provides a mythos that enables Zukofsky and other Jewish poets to enrich and clarify their personal visions of experience. Acknowledging that Zukofsky is a difficult poet, Hugh Seidman is particularly drawn to the clarity of "A"-12:

> But, in some of "A"-12, Louis gave us that leeway, he let in a little air in a way that he might not have done ordinarily and I, we, loved that. I once said, for example, that I had found the writings about his father incredibly moving and he told me that he himself had been moved when he read it back to himself.[9]

Combining the lyric and narrative modes, in "A"-12 Zukofsky tells a profound story with characters, setting, and action, and he also sings of his father's sanctity, love and courage.

Using the central intelligence or limited third person point of view, Zukofsky begins his father's story by showing him moving about through the Russian countryside and simultaneously by recording the wisdom of his inner thoughts:

> Reject no one
>   and
> Debase nothing.
> This is all-around
> Intellect.
>
> (A, p. 135–36)

Emulating the epigrammatic style of his father's rabbinic musings, the poet renders simple wisdom as lovely verbal music. Far from being "the most hermetic" of poets, Zukofsky communicates clearly to the reader. The Jewish heritage of wisdom and faith prompts him to tell stories and speak truths rather than create elaborate variations on the "void."

As the poet remembers his father's wisdom and faith, the tradition of the fathers speaks through Zukofsky's words:

> To get out of the world alive
> Despite despite—
> To live among ordinary men
> And yet be alone with Him;
> To greet profanity
> And from it draw the strength to live,
> Said the Baalshem—
> Thaew—as good as his name.
> To sing a michtam of David,
> To be alive, that is good.
>
> (A, p. 139)

The resolution of adversity in these lines shows the Jewish commitment to survive and keep the faith despite terrible vicissitudes. The poet also alludes to his father's exemplary Jewish life. The Baal Shem, "The Master of the Divine Name," speaks as a wise teacher. Reb Pinchos was his son's most essential teacher. The poet repeats his wish to sing psalms as David once did, and he affirms life.

There are many religious references in Zukofsky's verse. For example, he prefaces a brief sketch of his grandfather with a maxim on the sanctity of the Sabbath and then describes his grandfather praying in the synagogue and singing so stirringly at home that neighbors gather outside his windows. In this passage, the poet celebrates the holiness of the Sabbath, the Jews' day of rest and worship, the one day in the week when they can be spiritually replenished both in the synagogue and at home. The poet knows the Sabbath has helped sustain the Jews through centuries of oppression, or as the traditional saying would have it: "More than Israel kept the Sabbath, the Sabbath kept Israel." Having remembered his father and grandfather and their link to his son and to himself, the poet recalls God's commandment to the Israelites—recorded in Exodus—to make a tabernacle for the ark from shittimwood cut to specific dimensions:

> A voice out of the tabernacle—
> For the ark
> Shittim wood—the acacia.
>   (A, p. 141)

In Zukofsky's terse allusion to Scripture, he refers to the tabernacle, the portable sanctuary in which the Jews transported their Ark of the Covenant through the desert, and shittimwood, the type of tree—probably acacia—whose wood was used to make the Holy Ark.

After referring to various Greek mythological figures, the Virgin, a World War II battle, Stephen Hero, Aristotle, Philo, Jesus, and others, Zukofsky, the intellectual historian, returns to the poetry of his fathers with a discourse on creation, which resembles the commentary of The *Pirke Abot: The Wisdom of the Fathers*, one of the treatises of the Talmud, consisting of sayings of the rabbis:

In Hebrew "In the beginning"
Means literally *from the head*?
A source creating
The heaven and the earth
And every plant in the field
Before it was in the earth.
Sweet shapes from a head
Whose thought must live forever—
Be the immortelle—
Before it is thought
A prayer to the East
Before light—the sun later—
To get over even its chaos early.
    (A, p. 142)

Emulating the rabbis' aphoristic style, Zukofsky creates verse based on the art of talmudic discourse. In this instance, the poet starts with "In the beginning," the English translation of the first Hebrew word of Genesis, and then develops and exemplifies the ramifications of this concept through a series of images and metaphors with the verbal lucidity and music of poetry.

The poet then shifts to the voice of his grandfather telling his son, the poet's father, not to forget the Lord after going to the United States. When the poet names his son Paul after the anglicized version of his father's Jewish name, Reb Pinchos is not overly enthused about having the same English name as his grandson, but he agrees and blesses the child. As an example of how Zukofsky incorporates countless themes into his symphonic literary score, he immediately mentions Bach and says that if he, the poet, had been asked, he would have recited Kaddish for the composer, and then he quotes Einstein on simplicity:

> Everything should be as simple as it *can* be,
> Says Einstein,
> But not simpler.
>
> (A, p. 143)

Then, after he recalls the lines of the psalm his father often recited, the poet provides several sayings about the efficacy of learning and charity.

After more assorted thoughts and references, the poet presents an ironic portrait of Henry James, the expatriate aristocrat who looked at the new immigrants of the East Side with a condescending eye:

> I have just met him on Rutgers Street, New York
> Henry James, Jr.,
> Opposite what stood out in my youth
> As a frightening
> Copy of a Norman church in red brick
> Half a square block, if I recall,
> Faced with a prospect of fire escapes—
> Practically where I was born.
>
> (A, p. 148)

Something imposing and yet funny comes through Zukofsky's satirical comparison of James and the imitation Norman church. The irony continues as Zukofsky sees in James "The look of a shaven Chassid." Having ironically identified James with the Chassid, Zukofsky has the Chassid make a tongue-in-cheek request: "If you do not, Lord, yet wish to redeem/Israel, at least redeem the Gentiles" (A, p. 149).

After poking gentle fun at Henry James, Zukofsky alludes to the biblical Jacob's dream of angels going up and down a ladder with its top extending to heaven.

> There were angels going up and down a ladder.
> Standing over him a Voice:
> —I will give you the land where you sleep on stone,
> Seed the dust of the earth.
> (A, p. 149)

While Zukofsky's version is more condensed and less detailed than the scriptural one, the only real change occurs at the end of the poet's account when Jacob says that with God's help he will come back not, as in Genesis, to his *father's house* but, bearing bread and a coat, to his *father*.

In order to symbolize the theme of generations, the poet speaks of wood and recalls the acacia of the Ark of the Covenant, the spruce of his son's fiddle, and the wood's heart, which son and grandfather share, in addition to their names. The poet speaks poignantly to his son of his grandfather's deeply religious life based on songs, prayers, and often repeated words and gestures. Although Zukofsky does not compose his father-poetry in the form of continuous narrative, he does present key moments in Reb Pinchos' life.

As he remembers how his father sang on the Sabbath, the poet ponders the Jewish language of survival and faith in strange lands. He does this in lines beginning with an aphorism about the tenuous Jewish life in the Diaspora pictured by means of a simile of a hummingbird flying both backward and forward in order to endure (A, pp. 150–51). As he writes of Jewish rootlessness and alienation, the poet could be speaking of himself, his father, or the plight of Diaspora Jews in general. As we have seen, this theme of rootlessness and exile plays a prominent part in "Poem beginning 'the,'" as well as in "A."

In a long passage the poet describes his father leaving his family in Russia and journeying to the United States to do backbreaking work as a night watchman and as a worker in a men's shop. The poet sees his father in a heroic light, working at least fifteen hours a day except on Fridays when he quits before sunset, because, as he tells his boss, he must observe the Sabbath. Zukofsky creates a classic portrait of the Orthodox Russian immigrant, who maintains his simple, pious Old Country way of life in America:

> He rose rested at four.
> Half the free night
> Befriended the mice:
> Singing Psalms
> As they listened.
>
> (A, p. 153)

By showing how others, even strangers, respond lovingly to this loving man, the poet deepens and broadens the image of his father: "Everybody loves Reb Pinchos/Because he loves everybody" (A, p. 153). Reb Pinchos embodies, for his son the poet, the spirit of Israel's sacred past.

Even "Goodness dies," however, and the hummingbird, symbolic of the estranged but enduring Jew, "flies forward." Because records were lost or left behind in the Old Country, his own children were not sure what age, ninety-one or ninety-five, they should inscribe on Reb Pinchos' tombstone. Even the poet's father had forgotten his birthday. Almost all that he remembered and loved went into his religion, which sustained him both in Russia and in the United States. Zukofsky's father died resolutely and alone: "With such the angel of death does not wrestle—" (A, p. 155).

Finally, the poet pictures his father totally at peace in his synagogue:

> He opens the gates of the synagogue
> As time never heard
> Lifting up the voice.
> Actions things; themselves; doing.
>
> (A, p. 156)

Zukofsky identifies his father with the strength and sanctity of acacia, the wood of the Holy Ark, the wood of the synagogue, the wood of his grandson Paul's violin, the heart of the wood the generations share:

> Father to son to grandson.
> People carry a wood
> To him.
>
> (A, p. 156)

The wood shared by Reb Pinchos, the poet, and the poet's son Paul symbolizes the generations of fathers and sons and the sanctity of the Jewish family.

Zukofsky ends his encomium to his father with a series of rabbinic sayings concerning such questions as the value of Torah exposition, the nature of human character, and the relationship of body and soul. Rabbi Leib explains that actions are more important than Torah study:

> All a man's actions
> Should make him a Torah—
> So to light up
> Whether he moves or is still.
>
> (A, p. 159)

Combining the connection between Torah and life with complex insights and simple, clear language, Zukofsky develops Rabbi Leib's exposition of the relationship between body and soul. The latter believes the body, which is holy, must be in harmony with the soul; however, Rabbi Pinhas, whose name sounds like that of the poet's father, says the soul constantly teaches man. And when a disciple asks him why the soul is not in command, he answers that though the soul teaches, it does not reiterate.

In the convoluted lines that follow, the poet could well be speaking of the relationship between himself and his father:

> It is no small thing to
> > hearten men
> But the quiet cannot speak
> Unless a tie sustain their dead—
> That the pure body bear them up
> With their light it receives
> Pure oil beaten for lights,
> To glow—not to grovel.
>
> (A, p. 160)

In these lines the "quiet" poet suggests that imaginative memory of his father provides him with the light that enables him to effectively memorialize past wisdom and glory. Rabbi S then interjects that just as everything a man makes can teach, so what one says in this world is heard in the other. And so ends this talmudic treatise in the midst of an innovative modern work.

Although Zukofsky is not known for his devotion to social and political justice, "A" demonstrates the poet's concern for the poor and the oppressed. In "A"-1 the poet ironically contrasts the rich patrons of the arts, who leave the concert hall dressed in their finest, with striking miners, and he condemns those who exploit the workers:

> "We ran 'em in chain gangs, down in Argentine,
> *Executive's* not the word, use *engineer*,
> Single handed, ran 'em like soldiers,
> Seventy-four yesterday, and could run 'em today . . .
>
> (A, p. 5)

At the outset of "A"-8 the poet speaks of "Labor as creator," and later in "A"-8 he denigrates the mechanization of human energy and power. These and many other passages show Zukofsky's dedication to social and political justice. The complicating factor in Zukofsky's case is that his strong political interests are part of a dazzling orchestration of themes played at intervals throughout this long symphonic poem. While this complex structure allows the poet to strive for an overall thematic unity, it often prevents narrative and dramatic development of particular subjects and themes.

In addition to his powerful poetry about the exploitation of the working class, Zukofsky often aspires to sing his own psalms, "a song a/song in a strange land." Along with his memory of the patriarchal tradition, the poet invokes the words of the prophets:

> *Words commanded the prophets*
> *Did they not take hold*
> *of your fathers?*
> (A, p. 195)

This is one of several references in "A" to Zecharia in which Zukofsky speaks of the tradition of fathers and prophets. Zukofsky also refers to the Menorah, the seven-branched candelabrum of the temple signifying the seven days of creation.

As in "Poem beginning 'the'" and "A"-4, the sacred past is largely overshadowed by the dire exigencies of the present:

> But worse
> That men out
> Of the need of their nature
> Should try not to exist
> By blowing up ruins
> Of the Warsaw ghetto,
> Not beasts, a terror
> Howling "Sub-humans!"
> (A, p. 197)

In this case the poet describes the horrors of the Holocaust and the world's inhumane response to the plight of the survivors "in the ship *Exodus*." These thoughts fill the poet with rage, but looking at his son's hands, he affirms the strength of love that counteracts hate:

> For all actions
> Which passions determine
> Are determined better
> By a reason like love.
>
>   (A, p. 198)

Even as he is torn by remembrance of the Holocaust, the poet is inspired by Patriarchal memory to write with the wisdom and faith of his tradition.

At the beginning of "A"-13, Zukofsky provides a long series of aphorisms patterned after the biblical Proverbs. As he has already shown in "A"-12, Zukofsky is a master of the rabbinic maxim:

> Marriage is fast, wit
> Less than fate
> Look to love.
>   (A, p. 262)
> . . . .
> Man should not work
> At the same time
> With his mind and his body.
>   (A, p. 271)

These sayings bear a striking resemblance to those in the Hebrew Bible. A most unusual example of Zukofsky's use of Scripture occurs at the outset of "A"-15 where his words in English are patterned after the Hebrew of Job: "He neigh ha lie low h'who y'he gall mood" (A, p. 359).

I will conclude my discussion of Zukofsky with a passage from "A"-12 in which the poet evokes the voice and vision of the Hebrew prophets. While walking and talking with his son Paul, the poet thinks of the printing shop in the house on Cranberry Street where Whitman first printed *Leaves of Grass*. Not only does the poet often pass the historic house, but he teaches in the very building where Whitman edited *The Brooklyn Eagle* from 1846 to 1848.

After pondering that the mind sometimes enacts things centuries before it can explain them, the poet renders a vision similar to that of the horsemen on horses of four different colors, who range through the world, as depicted in Zechariah. When a voice asks what these creatures are, there is an inspired response, similar to that of the man in Zechariah and also echoing Eliphaz's third speech (Job 22:14):

>   —they walk
> To and fro
> Thru the earth—
> We have
> Walked
> To and fro
> And the earth
> Is quiet . . .
>   (A, p. 229)

Zukofsky's horses represent the spiritual grandeur of the ancient tradition and, more specifically, the splendor of the prophetic vision, which comes as a mysterious gift, bringing quiet to the earth.

After seeing the horses once again, the poet speaks humbly of the sacredness of prophecy:

> When
>   the eyes
>   have seen
> To everyone grass in the field
> My staff, even Beauty
> Shall say, I am no prophet.
>   HOLINESS
> Upon the bells of horses
>   In that day
>   (A, pp. 230–31)

Having remembered the heroic and devout life of his father and the psalms, proverbs, and sayings of the fathers, Zukofsky is witness to the prophetic voice and vision. As is so often the case with the American Jewish poets, memory and fire combine in a complex imaginative mixture. Far from being an obscure, hermetic, coterie poet, Louis Zukofsky proves to be, at least in his Jewish poetry, a writer of wisdom and vision blessed by the tradition he remembers.

Chapter 7

Allen Ginsberg

Prophet of Apocalypse

In his inimitable fashion, Allen Ginsberg has described an experience that changed his life. It began while he was in his East Harlem apartment reading Blake's "Sun Flower." Although he had often read this poem before without an intense reaction, this time he identified strongly with it. Suddenly he heard Blake's voice. It sounded as if God was talking to his son, the twenty year old poet Allen Ginsberg, in the year 1948. He knew almost immediately this was the reason to live that he had been waiting for. As the Creator's son, he now had a sacred mission never to forget the divine voice and vision. He saw evidence of divine creation and of heaven everywhere, and, perceiving a new cosmic consciousness, he awoke into a deeper sense of the real universe.

Hundreds of years after Ezekiel and Jeremiah, Allen Ginsberg became a poet-prophet enlightened by "a common key" to the universe, a key that his mother Naomi shares with him in "Kaddish." Although Ginsberg has been deeply influenced by oriental religion and by such poets as Blake, Whitman, Williams, and Pound, his Jewish memory and fire, as personified by his mother and by the Hebrew prophets, is the essential cause behind his famous prophetic poems. It was his memory of his mother's leftist politics, her fears of Hitler, fascism, and capitalism, her sense of exile from both her native Russia and from most of American society, her subsequent breakdowns and her visions that prompted Allen Ginsberg to perceive himself as an exiled Jewish poet-prophet, willing to risk madness and even death to sanctify his mother's suffering and to vindicate all personal consciousness as opposed to the impersonal machinery of modern industrial capitalism. His mission, then, was two-fold: to condemn capitalist America for destroying his mother and a whole generation of geniuses and to affirm the mystical knowledge that she and now he claimed to have and which he recognized in the saints of the Beat Generation.

Naomi imbued her son with her life of exile and suffering manifested in feelings of rage, shame, paranoia, and terror, which he could only resolve in his prophetic poems. Written as an elegy "For Naomi Ginsberg 1894-1956," "Kaddish" is modelled after the ancient Hebrew prayer for the dead, the mourner's Kaddish. When the mourner who prays for the departed says, "Let His great Name be blessed for ever and to all eternity," he or she invokes the establishment of God's messianic kingdom on earth, during which a great spiritual awakening, including judgment, resurrection, and immortality, will occur. Through this prayer the individual Jew is joined with the generations of Israel in affirmation of the faith. By basing his elegy to Naomi on the Hebrew Kaddish, the poet linked his destiny with the Jewish people and with the God of Israel.

Ginsberg started to write "Kaddish" in Paris in 1958 two years after his mother's death. About a year later, while taking metaamphetamine pills and listening to Ray Charles records, the poet began to look at a friend's bar mitzvah book and heard his friend read passages from the Kaddish prayer. This unusual combination of stimulants had a potent effect on the poet. After walking through the New York streets before dawn, he got home and wrote down a spontaneous and fragmentary series of memories concluding "with a death-prayer imitating the rhythms of the Hebrew Kaddish—'Magnificent, Mourned no more, etc.'" Because he discovered that he had not told the harrowing story of his family during the long years of Naomi's illness, he wrote what became the long narrative section, "sketching in broken paragraphs all the first recollections that rose in my heart—details I'd thought of once, twice often before—embarrassing scenes I'd half amnesiaized."[1]

With the help of drugs he finished most of the poem in one long sitting, lasting from early one Saturday morning until Sunday night. A week later the final section, beginning "Caw caw caw," came to him. Then it took him a year to revise and type the poem in a readable format. Although he was not sure he had written a poem, by 1963 he believed his prophecy signalled a triumph of the spiritual self over the impersonal, mechanical void threatening to destroy his worth as a human being and a Jew torn by exile, suffering, and guilt as he knew his mother Naomi had been. So he wrote a holy poem, "while chanting Kaddish the names of Death in many mind-worlds the self seeking the key to life found at last in our self."[2]

As "Kaddish" shows, it was Naomi who provided her son with the mystical key to the universe. Through his invocation of her memory, Ginsberg opened himself to prophetic fire. Writing in long lines resembling verse paragraphs broken by dashes, the poet re-creates the inspired moments he experienced before writing the poem. Then he pictures Naomi's arrival in America as a scared little immigrant girl, her years as wife and mother, her radical political ideals, and her subsequent life of suffering and madness, culminating in her mystical revelation, which dominates the poem:

> Toward the Key in the window—and the great Key lays its
>   head of light on top of Manhattan, and over the floor,
>   and lays down on the sidewalk—in a single vast beam
>   moving, as I walk down First toward the Yiddish
>   Theater—and the place of poverty.
>   (K, p. 8)

In "Kaddish," Ginsberg gets as far from the traditional iambic pentameter line and as close to prose as a poet can with the possible exception of prose poetry; however, as he describes his mother's mystical key to the universe, the poet's uncanny rhythms and images and his use of repetition and parallelism create a passionate and rhapsodic poetry.

In "Kaddish," Ginsberg writes not only about his Jewish family and culture—his ethnicity—but also of the Hebrew God, Adonai, whom he addresses in a series of staccato phrases and clauses:

> Nameless, One Faced, Forever beyond me, beginningless,
> endless, Father in death. Tho I am not there for this Prophecy,
> I am unmarried, I'm hymnless, I'm Heavenless, headless in bliss-
> hood I would still adore
>
> (K, pp. 11–12)

Calling for Naomi's redemption from the Wilderness in "God's perfect darkness" in long lines marked by parallel syntax and continual pauses, the poet offers God this poem as a sacred "Psalm" in honor of his mother. Both here and in his series of original "Psalms," as well as in his prophetic poems, Ginsberg identifies with the Hebrew prophets and psalmists.

While the poet sees God in lofty religious terms, Naomi's Lord is comic and bathetic, but also unforgettable:

> 'Yesterday I saw God. What did he look like? Well, in
> the afternoon I climbed up a ladder—he has a cheap cabin in
> the country, like Monroe, NY the chicken farms in the wood.
> He was a lonely old man with a white beard.
>
> (K, p. 23)

Naomi's matter-of-fact, prosaic, highly detailed depiction of God is ridiculous and funny in a characteristically Jewish way: blunt, expressive language; exaggerated comparisons and contrasts; Yiddish inflections; and a strange mixture of humor and pathos.

In the midst of this painful and even tortured poem, the poet creates through his mother's voice a comic portrait of God:

> 'I cooked supper for him. I made him a nice supper—
> lentil soup, vegetables, bread & butter—miltz—he sat down
> at the table and ate, he was sad.
> 'I told him, Look at all those fightings and killings down
> there, What's the matter? Why don't you put a stop to it?
> 'I try, he said—That's all he could do, he looked tired.
> He's a bachelor so long, and he likes lentil soup.'
>
> (K, p. 23)

Ginsberg deftly captures the Yiddish intonations of his mother's voice along with complex associations of idealism, madness, suffering, and humor.

Naomi is her son's muse, his Shekinah, the female manifestation of divinity as a Jewish "Communist beauty" destroyed by a terrifying society of machines and technicians, a society her son imaginatively condemns and transforms through prophecy as he searches for a poetic sanctuary for his mother and himself:

> O Russian faced, woman on the grass, your long black
> hair is crowned with flowers, the mandolin is on your knees—
> Communist beauty, sit here married in the summer among
> daisies, promised happiness at hand—
> holy mother, now you smile on your love, your world
> is born anew, children run naked in the field spotted with
> dandelions . . .
> (K, p. 29)

In his highly idealized, romantic portrait, the poet identifies his mother with nature, religion, and revolution, as if she is a mythic personage, but the romantic bubble soon bursts.

The poet describes another Naomi, who, while lying in bed with the scars of her various operations exposed and her body odors apparent, tempts her son with incest. Revolted by what he perceives and feeling at the brink of madness, he survives to recite the words of the Hebrew Kaddish in his mother's memory. Undaunted, Ginsberg presents all the sad, shameful, frightening details of his family life with the "kind of Bardic frankness prophecy" he believes Whitman called for. This means simply knowing "what you actually think & feel & every sentence will be a revelation—everybody else is so afraid to talk even if they have any feelings left."[3]

So the poet depicts his lonely vigils with his mother in their Paterson apartment while she screams her denunciations against Hitler and grandma. He tells about his trip to the rest home with Naomi; how he left her there, and as Naomi's lonely and guilty twelve year old son took the bus back to New York. He recalls his own first love for a Jewish boy, who later became a doctor, and he remembers how he planned to be a radical labor lawyer and then president or senator. Contrary to his youthful intentions, Ginsberg went on to become not only a poet but an avowed homosexual. Anyone who reads Ginsberg encounters the graphic details of his sexual affairs, which are part of his totally open and exclamatory celebration of his life. Such candor seems necessary to Ginsberg's identity as man and poet.

The poet describes his father Louis as a rather weak and passive man, who has been traumatized by his wife and has left most of the family responsibilities to Allen and his brother Eugene. After several terrible and demoralizing breakdowns, Naomi is permanently institutionalized and the father and his two sons go their own ways, but not before Naomi has wreaked havoc among them. There was the night she started vomiting and having convulsions, and the time she locked herself in the bathroom with a razor or iodine and Louis had to break through the "glass green painted door" to pull her out.

Ginsberg uses crucial details that can bring a scene to instant life. The last time he visits his mother in the hospital he describes her as a "small broken woman—the ashen indoor eyes of hospitals, ward greyness on skin—." She screams at him:

'You're not Allen—' I watched her face—but she passed by
me, not looking—
    Opened the door to the ward,—she went thru without
a glance back, quiet suddenly—I stared out—she looked old
—the verge of the grave—'All the Horror!'
                                      (K, p. 30)

Through unforgettably dramatic speech, details, and action, as well as natural and spontaneous rhythms, Ginsberg creates his own powerful brand of poetry without the traditional trappings of metrical verse.

Accepting the reality of his mother's tragedy and honoring her memory, Ginsberg not only survives his horrible ordeal; he becomes an inspired poet-prophet:

    O glorious muse that bore me from the womb, gave suck
first mystic life & taught me talk and music, from whose pained
head I first took Vision—
            (K, p. 29)

In his long bardic lines, the poet celebrates Naomi's radical vision despite the suffering and madness it entails. By doing so, he praises his Jewish heritage, which comprises not only the modern secular messianism of communism, socialism, and anarchism but the ancient religious messianism of the Hebrew prophets and psalmists.

At the end of the long second section, when the poet learns of his mother's death, he chants sacred names in conjunction with the names of those members of his family who along with him have suffered so much. After referring to Naomi as the biblical Ruth, Naomi, and Rebecca and his brother Eugene as King David the psalmist, the poet invokes his own Hebrew name:

> or Svul Avrum—Israel Abraham—myself—to sing in the wilderness toward God—O Elohim!—so to the end—2 days after her death I got her letter—
> Strange Prophecies anew! She wrote—'The key is in the window, the key is in the sunlight at the window—I have the key—Get married Allen don't take drugs—the key is in the bars, in the sunlight in the window.
> Love,
> your mother'
> which is Naomi—
> (K, p. 31)

As Naomi shows her son the mystical key to prophecy, the magnitude of the ancient Hebrew names, including Elohim and the patriarchs, and Naomi's crazy Yiddish realism create an uncanny and original revelation despite all the suffering, sickness, and violence, which the poet portrays so candidly throughout the long narrative of his years as Naomi's son. In the American "wilderness," Ginsberg aspires "to sing" like the prophets and psalmists "toward God."

In "Hymmnn," which concludes the long second part, Ginsberg comes through his painful ordeal to praise God and his mother in the spirit of the Kaddish prayer:

> In the world which He has created according to his will Blessed
> Praised
> Magnified Lauded Exalted the Name of the Holy One Blessed
> is He!
>
> (K, p. 32)

The traditional prayer begins, "Magnified and sanctified be his great Name in the world which he hath created according to his will." Emulating the Hebrew prayer, the poet mourns his mother's death and exalts God and, at least implicitly, the messianic kingdom as he blesses the presence of the divine in his mother's life and death and in everything that lives and dies.

In "lament," the poet utilizes a long, rambling free verse catalogue in which he repeats the phrase "only to" at the start of most lines, using parallel syntax to create an incantatory rhythm, In the first half of "lament," the poet recalls some of the graphic details of Naomi's breakdowns. Although these lines are shorter and more straightforward than those in "Proem" or "narrative," the effect is that of a jarring kaleidoscope of images. In the second half, the poet moves without transition from Naomi's madness to her vision of the key at the barred hospital window. While she listens to the Atlantic and waits to die, she sees the key that opens the door to the secrets of the universe and of divine creation. In this vision, which encompasses light and darkness, life and death, derangement and genius, Naomi once more gives her prophetic key to her poet-son. Accepting the key, "the living" son can, after turning the door and looking back see, "Creation glistening backwards to the same grave, size of universe, size of the tick of the hospital's clock on the archway over the white door—" (K, p. 33). In "lament," the poet repeats the movement of "narrative" from horror and madness to exaltation and wonder and sums up much of the essence of Naomi's life and spirit.

"Litany" consists of a series of syntactically parallel lines cataloguing many of the sordid details of Naomi's life and death. Resembling the strophes of Blake, Christopher Smart, Whitman, Hebrew liturgy, and the Prophets, the long free verse sequence produces a spellbinding incantation. Finally, in "fugue" a strange and horrifying voice speaks through the poet in a double refrain:

"Caw caw caw" and "Lord Lord Lord." As he listens to the frightening shrieks, the poet thinks of Naomi's spirit. Again, in parallel lines, the poet creates a mood of magic ritual as he brings the ineffable to life in words. As the Lord calls out through all of time and space, the empirical world and the poet's voice and imagination are subsumed by the frightening majesty of the final double refrain: "Lord Lord Lord caw caw caw Lord Lord Lord caw caw caw Lord" (K, p. 36). With this primal cry the poet concludes his elegy to Naomi. Although she antagonized and hurt everyone she touched, she was most destructive to herself, and yet she gave her son the magic key to the universe so that he might prophesy.

In "To Aunt Rose," Ginsberg takes another look at his mother's radical Yiddish milieu. The poem is about Naomi's sister Rose, whom the former had physically assaulted in "Kaddish." Although the poet was influenced by Naomi and Aunt Rose's affinity for leftist ideologies, he sees his aunt in a discriminating and comic light. Knowing with the benefit of hindsight that his relatives and their peers were largely ineffectual, he pictures Aunt Rose not as a heroic feminist radical but as Aunt Rose the flawed human being, whom he identifies with his adolescent sexual fears and inhibitions:

>—the time I stood on the toilet seat naked
>   and you powdered my thighs with Calomine
>   against the poison ivy—my tender
>   and shamed first black curled hairs
>what were you thinking in secret heart then
>   knowing me a man already—
>   (K, p. 46)

Here Ginsberg skillfully blends sensuous details and a tone combining irony, humor, and pathos. Along with Hitler, Emily Brontë, and Louis Ginsberg's out-of-print poetry books, Aunt Rose and the Jewish communists, anarchists, and socialists of the poet's youth are gone. When he remembers Aunt Rose in the hospital close to death, he recalls the long lost cause of the Spanish Republic.

Although it is in "Howl" that the poet unleashes his full fury against capitalist America for killing the dreams, ideals, and illusions of Naomi, Aunt Rose, and other activists he knew and admired as a boy, Ginsberg manages a number of political denunciations in several of the shorter poems in *Kaddish*, such as "Death to Van Gogh's ear!":

> Poet is Priest
> Money has reckoned the soul of America
> Congress broken thru to the precipice of Eternity
> the President built a War machine which will vomit and rear up
>   Russia out of Kansas
>   (K, p. 61)

As in the more well known "America," the solitary poet opposes the sinful nation and predicts the United States will fall, because it cannot tolerate its brilliant nonconformist saints, such as Einstein, Bertrand Russell, Chaplin, and Hart Crane, as well as Allen Ginsberg and his Beat friends. The poet condemns America as a "war-creating Whore of Babylon bellowing over Capitols and Academies!" (K, p. 65). Combining condemnation and bathos, horror and black comedy, realism and surrealism, as he does in passages of "Howl," Ginsberg renounces America's greed and lust for money and power, which are so evident in the abominations of Hollywood. Chastising evil governments, the poet-prophet is willing to die for his world-saving poetry.

To sustain and extend his consciousness as a visionary poet and prophet, Ginsberg has experimented with drugs, most explicitly in the poems named after the drugs which inspired them. In several of these drug poems and especially in the final three poems of *Kaddish*, the poet communicates directly with God. Unlike the poet-protagonist of "Kaddish," who, while emulating the psalmists and prophets, speaks to a majestic and transcendent God, the "I" of "Lysergic Acid" vehemently questions and challenges God and celebrates his own sacred individuality.

In "Magic Psalm," the poet invites the Lord to sexually assault him, so that he might prophesy:

> I am Thy prophet come home this world to scream an unbear-
>   able Name thru my 5 senses hideous sixth
> that knows Thy Hand on its invisible phallus, covered with
>   electric bulbs of death—
> Peace, Resolver where I mess up illusion, Softmouth Vagina
>   that enters my brain from above, Ark-Dove with a bough
>   of Death.
>   (K, p. 63)

The poet dares God to drive him crazy, to eat his brain and cock, and to "blind" him "with prophetic rainbows," so that he might see the invisible and speak the unspeakable as God's prophet with a magic key to the universe.

In "The Reply," the poet is "annulled," cancelled out by God, whose spirit enters into him:

> a dead gong shivers thru all flesh and a vast Being enters my
>   brain from afar that lives forever
>   None but the Presence too mighty to record! the Presence
>   in Death, before whom I am helpless
>   makes me change from Allen to a skull
> Old One-Eye of dreams in which I do not wake but die—
>   (K, p. 96)

Using "a dead gong shivers" as onomatopoeia and as a trope to convey the divine "Presence," Ginsberg shows that the price of divine possession, of total spiritual knowledge, is death of the body and of human consciousness. Comparing his own terror to that of Christ on the cross but unwilling to die, the poet desires to escape from this frightening and deathly realm back to the human world and the life which he has risked for this ultimate knowledge.

The last poem of the volume, appropriately called "The End," records the divine voice speaking through the poet as he returns from the world of God to the human world of sex, poetry, and music. "I am I, old Father Fisheye that begat the ocean, the worm at my own ear, the serpent turning around a tree" (K, p. 99). Reentering the human dimension of love and sex, seemingly delighted with his new life after surviving God's onslaught, the poet expresses sexual passion in the last line of the poem, "come Poet shut up eat my word, and taste my mouth in your ear" (K, p. 99). (Ginsberg dedicates the *Kaddish* volume to Peter Orlovsky with the same line.) The series of poems beginning with "Kaddish" and culminating in "Magic Psalm," "The Reply," and "The End" embodies Ginsberg's divine visions. At a time when God's presence is seldom felt even in the most sanctimonious settings, Allen Ginsberg, the strange and troubled son of Naomi, found the words and the way to bring God stunningly back to life.

While his memory of Naomi's tragedy inspired Ginsberg to emulate the messianic vision of the Hebrew Kaddish and the Prophets, it also influenced the writing of "Howl." In his most notorious poem, the poet condemns America and celebrates, not Israel, but his own chosen people, the saints of the Beat Generation. In a 1975 letter to the poet Richard Eberhart, Ginsberg provides an important clue to the poem: "What I didn't say to Eberhart: 'Howl' is really about my mother, in her last year at Pilgrim State Hospital—acceptance of her, later inscribed in 'Kaddish' detail." He also says that while he later came to believe in a Buddhist "emptiness," when he wrote "Howl," he still "believed in some sort of God and thus Angels, and religiousness."[4] Despite Naomi's apparent absence from most of "Howl," it is her memory that is behind the poet's apocalyptic vision.

Many readers of the poem have noticed its resemblance to the Hebrew Prophets. Eberhart finds it "Biblical in its repetitive grammatical build-up. It is a howl against everything in our mechanistic civilization which kills the spirit, yet it offers love as redemption."[5] Noting that "Howl" was influenced by the repetition of "He hath" at the beginning of lines in Jeremiah, Paul Portuges claims that Ginsberg is "writing a prophecy in the style of Jeremiah's lament, bemoaning the terrible treatment of his 'angelheaded hipsters' by a society built on ruthless destruction and doom."[6]

In "Howl," Ginsberg defies traditional literary analysis. Combining poetry, prose, autobiography, pornography, and "gibberish," he creates a powerful apocalypse. "Howl" became the most famous underground poem of the sixties and contributed to a new myth of the Beat Generation along with Kerouac's *On the Road* and Burrough's *Naked Lunch*. Because Ginsberg wasn't even sure at first he had written a poem but rather wanted to communicate his deepest and most private feelings to himself and his closest friends, it is indeed remarkable that "Howl" has become one of the most influential poems in English since Eliot's *The Waste Land*.

Ginsberg's own commentary reveals the extremely personal and perilous origins of the poem. Besides telling Eberhart that "Howl" is about his mother's last year in the mental hospital, he says, "A lot of these forms developed out of an extreme rhapsodic wail I once heard in a madhouse,"[7] referring to his mother's experience or to his own sojourn in the mental ward where he met the man to whom the poem is dedicated, Carl Solomon. The poet was determined to battle what he felt was a conspiracy by the capitalist war machine to destroy the psyches of those he loved.

In order to be true to his own experience and that of Carl Solomon, Naomi, the Beats, and others, the poet felt he must capture the natural flow of his mind by using not only the long line, catalogues, repetition, and so on, but also a concept he learned from Cézanne: "juxtaposition of one wo*rd* against another, a *gap* between the two words—like the space gap in the canvas—ther'd be a gap between two words which the mind would fill in with the sensation of existence."[8] By creating such gaps, the poet would encourage the reader to intuit the presence of God.

In the first section, the poet catalogues the exploits of the Beats, who, like Naomi, asserted their personal visions against the norms of sanity and success: "angelheaded hipsters burning for the ancient heavenly connection to the starry dynamo in the machinery of night" (H, p. 9). In "Howl," Ginsberg channels his Jewish memory and fire into his sanctification of the Beats and Carl Solomon, who have replaced his own Jewish family and the prophetic tradition. In long lines—each supposedly a single breath unit but saturated with imagery and breath—the poet alludes to the "ancient" spiritual origins of the Beats' resolve to experience revelation, even if this means they must be reborn in heaven or hell.

The poet of "Howl" delineates a way of life, which involves self-transcendence through drugs, sex, madness, and suicide, and its saints, who are driven to the ends of the earth in order to challenge the status quo. In the long first section in which almost every line begins with "who," Ginsberg presents an almost numbing proliferation of surreal and deranged images and associations of Beat existence with an incredible speed and intensity of enumeration. The problem is that these Beat events, including sexual perversion as well as a predilection for madness and suicide, are never rendered in depth but listed along with everything else in this catalogue of a living, breathing inferno:

> Who bit detectives in the neck and shrieked with delight in policecars for committing no crime but their own wild cooking pederasty and intoxication,
> who howled on their knees in the subway and were dragged off the roof waving genitals and manuscripts . . .
>
> (H, pp. 11–12)

Unlike "Kaddish," where he presents a family engaged in a tragic action and with the poet-son's point of view as the central focus, in "Howl I," Ginsberg offers a long, discordant catalogue of anonymous antics. Instead of individual characters, there is a "mad generation," which seldom talks or thinks.

Perhaps because not even the poet can take this crazy litany with total seriousness, he becomes sardonic and ironic about his own art toward the end of the first section: "who scribbled all night rocking and rolling over lofty incantations which in the yellow morning were stanzas of gibberish" (H, p. 13). It is only at the conclusion of the first section, as he remembers the "foetid halls" of the mental hospitals, that the deeply personal roots of "Howl"—the poet's lonely, tormented quest for prophecy in the aftermath of his mother's madness—come to the surface:

> with mother finally******, and the last fantastic book flung out of the tenement window, and the last door closed at 4 AM and the last telephone slammed at the wall in reply and the last furnished room emptied down to the last piece of mental furniture, a yellow paper rose twisted on a wire hanger in the closet, and even that imaginary, nothing but a hopeful little bit of hallucination—
>
> (H, p. 15)

As rendered in this incredibly long line, which resembles the broken verse paragraphs of the elegy for Naomi, the impassioned utterance of personal suffering, exile, and shame brings the reader back to "Kaddish" and Ginsberg's tormented, prophetic self.

At the end of the first part, Ginsberg articulates his aesthetic, beginning with a tribute to the "all powerful father eternal God," and praises Cézanne's method of juxtaposition, which is integral to the poem. Most forcefully and poignantly, however, he speaks of himself and his art:

> to recreate the syntax and measure of poor human prose and stand before you speechless and intelligent and shaking with shame, rejected yet confessing out the soul to conform to the rhythm of thought in his naked and endless head . . .
>
> (H, p. 16)

Ginsberg was right when he wrote to Eberhart that "Howl" starts "with a catalogue sympathetically and *humanely* describing excesses of feeling and idealization."[9] The Beat mythology of absurd gamesmanship never reaches the spiritual dimension of "the ancient heavenly connection" that the poet strives for in part one; however, Ginsberg is able to express his own vulnerable Jewish sensibility in his long, dynamic lines.

"Howl II" is the poet's denunciation of America, which he believes has destroyed Naomi and threatens the inspired vision he inherited from her. In his usually frank way, Ginsberg describes the details of composition:

> I had an apt on Nob Hill, got high on Peyote, & saw an image of the robot skullface of Moloch in the upper stories of a big hotel glaring into my window; got high weeks later again, the Visage was still there in red smokey downtown Metropolis, I wandered down Powell Street muttering, "Moloch Moloch" all night & wrote "Howl II" nearly intact in cafeteria at foot of Drake Hotel, deep in the hellish vale.[10]

Influenced by Naomi's extreme reactions to America, the prophets' religious condemnations of the unfaithful, and his own vision of Moloch, the evil angel, Ginsberg criticizes a society he cannot tolerate because he believes it destroys all expression of personal feeling and imagination.

"Howl II" is Ginsberg's most savage indictment of the industrial, technocratic society, the monster of mental consciousness:

> Moloch whose love is endless oil and stone! Moloch whose soul is
>   electricity and banks! Moloch whose poverty is the
>   specter of genius! Moloch whose fate is a cloud of sexless
>   hydrogen! Moloch whose name is the Mind!
> (H, p. 17)

The poet creates his incantatory effects through such means as parallelism and the catalogue, including the juxtaposition of the Blakean word "Specter" and the trope "cloud of sexless hydrogen." Ginsberg goes on to condemn America's many crimes against everything he stands for and loves. Because he castigates so convincingly, there is little left to save. Even survival seems out of the question in such a monstrous place. And so, after "Ten years' animal screams and suicides," the entire "Mad generation" smashes "down on the rocks of Time!"

Having confronted the monster that destroys individual experience and drives a generation of sensitive, intellectual madmen to suicide, Ginsberg creates a catalogue of mercy and praise for his mentally disturbed friend Carl Solomon:

> Carl Solomon! I'm with you in Rockland
>   where you're madder than I am
> I'm with you in Rockland
>   where you must feel very strange
> I'm with you in Rockland
>   where you imitate the shade of my mother
> (H, p. 19)

As the last line of this passage shows, the poet's memory of Naomi plays an important psychological function in "Howl." His sympathetic depiction of the Beats and Carl Solomon is instrumental in Ginsberg's attempt to come to terms with Naomi's madness and his own feelings of guilt and shame as her son, the gay Jewish poet-prophet, in the midst of a highly conservative and conformist society.

In defiance of America's merciless mentality, which condemns the least sign of nonconformity, the poet presents a mad surreal comedy of his friendship with Carl Solomon:

> I'm with you in Rockland
> > where you accuse your doctors of insanity and plot the Hebrew socialist revolution against the facist national Golgotha
>
> I'm with you in Rockland
> > where you will split the heavens of Long Island and resurrect your living human Jesus from the superhuman tomb
>
> I'm with you in Rockland
> > where there are twentyfive-thousand mad comrades all together singing the final stanzas of the Internationale
>
> (H, p. 20)

It is as if through the mask of his friend, Ginsberg has once again found a way to praise his Jewish mother's visionary politics, her psychosis, and her tortured prophecy of the key shining in the hospital window, which will unlock the secrets of the universe. He accomplishes this in lines combining comedy and tragedy, surrealism and absurdity, idealism and madness.

Ginsberg begins "Footnote to Howl" with a line consisting of "Holy!" repeated fifteen times and then goes on to proclaim that nearly everyone and everything is holy, including his mother in "the insane asylum." After condemning the United States and describing the demise of his generation of mad geniuses, the poet celebrates universal holiness. Influenced by Blake's prophetic proclamations and by Isaiah's celebrated lines, which have been recited during synagogue services for generations ("Holy holy holy is the Lord of Hosts:/the whole earth is full of his glory"), Ginsberg affirms the mystical consciousness of Naomi, the Beats,

Carl Solomon and "the supernatural extra brilliant intelligent kindness of the soul!"

Whatever formal imperfections the poet and his poem may be accused of, Ginsberg was able to enliven and energize the long free verse line through his gift for sustained lightning strokes of inspiration, utilizing catalogues, parallelism, repetition, surrealist images, and various structural devices. When he writes, as he does in "Howl II," from the deeply personal source of his Jewish memory of exile and suffering, magically transformed into the fire of prophecy, he is an unforgettable poet.

Several other poems in the *Howl* volume show the poet's Jewish penchant for radical politics and black humor without the passionate prophecy of "Howl" and 'Kaddish." "America" consists of a long series of end-stopped declarative sentences. While the theme of the poet's deliberately provocative address to America is serious—that his country should follow the poet's nonconformist example—the tone is often ironic and even comic:

> America why are your libraries full of tears?
> America when will you send your eggs to India?
> I'm sick of your insane demands.
> When can I go into the supermarket and buy what I need with my good looks?
> (H, p. 31)

Everyone knows Ginsberg is not good-looking, at least in the all-American mode, and he is not Catholic and will never be president of the United States; however, the comedy is balanced by the poet's memories of leftist Jewish political ideals that still stir him with passionate rage against the capitalists:

> America when I was seven momma took me to Communist Cell
>   meetings they sold us garbanzos a handful per ticket
>   a ticket costs a nickel and the speeches were free
>   everybody was angelic and sentimental about the workers
>   it was all so sincere you have no idea what a good thing
>   the party was in 1835 Scott Nearing was a grand old man
>   a real mensch Mother Bloor made me cry I once saw
>   Israel Amter plain. Everybody must have been a spy.
> (H, p. 33)

In this long, breathless verse paragraph, the poet re-creates his memories of radical Jewish politics in an ambivalent voice combining sentiment and irony. He then goes on to deride America for its cold war tactics, its obsession with communism, and its discrimination against Indians and blacks. He concludes by proclaiming that he is getting down to business in his own "queer" un-American way.

In "A Supermarket in California," while shopping for groceries along with families who are as alien to him as he must be to them, the poet turns for solace to Walt Whitman and speaks to Walt, who is also lost in the mundane supermarket setting. Both poets are alone in a society that neither appreciates nor understands them. In the concluding lines, Ginsberg captures his own sense of solitude, alienation, and fear. Because he is without the brotherhood of his Beat companions, he finds there is only the courageous and solitary example of Whitman:

> Ah, dear father, graybeard, lonely old courage-teacher
> what America did you have when Charon quit poling his ferry
> and you got out on a smoking bank and stood watching the
> boat disappear on the black waters of Lethe?
>
> (H, p. 24)

The final image of the poem suggests that much of the time the poet who challenges the American supermarket mentality must live in his or her own private hell.

Many of Ginsberg's poems since *Howl* and *Kaddish* do not embody the powerful revelations inspired by Jewish memory and fire but rather an eclectic myth of many gods, including Buddha, Christ, and numerous exotic and occult divinities. Even in the early poems, there is evidence of the poet's ambivalence toward his heritage. In the long drug poem "Aether," from *Reality Sandwiches*, he asserts that the notion of one God is absurd, "IT'S MAD!/GOD IS ONE!" (RS, p. 93). As his later poetry shows, he has turned from the Hebrew God of "Kaddish" to a long list of gods and idols; however, *Reality Sandwiches* also contains the visionary "Psalm III," addressed "To God," in which the poet acclaims the transforming power of the divine spirit. Along with his prophecies, Ginsberg has written a remarkable series of "Psalms," including "Psalm IV," a rare instance of a powerful poem inspired not by Naomi but by the poet's father Louis, whom Ginsberg depicts along with the Father-God, as he describes his East Harlem Blake vision. After the poet sees God's face and hears His magic voice speak of eternity, he imagines that his own father holds his poet-son in his "dead arms."

Along with "Howl," "Kaddish," and the sequence of visionary poems at the conclusion of the *Kaddish* volume, "Wichita Vortex Sutra" is one of Ginsberg's monumental prophetic poems. It is, however, prophecy in a new key. Gone are the strong overtones of Jewish culture: the anarchist and communist antics of Naomi and Aunt Rose, the Yiddish inflections, the black humor, the paranoia of the haunted immigrant mind. "Wichita Vortex Sutra" is not the prophecy of Naomi's son but of Allen Ginsberg, the famous Beat, Buddhist poet, nearing middle age, no longer invoking the sacred names of the patriarchs and the one Hebrew God.

Although his religion has become a cultish amalgam, Ginsberg somehow manages to plumb the depths of his soul to warn against the false bureaucratic language of war and the latent violence of the Bible Belt and all of America, while enunciating the redemptive power of the poetic image. The occasion of the poem is the poet's trip to Wichita by VW bus. While riding, Ginsberg speaks his poetry into a tape recorder, blending his own musings with the passing countryside and the radio voices. As in "Kaddish" and "Howl," the poet wants to prophesy once again from the depths of his loneliness and despair, to express his spiritual self.

Almost unconsciously the poet establishes a contest between the language of his lonely prophecy and the words of the preachers and the politicians of war. He shows there can be no true contest between the clichés of the war machine and the original poetic image:

> A black horse bends its head to the stubble
> > beside the silver stream winding thru the woods
> > by an antique red barn on the outskirts of Beatrice—
> > > > (PN, p. 117)

Resembling a lush pastoral scene depicted on tapestry, this striking image combined with alliteration and assonance is one of the splendid moments in the poem.

Both in form and content, "Wichita Vortex Sutra" bears the imprint of Williams and Pound:

> Language, language
> Ezra Pound the Chinese Written Character for truth
> > defined as man standing by his word
> > > Word picture :   forked creature
> > > > > Man
> > > standing by a box, birds flying out
> > > > representing mouth speech
> > Ham Steak please waitress, in the warm cafe.
> > > > > (PN p. 119)

The short, imagistic lines, the emphasis on word pictures, and the organic rhythms are essential components of the mature art of this poem that Ginsberg learned from his twentieth century American masters.

Although his art is more controlled than in his earlier prophecies, Ginsberg can still issue his fiery denunciations:

> Napalm and black clouds emerging in newsprint
> > Flesh soft as a Kansas girl's
> > > ripped open by metal explosion—
> > > > > (PN, p. 121)

Using poetic images instead of media double-talk to depict the killing in Vietnam, the poet condemns the United States and says it is time for him to "make this nation one body of Prophecy" (PN, p. 126). Emphasizing his own vulnerability and loneliness as well as the need for love, he searches the debris of language for the right words to proclaim a host of strange gods, and then he prophesies the end of the war and the start of a new era:

> I lift my voice aloud,
>   make Mantra of American language now,
>   I here declare the end of the War!
>   Ancient days' Illusion!—
>   and pronounce words beginning my own millennium.
>   (PN, p. 127)

Inspired by his various divinities and by the poetic word, Ginsberg prays for peace and for the memory of his mother:

> Proud Wichita! vain Wichita
>   cast the first stone ! —
>   That murdered my mother
>   who died of the communist anticommunist psychosis
>   in the madhouse one decade long ago
> complaining about wires of masscommunication in her head
>   and phantom political voices in the air
>   besmirching her girlish character.
>   (PN, p. 132)

In "Wichita Vortex Sutra," as in "Kaddish" and "Howl," Ginsberg is induced by the memory of his mother to create the fire of prophecy. Now that he has declared the war's end and moved the stone-faced denizens of Wichita to tears of love, mercy, and forgiveness, he concludes in Blakean fashion by evoking the souls "held prisoner in Niggertown," who are "pining" with love for the "tender white bodies" of the "children of Wichita!" (PN, p. 132).

Many of the poems in *The Fall of America* consist of a transcription of descriptive details and conversation spoken into a tape recorder while the poet and several friends ride across the United States. Although the description is sometimes incisive, the poems lack Ginsberg's transforming prophetic power, but there are moments of fire. In "A Vow," he says he "will haunt these States/ with beard bald head" and declares, "Common Sense, Common law, common tenderness/& common tranquility" are the "means in America to control the money munching/war machine, bright lit industry" (FA, p. 46).

In "A Vow," Ginsberg admonishes "Future bards" to "chant from skull to heart to ass/as long as language lasts" and thinks of the future of his own words:

> Not my language
> but a voice
> chanting in patterns
> survives on earth
> (FA, p. 87)

"Eclogue" reads like a journal or diary of rural counterculture practices and is laced with such magic names as Kerouac, Cassady, Olson, Leary, along with Nixon and Hoover, but there is also condemnation of America:

> In a thousand years, if there's History
> America'll be remembered as a nasty little Country
> full of Pricks, thorny hothouse rose
> Cultivated by the Yellow Gardeners.
> (FA, p. 147)

Even in this ambitious poem, however, Ginsberg seems to write more as a form of work "to ease the pain of living" than to shape the pain, suffering, and horror of his life into prophecy.

In "Jaweh and Allah Battle," from the volume *Mind Breaths*, Ginsberg criticizes the modern state of Israel and the Hebrew God as part of the world's continuous cycle of religious hatred and violence. The strongest hint of his earlier emphasis on Jewishness is in the sixth section of his poem about his father's burial "Don't Grow Old." Now not only the poet's anarchist and communist relatives are gone, including Naomi, but his father is to be buried in the midst of the urban wasteland:

> where there used to be a paint factory and farms
> where Pennick makes chemicals now
> under the Penn Central power station
> transformers & wires, at the borderline
> between Elizabeth and Newark, next to Aunt Rose
> Gaidemack, near Uncle Harry Meltzer
> one grave over from Abe's wife Anna my father'll be buried.
> (MB, p. 86)

The father whom the poet associated with the Father-God in "Psalm IV" goes to his death surrounded by omnipresent signs of industrial America, the "sphinx of cement and aluminum," which the inspired word of prophecy has not moved. Perhaps Ginsberg's memory of Naomi and his prophetic fire have faded in recent years, but not before the creation of "Howl," "Kaddish," "Magic Psalm," "The Reply," "The End," "Wichita Vortex Sutra," and other phenomenal poems. This son of Naomi has given his readers much of the "absolute heart of the poem of life" and revivified the ancient prophetic voice and vision in electrifying poetry.

Chapter 8

David Ignatow

Prophet of Darkness and Nothingness

For many years David Ignatow was a businessman, trying to survive and make a living in one of the few occupations traditionally open to Jews. His poetry reflects his intimate association with the business world and with the harried life of the workingman, who must subsist with neither artistic nor intellectual sanctuary. In one of his earliest published *Notebooks* entries, Ignatow describes an imaginary Jew to whom he bears more than a small resemblance:

> It is interesting that the Jew who is so bent on making money, prospering and aggrandizing position, status, should also have within himself the fanatic prophet of doom and corruption; should persist on one hand as businessman, buyer and seller, with all the rot it implies, and on the other hand scream from the rooftops his denunciations![1]

Under his businessman's hat, David Ignatow the poet has always burned with prophetic fire. When William Carlos Williams characterized the young Allen Ginsberg's poetry as "prose among whose words the terror of their truth has been discovered," he might have been speaking of Ignatow.[2] Unlike Ginsberg's long, frenzied lines filled with kaleidoscopic images, Ignatow's lines tend to be short, almost breathless gasps, barely audible emotional knots that embody the poet's prophetic utterances as he denounces evil and searches his bleak world for signs of humanity.

In a 1961 review, Denise Levertov described a fundamental conflict in Ignatow's verse: "The skeptic and pragmatist in him are inextricably linked with the longing for God in a way that is typically... Jewish. God is questioned, berated, pleaded with here as in the Bible, although in rhythms and in a vocabulary in no way Biblical." Although Levertov was commenting on an early stage in the poet's career, she was right to see him "as essentially a religious poet, one whose dominant underlying preoccupation is with the relations of God and man."[3]

Although he has never been part of a school or group of poets, Ignatow knew and admired the Jewish Objectivist poets, but it was William Carlos Williams who served as his mentor. Besides encouraging the younger poet, Williams inspired Ignatow through his pioneering efforts to revitalize the craft of American poetry via strict adherence to the visual image, colloquial American diction, and "the variable foot," plus other experiments with open forms. After some fifty years of poetic practice, Ignatow's faith in Williams' approach to craft has not wavered. In fact, Ignatow's short, imagistic poems can be read, in part, as an extension of Williams' theory and practice.

Despite his debt to Williams, Ignatow has brought his own heritage to the art of poetry:

> Through his projection of American life Williams has given the rest of the world a feel of itself also and now it is my duty to speak of myself and my mixed heritage, to speak of myself purely if I would perform the same feat myself as an American, a Jew and a world contemporary, a skeptic and a desperate believer in the One.
>
> (N, p. 276)

While he was growing up, Ignatow was given a traditional Jewish education and responded deeply to his heritage. In recent years he has questioned the concept of a personal God and turned to "the religion of physics joined with the mystery of the origin of energy."[4] He has come to believe that we must explore ourselves and the cosmos in a scientific way.

Although the poet recognizes that his religious insights of recent years are not traditionally Jewish, he can still see parallels:

> All this is by the way of saying that we are simply manifestations of the different forms that energy can take. It is a strikingly parallel concept to the belief in the Hebrew religion that all about us, including ourselves, is merely the show of God's handiwork, as the psalms have it. Therefore it can be said that in principle at least the two concepts are religious.
>
> (N, p. 227)

No matter how Ignatow explains his beliefs, Jewishness has played a significant part in his poetic consciousness as revealed in his preoccupation with fathers and sons; his depiction of suffering and humor; and his prophetic denunciations of the same dark, oppressive world that he searches desperately for divine illumination.

One of the sources of the poet's tragic and prophetic art is his hostile relationship with his father. Judaism has always been sustained by successive generations of fathers and sons, beginning with the patriarchs Abraham, Isaac, and Jacob. Contrary to the Freudian depiction of oedipal conflict, the Jewish son was taught to respect and venerate his father in order to keep the tradition alive. By rebelling against his father, the poet implicitly rebels against the tradition of the fathers. Unlike Reznikoff, whose art he greatly admires, Ignatow has not tried to preserve the Jewish past through imaginative memory. Rather, by depicting enmity between his father and himself and then the subsequent clash between himself and his own son, the poet has maintained a tragic link with the generations.

In his later poems Ignatow tends to take the part of both father and child and to empathize with the father more than he did in his early poems; however, even in "Brightness as a Poignant Light," from *Tread the Dark*, the father is a menacing figure:

> As I tread the dark,
> led by the light of my pulsating mind,
> I am faithful to myself: my child.
> Still, how can I be happy
> to have been born only to return
> to my father, the dark, to feel his power
> and die?
>   (TD, p. 3)

Although it is apparent that the poet identifies the father with darkness, authority, and death, the father might also symbolize the Jewish Father-God and the patriarchal tradition, which the poet-son has rejected.

In "Europe and America," from *Poems*, his first book, published thirty years before *Tread the Dark*, the poet describes the conflict between the immigrant father and his American-born son in metaphorical terms:

> My father brought the emigrant bundle
> of desperation and worn threads,
> that in anxiety as he stumbles
> tumble out distractedly;
> while I am bedded upon soft green money
> that grows like grass.
> (P, p. 49)

The metaphorical contrast between the poor, struggling immigrant father and his spoiled American son exists largely in the son's mind. Despite the alienation which the poem depicts, the metaphors are at least witty, if not funny: the peripatetic threads, the figurative bed of money that resembles grass, and so on. Nevertheless, the metaphorical contrast is not funny to the son who imagines it, because it shows how he is separated from his father by two different ways of perceiving the world. It is significant that the father and son never try to communicate; they bear their marked differences in silence.

The alienation between father and son in "Europe and America" can be felt in the son's later reaction to his father in "Prodigal Son":

> I went back for redress,
> I would show my father
> how much better I could act
> in his place, and when I had bound
> myself to his circumstance
> I found my only satisfaction
> in setting him
> adrift.
> (P. p. 134)

The son wants to show his father that he was wrong and to make amends; however, now that the son has achieved fatherhood, he can only feel pride in severing any ties with his father. The last three lines are characteristic of Ignatow's strategy of ending his poems with a sudden and emphatic tag. As if in a moment of revelation, which can be serious, ironic, or humorous, the tag clinches the poem's meaning. In "Prodigal Son," for example, the ending undercuts the rest of the poem. Ignatow's uncanny creation of irony and humor in the midst of serious and even tragic moments, his subtle shifts in mood and tone, come, at least in part, from Yiddish rhythms and inflections. The influence of Yiddish is more pronounced in the poet's comic poems, which I shall turn to later.

In 1938 the poet married the artist and writer Rose Graubart and they had a son, David. Ignatow's account indicates that David was adversely affected by his ambitious and frustrated father's neglect and bad temper. The son began to suffer from mental illness. When his condition grew progressively worse, he had to be hospitalized. The poet has written extensively about the meaning of this personal tragedy. "What has he done to deserve, rather what have I done to deserve his exile? He is like a mark upon me, the mark of Cain. Rather than my son he is more like a brother" (N, p. 245).

If there is a central experience in the poet's life, it is his relationship with his son, which has torn at his psyche, making him feel horrible guilt, because he blames himself for his son's affliction. Some of Ignatow's most effective poems describe his hospital visits to see his son. In "Sunday at the State Hospital" (P, p. 130), he sits across the table from his son, who is staring at his sandwich, which he cannot eat because he is so haunted by the past. In "I Can Be Seen," as he once again visits his ailing son, the poet emphasizes his feelings of guilt and shame:

> So long as I live
> I will be known for this.
> If I have been cruel
> than that was me,
> gripping the handbag
> as I stood waiting for you
> to come out of your ward.
> (P, p. 201)

As the poet explains in his *Notebooks* entries, there was not sufficient room in his life for poetry and his other responsibilities, so he had to sacrifice his son to the muse. Realizing that his intolerance might have caused his sensitive son's breakdown, the desperate poet finds God in his life.

Ignatow's earliest depiction of God is in a comic, metaphorical vein. Indeed, nature besieges the poet's divinity, who does not seem as formidable as the poet's own father:

> God stalks by stubble fields
> in a shivering garment of brown, wrinkled leaves,
> at the heels mud, on His face the weather,
> and in His hand a bunch of unripened torn-up grain.
> God, like a shriveled nut where plumpness
> and the fruit have fed the worm,
> lies sprawled beneath a tree,
> gaunt in His giving.
> 			(P, p. 8)

God's children are also harassed by nature and by such unfortunate socio-economic circumstances as the Depression. Yet these oppressed people can expect little help from Ignatow's vulnerable God.

A more forceful and serious vision of God, inspired by the poet's mentally ill son, appears in the group of poems in section three of *Say Pardon*:

> I felt I had met the Lord.
> He calmed me, calling me
> to look into my child's room.
> He said, I am love,
> and you will win your life
> out of my hands
> by taking up your child.
> 			(P, p. 141)

Only by loving his son can the poet find God's love in his life. Ralph J. Mills believes that this encounter "plainly indicates that the poet must deliver his life from the Lord." This means that the poet must not be concerned with "the realm of potential or idealized virtue" but rather with "the realized gesture of himself toward another person."⁵ Although Mills' reasoning seems plausible, the poem has a heightened style and tone, suggesting religious awe. What is apparent is that this skeptical contemporary poet has a prophetic meeting with God during which he is moved by God's words.

In "For the Living," the poet's God is closer to the Hebrew Lord of justice and judgment than the Lord of love and mercy in "I Felt":

> Said the Lord, I am humble
> of my powers and you
> who are proud I will let live
> as long as my humility abides
> which is forever—
> but I have proclaimed judgment
> against you.
> 			(P, p. 143)

Unlike the divinity of "Autumn Leaves," this God appears to have superhuman powers:

> God said, Have you finished my thinking?
> Now think yourself into stone
> and I will lift you
> and set you upon a mountain.
> 			(P, p. 143)

The stone could represent the tablets containing the Ten Commandments and thereby suggest that the Jew must devote himself to the laws and precepts of Judaism before God will provide His remedy. Only after the person whom God addresses loses his ego and becomes a stone, an inanimate object, part of nature imbued with faith, does God lift him up on the mountain.

Along with some emphasis on the omnipotence and stern judgment of the traditional Hebrew Lord, the poet also pays homage to his religion in a poem about his mother's burial:

> Over your mother's grave
> speak a prayer of bafflement,
> grasp the hand of the rabbi,
> nearest to steady you.
> He recites the prayer
> for you to follow unsteadily
> its meaning. You pray
> to the air.
>   (P, p. 144)

In his *Notebooks*, the poet calls the rabbi's reading of the psalms at his mother's burial "inspiring" and describes Judaism as a "poetic" religion. Although he compares himself unfavorably to the psalmists because he is not "God-inspired as they are," he believes that "this moral drive towards God, this religious context is from my upbringing" (N, p. 89).

In "The Rightful One," the God of love and mercy returns. He is announced by the poet's son, who has sought Him in his illness and who has inspired his guilty father to see Him as someone very close to himself.

> He had come. I saw Him standing,
> his hair long, face exhausted, eyes sad
> and knowing, and I bent my knee,
> terrified at the reality,
> but he restrained me with a hand
> and said, I am a sufferer like yourself.
>   (P, p. 145)

Rising to this rare occasion, the poet says he feels frustrated and remorseful. When this very human divinity asks the poet to show love and mercy to his son, the poet blesses his son and then feels free. This poem has the clear, simple language, the supple speech rhythms, and the remarkably consistent voice that the poet has almost always maintained. It has taken a long time for critics to see that Ignatow's consummate craft enables him to write profoundly within the framework of the short free verse poem.

Ignatow is not a confessional poet. Rather, he heightens and transforms deeply felt personal experience through his art into moments of revelation. These moments are prophetic because they show the poet's encounter with the forces of life and death, good and evil—and his quest for faith in a seemingly unredeemable world. Ignatow's poetry dramatizes the relationship between personal agony and religious meaning. Thus, no matter how much suffering the poet depicts, his poems retain some of the wonder and exaltation of the prophets and psalmists.

A significant mark of Ignatow's Jewishness is his belief in suffering as a source of meaning and "grace": "I deal with the entire range of experience given to each man in his life, as I seek through this apprehension of tragedy the saving grace, the cause for living in the act of serving tragedy itself."[6] It would be almost impossible for a Jewish poet to be unaffected by generations of suffering. Although he has written only occasionally of Jewish history, Ignatow is aware that the Jews have gone through hell:

> We came naked
> the ash smell upon us. We could believe
> it our bodies; no soul stirred in us—
> blackened tongues wilted upon the ground.
> We believed we were dead and in hell,
> piled bodies aspiring before us.
> Although we speak with the tongue of a witness,
> a voice we do not know from the fires, crackling.
> (P, pp. 28–29)

Referring to the Holocaust, Ignatow speaks for the Jewish people, "We," the victims and the survivors, who seek a new life in Jerusalem. Undoubtedly, "the ash smell" has influenced the poet's tragic world view. David Daiches had written that because the modern artist needs "an inwardness with suffering," the Jewish artist might have an advantage, since "he can draw on his own traditions of alienation, of suffering, of being on the *other* side of a dividing line, and use his knowledge to investigate and to project the nature of man."[7] Ignatow has certainly used his Jewish sensitivity to suffering in his art. In suffering he finds the "cry of the human" (P, p. 90).

New York City is this twentieth century poet's Babylon, a place so perverse and sordid, so lacking in decency and civility that the poet exclaims in a prophetic voice: "Come, let us blow up the whole business;/the city is insane" (P, p. 54). Ignatow is usually associated with Williams, but he has also been influenced by T. S. Eliot's dark urban vision and tries to mediate between them, "shaping my own poems out of an identity with Eliot's own problems while seeking for a resolution in the energy and freedom manifest in Williams' work."[8]

Although there is an echo of Eliot's bleak urban imagery in "Come!," the main energy of the poem derives from Ignatow's prophetic repudiation of the city's evils:

> Break down the sordid hospital,
> the cockroach-ridden restaurants,
> the whore-packed hotels
> and business buildings close by for convenience;
> the big night clubs and intimate ones
> in the cellars of old homes,
> where rats and vermin and dark dampness
> used to sport.
> (P, pp. 54–55)

Ignatow the businessman has become "the fanatic prophet of doom and corruption," screaming his denunciations against the sinful city as Jeremiah once did. The poet continues to build his detailed case against the city and its immoral inhabitants until he asks once again for its destruction and exclaims apocalyptically at the end: "But let us wipe out a few hundred million" (P, p. 55).

In "Communion," the poet challenges Whitman's idealization of America by beginning with an ironic description of the rapid rise of capitalistic society until there is nothing left but cemeteries. The poem concludes with another prophetic image of doom:

> It was then the gravediggers slit
> their throats, being alone in the world,
> not a friend to bury.
> (P, p. 67)

Although he has been influenced by Whitman's mystical optimism, Williams' empirical depiction of people and things, and Eliot's ascetic renunciation of modern life, Ignatow combines compassion and condemnation, rage and irony, dream and reality in a unique manner reverberating with echoes of ancient Hebrew voices.

While he criticizes and condemns the city and its citizens, the poet seeks for something to affirm; however, like many other Jewish poets and writers, Ignatow believes there is no escape from tragic reality. He also tends to be skeptical of grandiose intellectual schemes and designs. "No theory," he exclaims, "will stand up to a chicken's guts/being cleaned out" (P, p. 204). Ignatow's poetry is based on crucial moments of experience, "The highest poetry recreates the reality of the moment and in recreating assures itself of immortality, because it is in the process of recreating that poetry is most akin to reality" (N, p. 251). Over a long poetic career, Ignatow has developed his art commensurate to the task of shaping and forming crucial moments, which reveal the truth of life as he imagines it.

Some of the poet's most engaging poems picture dreamlike encounters with tragic strangers on the city's streets and show the need for love and mercy in a sordid world:

> Someone approaches to say his life is ruined
> and to fall down at your feet
> and pound his head upon the sidewalk.
> Blood spreads in a puddle.
> And you, in a weak voice, plead
> with those nearby for help;
> your life takes on his desperation.
> He keeps pounding his head.
> It is you who are fated;
> and you fall down beside him.
> It is then you are awakened,
> the body gone, the blood washed from the ground,
> the stores lit up with their goods.
>   (P, pp. 125–26)

In "The Dream," the poet's identification with the victim is so complete that he, too, becomes a victim, and then, as if awakened from a dream, he sees the sterile, materialistic city whose destruction he called for in "Come!" Again, Ignatow indicates his prophetic viewpoint in his renunciation of the unregenerate city and his identification with and merciful reaction to the suffering victim.

Because the poet skillfully combines a spellbinding mood and tone along with realistic details, "The Dream" has a mysterious element of depth. James Dickey has commented on the power of Ignatow's dreamlike parable poems: "What gives them their unique power is a kind of strange, myth-dreaming vision of modern city life, and the ability to infuse the decor of the contemporary city with the ageless Old Testament fatality of death and judgment."[9] Dickey shows yet again how Ignatow's poetry reflects his prophetic heritage.

In "The Dream," the protagonist's bond with the victim and the stern morality combining judgment and mercy are presented in a dynamic image. The dimension of myth or parable, which Dickey notes, is never tacked on but is suggested by the poet's use of rhythm, voice, mood, and tone as well as visual details. In addition, Ignatow's silences and gaps contribute a mysterious ambience, which accentuates the poem's crucial details. In showing how the protagonist endures one nightmare only to awaken to another, the poet has created a poem of surface lucidity that expresses deep awe and mystery.

In poem after poem the poet presents what Dickey calls the "strange, myth-dreaming vision of modern city life."[10] In "Say Pardon," the narrator is spat upon by a bum but summons the humility and grace to go on with his life. In "Moving Picture," the poet offers a frightening catalogue of the demise of two suicides whose worldly estate is devoured by a greedy and desperate society. "Off to the Cemetery" shows the violent, hopeless lives of Puerto Ricans for whom death seems the only appropriate resolution. In "The Appointment Card," the poet depicts a businessman and other subway riders who are devoid of emotional response to the knifer and his victim. Nothing matters. Even violence becomes ordinary:

> Let us continue to live humiliated
> and defeated because there is nothing to rebel against,
> the cause mundane, a life, another life, another death
> and defeat.
> (P, p. 166)

The businessman is lost in a society where nothing appears meaningful except money and other signs of materialistic success.

Even Ignatow, however, knows that tragedy and suffering are not all there is, because, as some of his poems show, there are also moments of joy and laughter, providing much needed comic relief. These moments seem Jewish in their bittersweet, sardonic humor. The poet's comic side can be evidenced in what might well be his best known poem. In "The Bagel," a man who has dropped a bagel as though "it were a portent" begins to run after it faster and faster in the wind until he "rolls down the street," resembling a bagel and "strangely happy" with himself. Although "The Bagel" has the dreamlike aura of so many of Ignatow's dark urban parables, there is almost no hint of pain, suffering, or degradation, and as the dream continues through to its buoyant conclusion, the rapidly accelerating rhythm and constant motion simulate the image of a man rolling like a bagel.

By countering any negative omens suggested by the "portent," the ending clinches the poem, emphasizing the man's unabashed happiness. The very use of "portent" gives the poem a prophetic tone. It is possible that the narrator is rolling toward some apocalyptic destiny. One could also surmise that the bagel symbolizes the narrator's affirmation of his Jewishness, or at least of Jewish cuisine; however, the poem is so resonant as a madcap dream, resembling a scene from a silent film, it might be best to stop playing detective and let the poem go on its own comic way. Never before has a bagel provided such happiness. It serves to remind us that there is a lighter, comic, joyous side to Jewish existence, which is largely missing from American Jewish poetry, and curiously surfaces in Ignatow's art despite his strong sense of being a sufferer.

Another poem showing Ignatow's flair for irony and humor is "Self-Employed." The point of this poem could be serious. Despite his disdain for his working conditions, the boss cannot fire himself. Indeed, this boss is genuinely perturbed and ready to quit. But he arrives at the truth of his situation in an incongruously funny way:

> You're fired, I yell inside
> after an especially bad episode.
> I'm letting you go without notice
> or terminal pay. You just lost
> another chance to make good.
> But then I watch myself standing at the exit,
> depressed and about to leave,
> and wave myself back in wearily,
> for who else could I get in my place
> to do the job in dark, airless conditions?
> (P, p. 216)

Although this experience takes place in the speaker's mind, it is dramatized as if the entire event occurred on stage, including speech, gestures, and deft comic timing, ending with the question, which, despite its wit, implies that the boss is his own victim. Jews have always had a proclivity for combining laughter and tears, for laughing at their problems, for seeing the ridiculous in the sublime and vice versa, and Ignatow brings this Jewish quality to his verse.

Ignatow's humor is revealed in the inflections of his voice and in the strange twists and turns of thought and feeling rendered in simple, highly expressive language. Skillfully using the Yiddish comic voice in "Nice Guy," Ignatow captures the conflict of the harried businessman, who wants to go to his friend's funeral but can't leave his business:

> I had a friend and he died. Me.
> I forgot to mourn him that busy day
> earning a living.
> (P, p. 217)

Somehow, this poem about death and conflicting loyalties is funny, because of the speaker's blunt, expressive language:

> He was a good guy,
> he meant well, only he had lost his teeth
> and had to swallow whole.
> He died of too much.
>
> (P, p. 218)

Although modulations of Yiddish diction, syntax, rhythm, and tone are evident in many of Ignatow's poems, Yiddish is most apparent in his comic poems.

There is something of the schlemiel in Ignatow's comic persona or mask, the man who has a proclivity for losing and being awkward; however, as Isaac Bashevis Singer, Peretz, and others have shown, the schlemiel or fool often has something of the saint in him. Diaspora Jews have had to develop a stoic, comic, passive mask in order to survive, and Ignatow wears this mask as well as the tragic and prophetic ones in his poetry. It is as if the poet will accept all the pain which comes his way and dares to be driven off the face of the earth. Almost miraculously, a note of irony and humor comes through.

Besides the tragic and comic poems, there is a third type of poem in which, by carrying on a dialogue within himself, the poet is able to achieve a meditative state of stillness and tranquility:

> I believe in stillness,
> I close a door
> and surrender myself
> to a wall and converse
> with it and ask it
> to bless me.
> The wall is silent.
> I speak for it,
> blessing myself.
>
> (P, p. 137)

In this poem, which suggests the image of a Jew praying (dahvening) to a wall, the wall symbolizes the ineffable in the world. When the poet blesses the wall, he blesses himself. Although prayer is only suggested, it dominates the rhythm and tone of the poem. In another poem of this type, "And Step," the poet carries on a dialogue with a stone and comes to know himself through the stone. In "Content," he addresses a mountain as a mountain and as nothing else.

I want to conclude my discussion of Ignatow's verse by studying his poems that probe darkness and nothingness. I have chosen most of these poems from *Facing the Tree* and *Tread the Dark,* but the three "Ritual" poems from *Rescue the Dead* are where I shall begin. These poems along with others signify, as Ralph J. Mills explains, "a decision to proceed from pain and abandonment and to live, though that entails an acceptance of existence as founded upon 'Nothing.'"[11]

At the outset of "Ritual One," the narrator enters a theater and overhears a father and son arguing on stage. This reminds the reader of the poet's painful father and son experiences. Perhaps because of strong personal associations, as he tries to take his seat the narrator feels close to insanity. He hears "doomed voices calling on god the electrode" (P, p. 224). Then he discovers to his horror that the audience and the players are waiting for him to break the neck of a strange man who has taken his seat. Although he is accustomed to the ritual slaughter of pigs and chicken for food, the narrator cannot willingly kill another human being at this early point in the psychodrama; however, the father and son leave their places on stage and try to force him to break the neck of the man in his seat. As violence becomes contagious, the narrator joins in, and the actors acknowledge his violent acts with a bow. He wonders if he should kill everyone and listen to the slowly fading applause. Returning to his seat, he sees children kicking each other in the groin.

This savagery continues in "Ritual Two." As children engage in a violent orgy, the narrator dances with the children, takes off his clothes, makes strange motions, and pretends to give away his money. Meanwhile, the children continuously chant, "Nothing, Nothing!" In the third "Ritual," the poet describes the narrator's reactions to the torture and murder of two children in England recorded on tape by the murderers. Having buried the child of innocence, who once existed within him, the narrator begins to ponder his own innate violence. Being a man capable of murder, he now exclaims, "I'm free."

Because the inhumanity of these poems is so uncharacteristic of Ignatow, I must believe his deranged, violent characters call out for the very love and mercy the poet affirms in most of his poems. The grotesque violence and sickness of this absurdist drama argue, at least implicitly, that "Nothing" is the very place at which man must find something, must leap beyond nothing toward faith. While the usual signs of the poet's Jewishness are missing, in these "Ritual" poems and other later works Ignatow has staked his poetic life on an uncompromising prophetic search for truth, watching and listening for spiritual signs and voices in a terrible wilderness.

In *Tread the Dark* and *Facing the Tree*, the poet continues to wander through his own personal wasteland, his own death in life, as if testing the void to see what it is really like. In "Going Down," from *Facing the Tree*, he descends into a hole in the earth and envisions his own burial. He says his apprehension about burial causes him to go down into the earth. In "Reading the Headlines," he declares he has a burial ground within himself where he buries the dead. Although he is lost and lacks energy to live, he has the dead as his companions. In "The Diner," Ignatow uses the prose poem format to create an absurd episode in a deadpan but humorous Kafkian style. The protagonist, who is so lost and confused he cannot even determine how he got ham and eggs instead of a sandwich, carries on a continuous debate with himself about his circumstances, until in the hilarious last stanza, he decides it is not only possible he made the ham and eggs; he is, indeed, the owner of the diner.

In another prose poem, "The Assassin," a man who stares into a gun barrel describes his remaining instant on earth before the killer pulls the trigger. "Thinking" depicts a man, like Jonah, trapped inside a fish, who ponders all the macabre possibilities of his fate, such as being swallowed by a bigger fish, and then surmises it is the very right and freedom to think that has caused his demise. In yet another poem about fathers and sons, "In a Dream," the poet at fifty encounters himself at eighteen outside his father's house, and the older self advises the younger self that life will not turn out the way he wants it to. He will want to hurt his elders, and they will be shocked and distressed. After all this advice, the eighteen year old self tells the fifty year old self to go to hell and walks away. Whether in the prose poem or the short lyric, Ignatow has learned how to use narrative techniques as well as the image to render his parables of a tragic world, which is also absurd and surreal.

As if to show that he has lost none of his poetic energy with the years, many of Ignatow's poems in *Tread the Dark* are powerful and apocalyptic. The poet continues to explore a world dominated by death and nothingness. In an untitled prose poem, the twenty eighth poem in the volume, Ignatow says he is "dreaming of the funeral of the world." After having buried himself, it is time for the poet to bury everyone else.

In another untitled prose poem in *Tread the Dark*, the poet provides the reader with a clue to his unusual and disturbing vision:

> I would like to become nothing for the pleasure of the great leap beyond being that becoming nothing alone can achieve. I can become nothing because I am something and I am something because it can lead to nothing. Can I ask of my life more than that it bring me to its transcendence, that I should be in search of it, as the work of being itself?
>
> (TD, p. 63)

Ignatow's relentless search for meaning in a world of nothingness and horror resembles the existential Jewish theology of Richard Rubenstein in *After Auschwitz*:

> No people has come to know as we have how deeply man is an insubstantial nothingness before the awesome and terrible majesty of the Lord. We accept our nothingness—nay, we even rejoice in it—for in finding our nothingness we have found both ourselves and the God who alone is true substance.[12]

Ignatow combines the stern morality and apocalyptic vision of the prophets with elements of absurdism and surrealism and a dark existentialist philosophy, which has resulted from unbelievable genocide in this century. His art renders with solemn power the contemporary Jew's "absurd, tragic, and free" situation, and suggests, as Rubenstein postulates, that "The limitations of finitude can be overcome only when we return to the Nothingness out of which we have been thrust. In the final analysis, omnipotent Nothingness is Lord of all creation."[13]

In Ignatow's poetic universe, however, nothing is not an end in itself. It is part of the poet's imaginative vision but not all of it. In the tenth poem of *Tread the Dark*, he falls into oblivion:

> I hear breathing
> Something must be said
> of nothing
>
> I am as queer as the conception of God
> I am the god and the heaven
> unless I scatter myself
> among the animals and furniture of earth
>
> (TD, p. 10)

Nothing will not suffice, the poet concludes, and then draws an analogy between his own strange fate and that of the divine. It is as if the poet has to imagine his own nothingness and death before he can conjure the full spiritual dimensions of his life.

Although Ignatow may now believe "There is no other universe than I am, no other power but I am made of the same materials as the stars and space,"[14] he still expresses the awe and wonder toward creation that the psalmists and prophets once did. In his own solitary, rebellious way, he is involved in a religious quest similar to that of the biblical poets. Although the terminology has changed, the essence of the ancient vision remains:

> I want to be buried
> under the angel of a tree
> among the cherubim of grass
> and the lion of the wind softly
> in my ear and the lamb of the rain.
>
> (TD, p. 70)

In this passage the poet's language echoes the sanctity and grandeur of the psalmists. "A Meditation" also resounds with the exultation, awe, and mystery of biblical poetry:

> I want to sacrifice myself
> I want to be God's confidant and right hand
> I want mercy and pity and love and gentleness
> and warmth and honor and blessing and victory
> over my sadness
>
> (TD, p. 44)

I believe that in these poems from *Tread the Dark* Ignatow emerges as a prophet of darkness and nothingness with a deeply spiritual vision, which he has not yet fully articulated, but he is undoubtedly working to find the right words.

In "Kaddish," one of his most impressive recent poems, Ignatow combines an elegy for his mother with a hymn to Mother earth:

> Earth now is your mother, as you were mine, my earth,
> my sustenance and my strength,
> and now without you I turn to your mother
> and seek from her that I may meet you again
> in rock and stone. Whisper to the stone,
> I love you. Whisper to the rock, I found you.
> Whisper to the earth, Mother, I have found her,
> and I am safe and always have been.
>
> (WTE, p. 40)

Besides its incantatory rhythms, this poem is dynamic because the poet unites his hymn to the earth as primal source with his expression of love for his mother. It is significant that Ignatow, like Ginsberg, entitles his elegy for his mother after the Jewish mourner's Kaddish, which never speaks of death but affirms God and His messianic kingdom with its hope of immortality.

And so I shall leave the poet poised in prayer over his typewriter, this avowed agnostic, who in his preoccupation with fathers and sons, his immersion in suffering and tragedy as well as his proclivity for humor, and his prophetic quest for truth in darkness and nothingness reveals himself to be a profoundly Jewish poet. So much of the meaning of David Ignatow's poetry comes from his struggle to adapt the tradition of the prophets to his own vulnerable American life, a dangerous but inspiring mission for "an American, a Jew, and a world contemporary, a skeptic and a desperate believer in the One" (N, p. 276).

Chapter 9

Philip Levine

Prophet of Oneness

In "The Turning," one of Philip Levine's early poems, the narrator describes himself as a man who having examined himself thoroughly finds nothing to bless or to give. At the end of the poem he declares, "The first Jew was God; the second/Denied him; I am alive."[1] These lines reveal Levine's tough, even cynical individualism but also his remembrance of the Jewish heritage, which is at the source of his vision of human oneness. The complex expression of Jewishness in Levine's verse begins with passionate evocation of exile and suffering in *Not this Pig* and *They Feed They Lion* followed by the poems of *1933* in which he elegizes his Jewish family. In *The Names of the Lost*, *Ashes*, and *Seven Years from Somewhere*, the poet combines his lament for the lost world of his fathers with elegiac praise of the Spanish anarchists, whose vision resembled the Hebrew prophets' injunction to establish God's kingdom on earth.

In 1933 when the poet was a five year old boy, his father Harry died. The father and son relationship is a predominant motif in Levine's poetry, and one can only surmise that the poet's need to keep alive his father's memory is a major force behind his art. The poet's father and his mother were born in Russia. Levine's mother came to the United States when she was eight. His father left czarist Russia for England and served in the English army during World War I. While running a prisoner of war camp for the British in the Middle East, Harry Levine deserted and came to the United States after the war.

Born and raised in Detroit, Levine uses this grimy, seething, racially troubled, industrial city as the setting for many of his poems. While in Detroit, the poet worked in factories, and he has never forgotten the workers:

> these were the men and women I met as an industrial worker and bum in America; they were mainly Southerners—so many of whom had come to Detroit in my boyhood to find work—and they were closer, I believe, to some great truths about people, to the truth that we are the children of God, and that we were meant to come into this world and live as best we could with the beasts and the trees and plants and to leave the place with our love and respect for it intact, and to leave it our selfs [sic].²

Although Levine is from the city and writes extensively of urban life, he is also attracted to nature and to rural people. In both the city and the country, he finds suffering and even terror but also grounds for belief in the courage, endurance, and glory of the human spirit.

While living in Detroit, the poet may have met people who inspired him, but he also learned about racism and anti-Semitism and he became angry and afraid

> Coming from a Jewish household, I had a very heightened sense of what fascism meant. It meant anti-Semitism; it meant Hitler. I mean he was like the king fascist. And then there were these minor league fascists, but they essentially meant the same thing. And I saw the threat reaching right into my house and snuffing me out if something wasn't done to stop the advance of fascism. And Detroit was an extraordinarily anti-Semitic city.
> (DA, pp. 92–93)

Levine's fear and hatred of fascism and of anti-Semitism in any form have affected his way of seeing the world.

"Saturday Sweeping" describes a man cleaning his apartment. The narrator talks of factories, workers, and his own loneliness. Then he imagines who might come to the door. Among the candidates are "the great talking dogs/that saved the Jews" (L, p. 31). In an interview, Levine describes the personal experience behind this reference:

> The "I" in the poem, the "me," is looking forward to what's going to come in Detroit. He's alone, he's got this apartment, he's sweeping it out. He talks about the isolation of each life in this little apartment. He says "If anybody knocks on your door, it will be this, it will be that, it will be the great talking dogs that saved the Jews." Well, that was a little story I was told as a child. My grandfather would put me to bed with little tales. One of them was about a talking dog who would be privy to the secrets of the mad Russian murderers, and then come and warn the Jews.
>
> (DA, p. 46)

Over the years Levine has come to believe that nations and governments are responsible for the violent oppression that has plagued the Jews and other peoples throughout the world and he has been attracted to anarchism.

During several long sojourns in Spain, Levine identified with the people: "In a year I began to become Catalan in a small way. I felt a great sympathy for the people; they looked familiar to me. I think half of them are Jews anyway, and they look very Jewish. They look a lot like me" (DA, pp. 4–5). The poet became increasingly interested in Spanish anarchism and its leaders previous to and during the Spanish Civil War, such as Francisco Ascaso and Buenaventura Durruti. Many of Levine's poems have been in honor of these men and their cause. The basic tenets of anarchism are violent opposition to all forms of governmental control; the belief that only individual freedom can lead to liberty for all; and the concept that work should be shared equally and should be the basis for political and economic rights and privileges. The Spanish anarchists controlled two large syndicalist unions: the CNT and the FAI. These unions advocated control of government and industry through direct action, such as strikes and sabotage, and the implementation of planned anarchist communities.

Anarchism is part of Levine's Romantic vision: "My religious anarchism at times overwhelms me and my writing becomes more frankly romantic—that is it asserts defiantly the boundless possibilities of the human, the unique holiness of animals and plants."[3] Paul Zweig believes that Levine is among those American poets who have imagined "religion turned loose from the rituals of orthodoxy; religion freed from the anti-worldly, anti-sensual prison of churches and institutions":

> American poets too have begun to create a new language of revelation. It is a syncretic language, gleaned in Oriental cults, American Indian songs, the Kabbala, the subversive, messianic strain of Christianity and Judaism. However spurious it may seem in the hands of lesser poets, at its heart, it is a deeply "pagan" language, which declares that all orders of experience, all the orders of perception, are one.

According to Zweig, "Philip Levine's work belongs to this new research of language and feeling."[4]

Levine's radical idealism has its precedent in the long history of Jewish devotion to social and political justice. Socialism, communism, and anarchism can be seen as secular manifestations of Jewish religious principles and practices. As Will Herberg's account reveals, it is no accident that many of the originators and leaders of these movements were Jewish:

> The passion for social justice runs through Judaism from the earliest writings to the present day. No modern attack upon economic exploitation can equal in earnestness and power the denunciations of the prophets against those who "grind down the faces of the poor." No modern warning against the evils of authoritarianism is so arresting as the words of Samuel rebuking the people of Israel for desiring to subject themselves to the yoke of kingship. And the numerous rabbinical provisions protecting workers against their employers and helping to mitigate the lot of the poor, the friendless and the underprivileged are a sign that the original biblical impetus was not lost in later Judaism.[5]

Although such poets as Ginsberg, Rukeyser, and Levine challenge their tradition, they also give it new imaginative life by reasserting in their art the prophetic ideals of freedom, justice, and glory for all.

The one continuous element in Levine's poetry deriving from his Jewish heritage is his concern with exile and suffering. In "Baby Villon," the last poem in *Not this Pig*, the poet-protagonist describes meeting the tiny ex-prize fighter Baby Villon, who speaks of himself to the narrator as a ubiquitous but plucky victim:

> He tells me in Bangkok he's robbed
> Because he's white; in London because he's black;
> In Barcelona, Jew; in Paris, Arab:
> Everywhere and at all times, and he fights back.
>   (NTP, p. 80)

In this catalogue of parallel references, the narrator draws a general portrait of the victims of discrimination.

After he inquires about the poet's father, Baby Villon evokes through suggestive details the loss of his father and brother during the Algerian war for independence:

> The windows of the bakery smashed and the fresh bread
> Dusted with glass, the warm smell of rye
> So strong he ate till his mouth filled with blood.
> "Here they live, here they live and not die,"
>
> And he points down at his black head ridged
> With black kinks of hair. He touches my hair,
> Tells me I should never disparage
> The stiff bristles that guard the head of the fighter.
>   (NTP, p. 80)

Holding the poet in his arms, this tiny man of pain and courage epitomizes much of the suffering, exile, and perseverance of the human spirit, which underlies Levine's art.

In his book of interviews *Don't Ask*, Levine describes giving a poetry reading in Wisconsin and meeting Abraham Chapman, the distinguished editor of the anthology *Jewish-American Literature*, who asked the poet to read "Baby Villon" and told him it was a Jewish poem. The poet's commentary about the poem and the Jewish people shows his agreement with Chapman:

> I saw what he meant: it is a celebration of courage and integrity and the difficulty of life wherever it takes place. We were a people scattered all over the world who knew what it was to be scattered all over the world. We knew what it was to be underdogs and to survive in the face of the enmity and disrespect of others. We knew we were a noble people no matter what anyone told us to the contrary. Our great cultural heritage was that we could feel the suffering of any people and know that any people was as good as any other.
>   (DA, p. 143)

The poet's eloquent analysis of "Baby Villon" is a declaration of his Jewishness. In poem after poem he writes about those who suffer and fight back and refuse to yield to the terrifying demons of the earth.

Levine has also written about his own experience of exile and suffering as a stranger in America, most notably in the sequence "Silent in America." In the first of eight sections, the speaker expresses an extreme sense of dislocation and chaos:

> Since I no longer speak I
> go unnoticed among men;
> in the far corners of rooms,
> greeted occasionally
> with a stiff wave, I am seen
> aslant as one sees a pane
>
> of clear glass, reflecting both
> what lies before and behind
> in a dazzle of splendid
> approximations.
>   (NTP, p. 43)

This is vintage Levine: lucid, rhythmic, colloquial, and dramatic. Levine is able to create a vivid scene with a few strokes of his pen. In clear and natural language, the poet skillfully uses an extended simile and highly accentuated speech rhythms to dramatize his feelings of being lost in his own country, of being a marginal man, a man without a sense of identity.

Lost in America, the poet is surrounded by discrimination and violence:

> For a black man whose
> name I have forgotten who danced
>   all night at Chevy
>   Gear and Axle,
>   for that great stunned Pole
> who laughed when he called me Jew
>   Boy . . .
>   (NTP, p. 48)

Until the Pole's anti-Semitic slur, Levine never mentions his Jewishness. Now, whether he likes it or not, he has been branded by another as a Jew, so, at least in a negative sense, he has a Jewish identity. As Hitler and others have shown, there are always those who will settle the thorny questions of Jewish identity.

Perhaps because of his inadequate sense of self, the poet tries to live imaginatively through others. For example, he reacts so strongly to a stranger in a Los Angeles bar he almost weeps, and then he makes a vow:

> Let me have
> the courage to live
> as fictions live, proud, careless,
> unwilling to die.
> (NTP, p. 50)

This vow reflects Levine's urge to identify with the pain, suffering, and loneliness of others as a literary communion, a way toward fellowship for the wandering Jewish poet, alone and speechless. It also reflects the ardor and restlessness of the Levine persona or mask, a man who wants to break through all masks to be close to the heart of life. At the poem's conclusion, the poet invites others, including the reader, to join him in his lonely and silent American odyssey.

Levine's preoccupation with suffering, exile, and injustice continues in *They Feed They Lion*, a remarkable book filled with rage against the sins of a society that victimizes many of its citizens. Some of his best work is in the book's second section. His principle subjects are the factory workers of Detroit, mostly black and white rural Southerners, who showed the poet how to see more deeply than he had previously thought possible both the horror and beauty of the world.

In the initial poem, "Cry for Nothing," the poet pits the human attempt to speak one's name, to declare one's humanity, against the dehumanizing forces that say "no" and cause the speaker to declare "nothing" at the end:

>   Say
>   Your name to stump,
>   to silence, to the sudden wings
>   of the air, say
>   your name to yourself.
>   It doesn't matter cause
>   it all comes back
>   a red leaf prick
>   in your crotch, burr balls
>   tapping at your ankles
>   with their Me! Me!
>   (L, p. 17)

Levine uses colloquial diction and rhythms very effectively here. Emulating the speech of the workers, he utilizes constant alliteration of s in the first four lines and parallel syntax in lines six through ten. In lines eight, nine, and eleven, he mixes highly stressed rhythms with assonance and alliteration.

As the poet wonders what happened to the once mythic nature of this northern place that became the factories and foundries of Detroit, he sees a brown-skinned child staring at him while he waits in his car for the traffic light to change. As if transfixed by her "frozen eyes," the poet sees a living inferno:

>   The charred faces, the eyes
>   boarded up, the rubble of innards, the cry
>   of wet smoke hanging in your throat,
>   the twisted river stopped at the color of iron.
>   We burn this city every day.
>   (L, p. 21)

With horrifying images suggesting the degradation of the Holocaust, Levine pictures people who have been devastated by forces beyond their control. The overall impression of this passage is that of a smoldering prison where death in life is the primary punishment. Because the people have been dehumanized by terrifying circumstances, their human features have become inanimate. They resemble the ruins of abandoned and wrecked buildings. The last line condemns all who refuse to acknowledge these victims of man's inhumanity to man.

The images of these individual poems cumulatively symbolize a strange, almost indefinable force. For example, the opening lines of "Detroit Grease Shop Poem" later reappear in altered form in the first stanza of "They Feed They Lion":

> Four bright steel crosses,
> universal joints, plucked
> out of the burlap sack—
> "the heart of the drive train"—
> the book says.
> (L, p. 22)

After the poet describes himself at work among his grease shop peers, he concentrates on a raindrop leaking through the roof that lands on the arm of a worker, who sees it as "rare or mysterious," as if it were a drop of water or a meteor flaming on his flesh. In the midst of automotive parts, there are crosses. At the center of a U Joint is a part called a cross, which is shaped like a cross.

The poet sees spiritual signs, including angels, in Detroit's industrial wilderness. As he describes a scene of domestic conflict, he hears angels sigh from the shirts a woman irons. In the second of the Detroit "Angel" poems, the troubled protagonist declares that angels saved him from his dangerous surroundings. Garbage, snow, and old cars are all blessed by angels.

It is paradoxical that angels are so prevalent in the secular poetry of this century. Even Wallace Stevens, whose "Sunday Morning" includes the most eloquent rebuttal of Christianity by a modern American poet and who in that same poem and other works advocated a personal and hedonistic religion of the earth, had his "Necessary Angel of Reality." It is more likely, however, that Levine's angels were inspired by the angels of Alberti, Blake, or Rilke. Although they have been largely concealed from Hebrew Scripture, angels and demons can be found in rabbinic literature and in Jewish mystical and occult writings.

In the Detroit poems, the poet molds powerful realistic details, action, and speech into a vision of lamentation and praise. The fourth of the "Angels of Detroit" poems concerns the angel

Bernard, who believes that only divine redemption might, beyond momentary pleasures, heal the heat and flames of his earthly suffering:

> He wants it all tonight.
> The long hard arms of a black woman,
> he wants tenderness, he wants
> the power to die in the
> chalice of God's tears.
>
> (L, p. 26)

As he cries himself to sleep in his unkempt hut, angel Bernard still seems trapped by his worldly existence. Nonetheless, no matter how arduous he shows life on earth to be, Levine affirms survival. Salvation must come from a prophetic commitment to mortal life.

The sixth "Angel" poem begins with the last factory shift and a catalogue of plants. The earthy plants are superseded by the toilets, rats, and maggots of the factory, which the last shift is about to leave. In the midst of squalor, the workers lie down with the angels. The poet's prophetic fire originates from his almost brutal enunciation of poverty and suffering. Levine affirms the workers' angelic hope in the midst of grease and flames.

In "An Afterthought: 'They Feed They Lion,'" Levine speaks of his life as a factory worker in Detroit during the Korean War. "Day by day I lived a life that would later become my poetry, but I didn't know it then." It was in the factories that the poet met the workers who profoundly changed his life:

> I found them a very hardy people, physically and morally. They lived by strong codes of decency and honor, yet they were warm and giving to me, an educated outsider, as though our common condition made us brothers and sisters. I was awed by their rebelliousness; it seemed to spring from a powerful faith in their own worthiness as men and women, as children of God.

Levine's imaginative remembrance of these workers inspired one of his most powerful poems:

Whether they voiced their angers or their hopes, their words shuddered and leaped like living things. I'd never before heard people speak with such authority. I kept my ears open, for even then I was a poet. "They Feed They Lion" is their poem. The rhythm, grammar, and details are theirs, as I remembered them fifteen years later, in 1968 when the country seemed to be hanging on the edge of civil war with millions of insulted people ready to burn their prisons. I tried to pay my small homage.

Levine's empathy for the workers' dignity, courage, and honor in the midst of "hell" is integral to the apocalyptic vision that he renders in "They Feed They Lion."

Symbolizing the workers' sense of the world's horror and beauty and Levine's rage at the terrifying energy that devours human hopes and aspirations, all the industrial and rural images of the Detroit poems merge in a unique poem of revelation, "They Feed They Lion." The lion is the final and crucial reference in each of the five stanzas. The poet says he was influenced by a passage in Christopher Smart's "Jubilate Agno," where the lion roars itself into being. He might also have been moved by the lions of the twenty second psalm: "Ravening and roaring lions/open their mouths wide against me." The psalmist envisions a dying man confronted by his enemies. And the man cries out, "My God, my God, why hast thou forsaken me."

Levine does not directly address the Lord in his poem, but the voice of "They Feed They Lion" does convey the wonder and terror of the human spirit confronted by an ineffable force. Levine's lion symbolizes an awesome power which both creates and destroys. This raging force grows from grease, slime, acid, trees, fences, and old cars. Paul Zweig stresses that Levine "has learned to focus intensely on the 'correspondences' which bind together different orders of experience." In Zweig's view, "Stones and forests, the conflagrations of poverty, the Spanish landscape, the inhumanity of urban America, are yoked together into a structure of revelation which becomes the real subject matter of Levine's poetry."[6]

The poet imagines the industrial workers' vision of the earth, but he does more than synthesize the imagery of the previous poems in the sequence. All the rage, pity, and wonder he has expressed at the mysteries of the world culminate in the concluding stanza:

> From my five arms and all my hands,
> From all my white sins forgiven, they feed,
> From my car passing under the stars,
> They Lion, from my children inherit,
> From the oak turned to a wall, they Lion,
> From they sack and they belly opened
> And all that was hidden burning on the oil-stained earth
> They feed they Lion and he comes.
>
> (L, p. 34)

What Levine is inspired to prophesy in this poem is the dreaded force flowing through all beings that are born, suffer, and die, a majestic force which makes all the earth's creatures holy and yet devours them, their hopes and ideals. This kingly lion of the earth is an awesome imaginative creation.

In "Angel Butcher," Levine envisions a ritual murder. The speaker, who works at a slaughter house, describes meeting Christophe (Christ bearer). After answering the latter's questions about the deadly machinery and sharing mutual disappointments, the narrator prepares Christophe for death. Christophe is willing to die to atone for the human sin of slaughtering animals. Christophe's wrist resembles a hen's throat. The slaughterer feels "blood thudding in the ring/his fingers make." As he prepares for his death, Christophe smiles and "looks down" at the "dark valley where the cities/burn":

> When I hit
> him he comes apart like a
> perfect puzzle or an
> old flower.
>   And my legs
> dance and twitch for hours.
>
> (L, p. 33)

At the end, as the slaughterer agonizingly dances in response to Christophe's death, there is great power to Levine's words. He pictures this scene of ritual suffering and death with a visionary intensity.

In 1933 the poet turns back to the memory of his Jewish family. Beginning with his early poems, the poet's remembrance of his father and grandfather is a constant theme in his verse. For example, in "Who Are You?" from *Not this Pig* the father addresses his son, who is only six years old, and calls attention to some of the problems and conflicts the boy faces as a young American Jew. He wonders how his son will react to anti-Semitic remarks, because he is being raised in an assimilated manner complete with Easter eggs and the Sunday funnies.

As he sees his face mirrored in his son's face, the father invokes Israel's ancient heritage:

> To see your face in mine,
> My father's face as well,
> As well as I remember
> Marked with the mark of Cain
>
> Somewhere beyond the Flood
> We wandered hand in hand
> In a country we remember
> Somewhere in our blood . . .
>
> (NTP, p. 35)

In language marked by its religious grandeur, the father remembers the tradition which he and his son share: the ancient land of Israel and centuries of Jewish exile. It is this mythic country of the blood that Levine and the other American Jewish poets of memory and fire consciously and unconsciously commemorate in their art.

Levine chooses the year of his father's death as the title of his next book. In *1933*, the poet memorializes his father, mother, grandmother, grandfather, uncle, and other family members. It is almost as if in these elegiac tributes the poet evades the white heat of his earthly vision to find solace in the spiritual world of the dead.

In "Zaydee," the first poem in the volume, the poet pictures his grandfather with the enigmatic signs of mock-divinity:

> I held the spotted hands that passed over
> the breasts of airlines stewardesses,
> that moved in the fields like a wind
> stirring the long hairs of grain.
>
> Where is the ocean? the flying fish?
> the God who speaks from a cloud?
> He carries a card table out under the moon
> and plays gin rummy and cheats.
>
> (1933, p. 3)

In the first stanza, the grandfather's magical hands move gracefully over flesh and fields. The series of rhetorical questions in the next stanza indicates that if God still exists he resembles the card-playing grandfather. In this reduction of God from mythic and religious splendor to humble human proportions, the poet writes with discordant irony and humor. His Lord is similar to Naomi's portrait of God as a hungry old bachelor in "Kaddish" and Ignatow's suffering Lord in "The Rightful One," who tells the overwrought father to bless his son.

The texture of "Zaydee" has always reminded me of the heavily stressed rhythms, constant repetition, and dreamlike images and leaps of association in Roethke's "The Lost Son." Levine is a sophisticated poet, who has assimilated a number of influences, such as Blake, Whitman, Smart, Williams, and Roethke. I am not implying that "Zaydee" or other poems in *1933* are derivative; however, the form and content of Levine's art changes significantly in these poems of memory.

In "Goodby," the poet describes his relatives anxiously gathered for a funeral—presumably the funeral of his father. When the young son visits the open grave, he begins to dream. Near a pond and white ducks the grandfather cleans the boy's ears with a match and handkerchief, and he also holds an amber jar to a woman's nose. At the poem's conclusion, the son encounters a sparrow, which he notices outside his window. When the sparrow says "Come here," the boy goes to an alley and sees a peddler's cart piled high with refuse:

> I saw the sheenie-man pissing
> into a little paper fire
> in the snow, and laughed.
> The bird smiled. When I unlatched
> the window the bird looked back
> three times over each shoulder
> then shook his head.
> He was never coming back inside,
> and rose in a shower
> of white dust above
> the blazing roofs
> and telephone poles.
> (1933, p. 61)

The message is summed up in the last two lines of the poem: "It meant a child/would have to leave the world" (1933, p. 61). In this sustained visionary passage, Levine writes with dramatic concentration of detail, gesture, and association. Big city factories, oppressed workers' lives, rage against injustice, the whole harsh social fabric of *They Feed They Lion* has been replaced by the son's nostalgia for the lost world of the fathers symbolized by the sparrow, which flies away from the mortal world and rises up toward spiritual wholeness, understanding, and peace.

"Uncle" celebrates a man who is closer to the Jewish tradition than anyone else in Levine's verse. In his description of his uncle, the poet combines sacred and profane references:

> I remember the forehead born
> before Abraham
> and flecked with white paint . . .
>
> Prophet of burned cars
> and broken fans, he taught
> the toilet the eternal,
> argued the Talamud
> under his nails.
> (1933, p. 62)

The poet admires this simple man, who personifies the Jewish heritage in an unassuming way. At the end of the poem, the poet refers to the yahrzeit candle lit in his uncle's memory burning in the glass of fat. Because he combines the earthy sensibility of the workers with the spirit of his religious tradition, the uncle is a unique personage in Levine's work.

In "1933," the volume's title poem, there is no chronological time, because past and present are part of an all-encompassing vision uniting the living and the dead, light and dark, reality and imagination. In a moment of revelation, the poet sees his father and other departed souls in a luminous spiritual light. Through most of "1933" the poet speaks to his dead father. He explains that the world has changed considerably since his father went away and he, the son, now has his own tall son.

Then the world undergoes a strange and terrifying metamorphosis; however, the poet is able to purge his fear of death by imagining the dead are somehow reborn:

> In the cities of the world
>   the streets darken with flies
>   all the dead fathers fall out of heaven
>   and begin again . . .
>   (*1933*, p. 66)

Enduring an odyssey as terrifying as death itself, the poet believes the dead fathers are resurrected in his apocalyptic vision.

After encountering a number of frightening dream images, the poet sees his mother, his two brothers, and his wife through the burning darkness. As he has so often before, he remembers his boyhood and his father, who writes in a black book and pays his debts. Then, says the poet, "I would be a boy in worn shoes splashing through rain" (*1933*, p. 67). The dead father lives again because of the transforming power of the son's art.

In "Hold Me," the final poem of *1933*, the poet praises the dead once more in a way reminiscent of "Zaydee" and "Goodby." The fourth and fifth stanzas of "Hold Me" are particularly analogous to the fourth and fifth stanzas of "Zaydee":

> Was I dust that I should fall?
> Was I silence that the cat heard?
> Was I anger the jay swallowed?
> The black elm choking on leaves?
>
> In May, like this May, long ago
> my tiny Russian Grandpa—the bottle king—
> cupped a stained hand under my chin
> and ran his comb through my golden hair.
>
> <div align="right">(<i>1933</i>, p. 68)</div>

In both poems the grandfather, who comforts the grieving son, is given mock-divine attributes, symbolized in "Zaydee" by his omnipresent hands and by the "stained hand" that comforts the boy in "Hold Me." As in a number of the *1933* poems, Levine combines elevated and coarse language and imagery ranging from "horse turds" to stars.

In the stirring climax, the poet enters the spiritual realm of death to join his fathers:

> I am the eye filled with salt,
> his child climbing the rain, we are
> all the moon, the one planet, the hand
> of five stars flung on the night river.
>
> <div align="right">(<i>1933</i>, p. 68)</div>

This passage epitomizes Levine's temporary search for sanctuary beyond the earth's raging inferno.

In many of his poems since *1933*, Levine combines his lament for the lost world of his fathers and his prophetic rage at suffering and oppression to commemorate the Spanish anarchists and their revolutionary ideals:

> Let me be clear. When I refer to myself as an anarchist I do not mean to invoke the image of a terrorist or even a man who would burn the deed to his house because "property is theft," which I happen to believe is true. I don't believe in the validity of governments, laws, charters, all that hide us from our essential oneness. "We are put on earth a little space," Blake wrote, "That we may learn to bear the beams of love." And so in my poems I memorialize those men and women who struggled to bear that love.
>
> (DA, p. xi)

While he is aware of the anarchists' use of violence, Levine believes in their glorification of equality and oneness.

"To P.L., 1916–1937" is about a man (a soldier, not the poet,) who suffered and died for the anarchist cause. In this and other elegies to the anarchists, the poet honors a secular faith, which he believes anoints its heroes and martyrs with holiness. Although the soldier of the Republic is dead, he lives on. A peasant woman who discovers his corpse, takes his boots, gray socks, and knife and utilizes them in her own life. Because she is haunted by P.L.'s fists, which resemble faces and symbolize, as hands often do in Levine's verse, the human spirit or soul, the woman blesses the soldier. Later she gives his boots and socks to a nephew. Although P.L.'s corpse has been abandoned, his life of dedication to the anarchist cause survives, because his few possessions are still of use to the living.

"On the Murder of Lieutenant Jose Del Castillo by the Falangist Bravo Martinez, July 12, 1936" resembles the elegy for "P.L." While the poem pictures the details of the soldier's violent death, it also conveys his sanctity. Levine has a remarkable gift for rendering experience in action. He captures the soldier's death detail by detail with the precision of video tape in slow motion, but he also reveals that the lieutenant has found a new life, not in heaven, but rather "in his eyes/slowly filling with their own light" (NL, p. 54). The soldier's death is the culmination of his commitment to a secular religion of human brotherhood, a religion not of spiritual sanctuary but of the beauty and terror of the earth.

In still another elegy for the anarchists, "For the Fallen," the poet stands in the graveyard called Montjuich, which means, "the hills of Jews" or "the hill of Jove," where the anarchists are buried. The sounds of the sea and the factories have been replaced by the noise of traffic. As the poet prays for the lost anarchists and their revolutionary faith, he looks at his pristine hands, which have never been scarred by violence. Then he imagines the great sense of loss felt at the funeral of Durruti and Ascaso by their followers. While the poet conducts his lonely vigil, he realizes that nothing remains but words and symbols of the human spirit surrounded by death.

Montjuich provides both the title and setting of an elegy for Ferrer-Guardia. After depicting Ferrer's murder and his crude burial among stones, the poet celebrates the community of faith shared by those who fought against the overpowering forces of nature and the state. Armed with their secular faith and their prophetic vision of the future, the anarchists valiantly opposed the tyrannical forces of the world. Because their secular beliefs were consummated in their lives on this earth, the anarchists were not beholden to a transcendent God. Levine honors those whom he believes asserted the valor of the human spirit against tyranny and oppression.

In "Ashes," the poet broods over the plight of the poor and oppressed, those who suffer so much and are exploited for the sake of others. Yet any movement toward a better life for society's victims and any individual affirmation of the human spirit is devoured by the same antagonistic forces Levine has continuously raged against:

> You can howl your name into the wind
> and it will blow it into dust, you
> can pledge your single life, the earth
> will eat it all, the way you eat
> an apple, meat, skin, core, seeds.
> (A, p. 63)

Instead of improved conditions, the workers are greeted by another new day of backbreaking labor followed by other such days until they die. To believe in a better world requires that you pray to a great king "to become all you'll/never be," such as "a small hurtling flame across the sky" (A, p. 64).

In "Francisco, I'll Bring You Red Carnations," written in memory of Francisco Ascaso, the poet again visits the cemetery and recalls the exploits of Durruti, Ascaso, and Ferrer-Guardia. After describing Ascaso's heroism, the poet speaks of Barcelona to the dead anarchist and tells him the old city has been replaced by a modern hell. Despite the death of the anarchists, their dream of the holy kingdom lives on in the hearts of all who know and remember, including the poet, who promises to return across the ocean to Ascaso's grave once again bearing red carnations.

Phoebe Pettingell believes that in "Francisco" Levine "makes the witness of the anarchist Ascaso a brilliant symbol for man's unquenchable spirit," but she also surmises that "the martyrs are merely aspects of Levine's death-haunted imagination":

> Paradoxically, this refusal to dissociate oneself from the suffering of others is an affirmation of as much wholeness as we can hope to achieve. Levine doesn't ever want to forget his dead; often we catch him pouring salt in his wounds to insure the scar, "When the Day of Atonement came I did not/bow my head or bind myself at wrist and brow/because I knew I would atone," he insists, meaning that this life always exacts reparations, is, in fact, a perpetual Yom Kippur.[7]

In "Francisco" and other elegiac poems, Levine writes of the anarchists and their cause with a religious passion.

The poet's urge to identify with the Spanish anarchists comes in part from his own feelings of exile and rootlessness, his search for a people, a community, in place of the lost country of his ancestors. In the title poem of *Seven Years from Somewhere*, he describes a remote encounter with a band of Berber shepherds, whom he admires because they are noble and primitive men of the earth, unspoiled by civilization and its discontents. It is not for them to question who they are or where they live. When one of the shepherds shakes his hand, the poet is moved, and he refers to this gesture symbolically at the end of the poem.

Longing for the shepherds' unity of being, the poet wonders how he can return to a land where there is

> ... no old city
> cupped carefully in
> a bowl of mountains,
> no one to take this hand,
> the five perfect fingers
> of the soul, and hold it
> as one holds a blue egg
> found in tall grasses
> and smile and say something
> that means nothing, that
> means you are, you
> are, and you are home.
> (7, p. 70)

Once again Levine uses the hand to symbolize the human soul, and here in the handclasp with the shepherd there is a communion of souls in a place signifying a human community amid nature's beauty and permanence.

In several of his best poems of recent years, Levine merges the spiritual faith of the Jewish people and the secular faith of the anarchists. In both systems of belief there is prophetic rage at suffering and injustice and affirmation of human freedom and oneness. In his poem based on a drawing of the Rabbi of Auschwitz by Flavio Constantini, the poet recalls the horrifying specter of suffering and death. The only solace is the courage and dedication of individual people and their link to others. When the poet looks at the rabbi, he sees that the rabbi's face resembles his own with eyes that are opened to death:

> He has these
> long tapering fingers
> that long ago reached
> for our father's hand
> long gone to dirt, these
> fingers that hold
> hand to forearm,
> forearm to hand because
> that is all that God
> gave us to hold.
> (A, p. 56)

In poem after poem the message is the same. Man suffers and is holy. If God exists He is not apparent and can be best realized in human spirituality as symbolized by the hand, which joins one person to another. Man must commit himself to justice and brotherhood, as the anarchists and Hebrew prophets did.

Levine believes the greatness of the Jewish tradition lives on in revolutionary commitment to social and political justice, but he also knows that universal peace and justice will come neither easily nor soon. In "The Face," the poet meets his father in a hotel room in Spain and compares his own vigil with that of his father and his ancestors. What those generations share is the human quest for freedom, justice, peace, and love, symbolized by their hands reaching through space and time.

In "The Red Shirt," the poet merges his love for the anarchists, whose red shirt he wears, with his innate and vital Jewish knowledge of the biblical tradition and his longing to "come home" to his "father":

> This is the red shirt
> Adam gave to the Angel
> of Death when he asked
> for a son, this
> is the flag Moses
> waved 5 times
> above his head
> as he stumbled
> down the waves
> of the mountainous sea
> bearing the Tables of 10 . . .
>
> (A, p. 51)

This poem derives from the poet's experience, his love for the Spanish anarchists, and his intuitive expression of his Jewishness in a way that is true to him, a unique way of seeing and singing the world for this prophetic poet who rages at the earth and envisions oneness and glory for all its people.

Chapter 10

Howard Nemerov

Prophet of Divine Signatures

While Ginsberg, Ignatow, Levine, and Rukeyser have all been influenced by Blake, Whitman, Williams, and other Romantic and visionary writers, Howard Nemerov has never seriously challenged the formal mastery of Yeats, Eliot, and Auden or the authority of the New Critics, who advocated a highly sophisticated poetry of irony, wit, ambiguity, and paradox. Although Nemerov has come to value clarity more than ambiguity, he admits that the guiding principles behind his early verse still leave their mark. Because of his penchant for irony, paradox, and wit that borders on cynicism, Nemerov sometimes gives the impression of being a satirist or parodist without his own deep commitments.

In "Debate with the Rabbi," the narrator's sardonic humor precludes any genuine debate with the earnest rabbi:

> We are the people of the Book, the Rabbi said.
> Not of the phone book, said I.
> Ours is a great tradition, said he,
> And a wonderful history.
> But history's over, I said.[1]
>
> (CP, p. 271)

Nemerov uses the dialogue format and cadence of Yeats' "Crazy Jane" poems; however, unlike Crazy Jane, who challenges the priest's churchly authority by ardently espousing physical love, Nemerov's acerbic narrator defends little but his own wit and irony.

Nevertheless, this one poem does not begin to tell the full story of Nemerov's response to his Jewish heritage. Beneath the sometimes light and stylized surface of his poetry, he presents a deeply tragic vision of man, who appears to be the victim of divine malevolence, while searching in nature for positive signs of God's influence. Nemerov has brilliantly utilized Scripture to augment his insights into the relationship between human tragedy and divine will. His view of nature as a spiritual text to be read, interpreted, and prayed to with the artistic aid of poetry resembles the Jewish veneration of the Torah, the ancient Book of Life, which contains the text of God's laws and teachings, and has been read, interpreted, and prayed to for centuries.

Nemerov's description of his poetics shows his religious purpose:

> Poetry is a kind of spiritual exercise, a (generally doomed but stoical) attempt to pray one's humanity back into the universe; and conversely an attempt to read, to derive anew, one's humanity from nature, nature considered as a book, dictionary and bible at once. Poetry is a doctrine of signatures, or presupposes that the universe is such a doctrine whether well written or ill . . . [2]

Using the Bible as the religious basis of his "doctrine of signatures," Nemerov reveals the divine voice and will upon the sacred scroll of life in three movements: a tragic vision of man as a victim of exile and suffering and of the Lord's machinations; the role of Jesus as inspired prophet and the agonizing Jewish response to Jesus; and the revelation of God's word in nature. As a poet of fire in the prophetic tradition, Nemerov believes, "The purpose of poetry is to persuade, fool, or compel God into speaking."[3]

Nemerov has been well aware of Yeats' dictum "In dreams begin responsibilities," and he has faced up to the most frightening of his dreams. For example, in the early poem "The Frozen City," he presents an apocalyptic vision of the sinful city:

> This was true. Moving, I saw
> The murderer staring at his knife,
> Unable to understand, and a banker
> Regarding a dollar bill with fixed
> Incomprehension. Queerest of all,
> Children rolled skulls in the street,
> The sound of their light laughter
> Contrasting strangely with their
> Gangrenous flesh and the
> Convulsive motions of their limbs.
> (CP, p. 6)

In this scene, which expresses moral revulsion at those deprived of spiritual values, Nemerov suggests that the sinful, guilt-ridden adults are haunted by their avenging children. The poet depicts the modern materialistic city and its inhabitants as a frozen inferno waiting for redemption, but when the sun burns away the ice, the dead are quickly reborn to their self-aggrandizing lust:

> The dead arose,
> And began with spastic hands
> To gather money from the streets:
> As though ravaged by intolerable
> Heat of life, people ran to the cool
> Marble vaults of bank and tomb
> And threw themselves upon the cold
> Gold or earth, it seemed for
> Sovereign unredeeming solace.
> (CP, p. 7)

Although the poet has been influenced by Dante and Eliot, the prophetic intensity of his condemnation of godless materialism is an essential factor in "The Frozen City."

"The Scales of the Eyes" is another macabre dream sequence picturing a world devoid of religious faith and community. Unlike most of Nemerov's poems, "The Scales of the Eyes" has neither narrative nor dramatic continuity and no coherent development of character, action, and time:

> Cold winter, the roller coasters
> Stand in the swamps by the sea, and bend
> The lizards of their bones alone,
> August of lust and the hot dog
> Frozen in their fat.
>   (CP, p. 110)

Coming close to a surrealist art of subjective dream experience, the poet imagines a dark night of the soul so relentless and bitter that the reader feels surely salvation must be at hand; however, the only hint of resolution is the act of awakening from the nightmare at the end. As in "The Frozen City," the poet envisions the derangement and horror of the modern secular city and the imprisoned narcissistic mind.

Even when he mixes wit with seriousness, the poet is often critical of human existence. Reminiscent of Auden's "The Unknown Citizen," "The Life Cycle of Common Man" coldly itemizes the lifetime consumption of an average and anonymous man:

> Roughly figured, this man of moderate habits,
> This average consumer of the middle class,
> Consumed in the course of his average life span
> Just under half a million cigarettes,
> Four thousand fifths of gin and about
> A quarter as much vermouth; he drank
> Maybe a hundred thousand cups of coffee,
> And counting his parents' share it cost
> Something like half a million dollars
> To put him through life. How many beasts
> Died to provide him with meat, belt and shoes
> Cannot be certainly said.
>   (CP, p. 221)

Although the limpid, prosaic style of the poem differs markedly from the surrealistic complexity of "The Frozen City" and "The Scales of the Eyes," this simple account of one citizen's consumption adds up to a grotesque indictment of the common man's quiet desperation. Behind the casual blank verse movement of these lines is the poet's prophetic loathing of human life devoid of spirituality.

As part of his prophetic quest to "compel God into speaking," Nemerov has turned to the Bible to dramatize the complex relationship between man and God. Several of these poems concern the story of Lot, the son of Abraham's brother Haran, who went to Canaan with Abraham but later moved to Sodom. According to the account in Genesis, Lot brought home two strangers one night and protected them from an angry mob. The strangers turned out to be angels dispatched by God to destroy Sodom and Gemorrah. Although Lot, his wife, and two daughters followed the angelic order to leave Sodom, Lot's wife, despite the angel's warning, looked back and was turned into a pillar of salt. Believing they were the last of humanity, Lot's daughters seduced him. The elder daughter bore a son named Moab, forefather of the Moabites. The younger daughter gave birth to Ben-Ammi, from whom the Ammonites are descended.

"Lot's Wife" is a monologue spoken by the woman who looks back and becomes a pillar of salt. In skillfully crafted six line stanzas written in an irregular iambic trimeter varying from line to line, Nemerov dramatizes the plight of this victim of God's unyielding power:

> I have become a gate
> To the ruined city, dry,
> Indestructible by fire.
> A pillar of salt, a white
> Salt boundary stone
> On the edge of destruction.
>
> (CP, p. 41)

In both the third and fourth lines, the poet adds an extra syllable to the iambic trimeter pattern, beginning with three syllables in the first foot, and the sixth line is hardly scannable. The frightening metaphor of divine power and human degradation takes precedence over metrical regularity.

Others try to escape, but because they look back are swiftly punished. Still others "escape/By looking back." The implication is that many besides Lot's wife have not been able to follow the divine commandment. The obscure second reference to "escape" might indicate that Lot's wife and others face a dilemma, because what lies ahead and what they leave behind are equally bleak. The inference of "Lot's Wife" is that man must suffer a cruel fate brought about by a seemingly arbitrary and authoritarian power.

In "Lot Later," while Lot tells his own story in a casual and naive voice, he must endure grievous circumstances. Lot may not fully understand the meaning of his tribulations, but he intuits that he has been victimized by a divinity who acts in baffling ways. He wonders why he has been picked to be a leading actor in such a mad tale:

> I've always been
> Honest enough for this world, and respected
> In this town—but to be taken by the hair
> Like that, and lifted into that insane story,
> Then to be dropped when it was done with me . . .
> I tell you. I felt used.
>   (CP, p. 263)

Although Lot may be comic as well as tragic, the point is that he is God's plaything.

Nemerov goes out of his way to portray Lot as an ordinary man without malice. So why should his town go up in flames, his wife be turned to a pillar of salt, and his own daughters seduce him? Lot knows the answer, "I was in the hand of God, and got me boiled" (CP, p. 267). Given his bizarre circumstances, it is no wonder that Lot is quizzical about the meaning of his life and of the Lord's designs:

> And I did this? Or this was done to me,
> A foolish man who lived in the grand dream
> One instant, at the fuse of miracle and
> The flare of light, a man no better than most,
> Who loves the Lord and does not know His ways . . .
>   (CP, p. 267)

In a supple, effortless blank verse line with very little modulation, the poet shows that Lot's faith must withstand an incomprehensible and unfriendly God, who offers little hope of salvation.

It was obviously not by accident that Nemerov chose to retell the story of Saul, one of the most tragic characters in the Hebrew Bible, in En*dor*, his one act poetic drama. Given the strict requirements of dramatic form, Nemerov wisely concentrates the action on Saul's meeting with the woman at Endor. Despite his prohibition against witchcraft and magic, Saul convinces the witch to summon the prophet Samuel's spirit from the dead. Saul's relations with Samuel have suffered, because he has not waited for Samuel at Gilgal and has made the burnt offerings before battle himself. Even more significantly, Saul has spared Agag, the Amalekite king, despite Samuel's command to show no mercy to the enemy. After Saul tears Samuel's robe, Samuel calls it a sign that the Lord has torn Israel from Saul. Even Samuel's spirit is merciless and predicts that the Israelites will be defeated and Saul and his sons killed. The terrified Saul falls to the ground.

Nemerov emphasizes the episode at Endor, but he draws upon Saul's tragically flawed character, so apparent in his conflict with David and with his own son Jonathan. The entire emotional range of the biblical narrative is implicit in the poet's condensed presentation. Nemerov stresses God's antagonism toward the Jewish king, but he adds his own handiwork to Scripture by complicating the action, creating several key characters (the commander and the minister), and illuminating the characters' reactions to divine foreknowledge of their downfall.

The Saul of *Endor* is haunted by the feeling that God is his enemy: "But now/God moves in darkness over against me" (CP, p. 279). Although Saul knows he lost God's favor when he did not kill Agag, he is determined to discover what his destiny will be against the Philistines. He calls upon the woman to bring Samuel's spirit back from the dead so he might prophesy the future.

Reinforcing the central action of Saul's fate, the minister and commander debate about whether or not man should know his future. The Machiavellian minister senses that he is being manipulated by God:

> It is as though the end already exists
> Out there, blindly, in darkness, while we,
> Like blind men, stumble toward it.
>
> (CP, p. 284)

Nemerov has created the commander and the minister to show how lesser men than Saul react to divine fate.

Turning to the witch, the brooding Saul expresses his apprehension:

> Already I suspect, and come to you
> For visible certainties. It is not death
> We fear, but going to
> Forsaken actions, while God laughs in hiding.
>
> (CP, p. 288)

Although the poet does not dramatize Saul's cruel behavior toward David, it is apparent that the king is a deeply flawed man, but he is also a tragic victim, who suffers terrible pain and humiliation because of his merciful reaction to the conquered king. Nemerov renders the tragic action of Saul's downfall that stems from a single moment of hesitation to carry out God's command.

Even when Samuel is magically reborn, he does not bring good news:

> Out of your disobedience, Saul, it came,
> Because you turned in the hand of power, because
> You did not His vengeance and execution of Amalek,
> Therefore the Lord has splintered you against a stone
> And taken another instrument.
>
> (CP, p. 292)

Nemerov's rich figurative language complements the sparsely written biblical narrative. By dramatizing Saul's downfall and death through the witch's rendition of the future, Nemerov accentuates the absurdity and tragedy of Saul's fate. Now Saul realizes what God knows, but he must still live out his life and death.

Nemerov has always been fascinated by time, and in *Endor* he dramatizes the complex interrelationship of past, present, and future. After the play within a play of the witch's prophecy ends and the fire fades, the action returns to the present. Foreknowledge only adds to Saul's agony: "But to have torn open the mercy of time/And seen a corpse in a pit" (CP, p. 303). While preserving the integrity and grandeur of Scripture, Nemerov shows the tragic suffering of the Jewish king and the chilling ramifications of man's vulnerability in a world dominated by God's autocratic rule and swift judgment.

Saul cannot help but wonder if he has lived out a dream plotted by divine fiat and caused by his refusal to kill the conquered king of Amalek. Although Saul has contributed to his own downfall, he knows that the Lord's ways are harsh and irrevocable. Having come to some understanding and acceptance of his fate by the play's end, Saul soothes his pain with wine and prepares to do battle. The dream that predicted the future is over. Now men must endure the present. The witch has the last word: "The fire dies in daylight now, and men/Wake from their dreams into the mercy of time" (CP, p. 317). Not only has Nemerov shown the ability to write a viable poetic drama; he has utilized the resources of both poetry and the stage to prophetically reveal God's voice and His powerful intervention in man's world.

Nemerov once again "compels God into speaking" and dramatizes the human tragedy in C*ain*, a brief one act poetic drama. *Cain* is not as technically convincing as *Endor*. The poet has trouble differentiating between his characters and the poetry can sometimes be unconvincing. "That's easy for a winner to say" (CP, p. 321), the jealous Cain responds to Abel. Despite the play's shortcomings, it treats the same fundamental issues as *Endor*. Along with lucid language and straightforward surface action, there are complex undercurrents, because the manifestations of divine power in human lives are subtle and mysterious.

Since the jealous Cain will not accept the fact that God prefers Abel's offering, he murders his brother. Therefore, the Lord punishes Cain by making him wander over the earth. The poet adds to the biblical text by making Adam and Eve significant characters in the action. Cain blames his fate on his parents' sin, but his father tries to rationalize the expulsion from Eden as the beginning of human civilization and progress.

Adam even goes so far as to say, "Sometimes I could bless that serpent!" (CP, p. 327). This is a significant reference, because there is a strong suggestion in the play that God is, in fact, the serpent who tempted man to sin. Throughout Nemerov's poems based on Hebrew Scripture, God appears to be a prime cause of human sin and suffering.

Cain is an intelligent man who skillfully refutes Adam's sophistry:

> But if a man, even if not a very good one,
> Is turned away by his God, what does he do?
> Where does he go? What could he do
> Worse than what is already done to him?
>
> (CP, p. 328)

Refusing to accept his fate, Cain questions divine authority, and God comes down to encounter Cain.

God asks Cain what he wishes to know, and Cain questions why God will not accept his offering. God explains that a man must accept things as they are. If he cannot accept his circumstances, then he must change them: "All things can be done, you must only/Do what you will" (CP, p. 331). Although the Lord warns Cain that any attempt to change his destiny may be fruitless, He compels Cain to act, because He indicates that anything one wills can be accomplished. The proof of divine influence is that almost immediately after God exits with a clap of thunder, Cain picks up Abel's knife, and when the latter returns Cain murders him.

Once again God seeks out Cain. Instead of showing pity, compassion, or stern rebuke, God reacts subtly and ironically by asking a series of rhetorical questions. He inquires whether Cain thinks he has changed things, and the latter responds that having acted decisively he has at least changed internally, because he now feels in command of himself. When Cain questions his exile, God becomes philosophical. He implies that men must adjust to the loneliness and complexity of their new lives outside of Eden. After Cain cries out that he will be killed by strangers, God tells him of the protective mark.

Then, as if to reinforce Adam's rationalization of sin and exile, God tries to bolster Cain's ego by claiming that despite his cruel fate he has introduced his fellow men to the promise of power. Nemerov's God engages in complex thought and action. He even goes so far as to reveal that He is the cause of human sin, "I was the serpent in the Garden" (CP, p. 336). Cain realizes that God's Manichean machinations are contradictory and inscrutable:

> I can believe that, but nobody else will.
> I see it so well, that You are the master of the will
> That works two ways at once, whose action
> Is its own punishment, the cause
> That is its own result.
>
> (CP, p. 336)

Cain rejects God and accepts the full burden of his fate. When Adam discovers Abel's corpse, he threatens to punish Cain, but he relents because of the divine mark. Adam, too, begins to recognize the divine part in man's destiny, and he says that Cain's crime "is somehow the Lord God's doing" (CP, p. 339).

Eve identifies so fully with her son that she first proposes they curse God and die and second that Cain should kill his parents for victimizing him with their own sin. Although he refutes his mother's desperate proposals, it is apparent that Cain views both God and Adam as his adversaries. After Cain departs to wander among strangers, marry, and build a city, Adam and Eve are alone. Adam becomes nostalgic about Eden, but Eve recalls the angel's sword, which guards the tree of life, and she refuses to believe they can go home again. Alone in the dark human world, which they have helped to bring about, they take courage from their love and speak of a new beginning. In both *Endor* and *Cain*, Nemerov has chosen to base his reading of man's dangerous and difficult fate and God's ominous presence on Hebrew Scripture and leaves little hope for man's redemption from suffering and exile.

Beyond his tragic Jewish vision of man as the victim of unredeemable suffering and exile, Nemerov probes and questions the ramifications of Christ's messianic mission. The poet has revealed that as a young man he was emotionally attracted to Christianity:

> Being with the whole family, living and dead, is identified with Jewishness, while the lonely and absurdly exalted pseudomysticism of the second, where death gets landscaped romantically, belongs to Catholicism. I am not a Catholic, but came close to being converted at least once while in college, on some such foolish ground as that it was a much more artistic and beautiful religion than Judaism (red hats and old masters, I guess) . . .
> (JFL, p. 122)

Perhaps because of his ambivalence toward the harsh Hebraic vision rendered in *Endor* and *Cain*, Nemerov is particularly sensitive to Christ's martyrdom. In a series of poems based on a dramatic Jewish-Christian dialogue, he tests the Jew's proud and defiant resolve to survive without Christ's intervention.

In several poems, the poet alludes to the Wandering Jew who, according to legend, was condemned to wander until Judgment Day because he mocked Christ on the day of Crucifixion. In "A Song of Degrees," the poet describes the Wandering Jew's courage and fortitude, which are indicative of Israel's survival throughout the ages:

> Foot and hand hardened to horn,
> Nose but a hook of bone, and eyes
> Not liquid now but stone—I
> To myself violent, fiercely exult
> In Zion everywhere.
> (CP, p. 54)

While he is haunted by the suffering and exile of the Jews and the harsh ways of the Jewish God, Nemerov cannot finally believe in the Christian version of divine salvation. Despite his admiration for Christ, the poet affirms the will of Israel to survive without a messiah, but not before writing several poems that pit the two religions against each other.

In "Ahaseurus," Nemerov again writes of the Wandering Jew but in a more subtle and complex presentation of the Jew's dilemma than in "A Song of Degrees." The poet structures the poem around a debate within the protagonist's mind between Christian and Jewish doctrine. Each of the thirty seven quatrains consists of a triple rhyme plus the refrain of the fourth line. While the first three lines are in iambic pentameter, the fourth line is in iambic trimeter.

The Jew is painfully aware of Christ's attractions, but despite his urge for salvation he mocks Christ:

> What is it happens then? Will I give in,
> Sit on a darkened planet, hand on chin,
> And cast away the great weight of my Sin?
>   Was ever grief like mine?
>   (CP, p. 172)

Although he refuses to believe in Christ, Ahaseurus sees himself and Jesus as brothers in suffering: "I suffered Time as He Eternity" (CP, p. 172). While the Jew suffers the tragedy of the mortal world, Jesus is the hero of spiritual time. Despite Ahaseurus' misgiving about the Jewish God and his sympathetic view of Jesus, he maintains his Jewish faith.

In "Nicodemus," the conflict between the Jew and Christ, which takes place in Ahaseurus' mind, is rendered as an actual debate. Although most of Nemerov's biblical poems are based on Hebrew Scripture, "Nicodemus" is drawn from the Fourth Gospel, which tells of a Pharisee who met Jesus by night, defended him before the Sanhedrin, and later gave him his last rites. According to scholars, the meeting between Nicodemus and Jesus might have occurred in the Garden of Gesthemane. Jesus advocated his new faith, and Nicodemus tactfully questioned the prophet. Some traditions believe Nicodemus may have become Christ's follower.

While the writer of the Gospel emphasizes Christ's answers to Nicodemus' questions, Nemerov bases his poem on the latter's subtle interrogation of Christ:

> Rabbi, all things in the springtime
> Flower again, but a man may not
> Flower again. I regret
> The sweet smell of lilacs and the new grass
> And the shoots put forth of the cedar
> When we are done with the long winter.
>
> (CP, p. 55)

With grandeur Nicodemus refutes Christ's doctrine and then, after reaffirming his Jewish faith, he asks to return to Israel:

> Rabbi, let me go up from Egypt
> With Moses to the wilderness of Sinai
> And to the country of the old Canaan
> Where, sweeter than honey, Sarah's blood
> Darkens the cold cave in the field
> And the wild seed of Abraham is cold.
>
> (CP, p. 56)

Besides his eloquent reenactment of the debate between Nicodemus and Jesus, Nemerov shows his rare ability to enrich his ancient source through vivid imagery and figurative language.

"To the Babylonians" marks one of the rare instances where the poet is openly skeptical of his Jewish heritage. Specifically citing the misfortunes of Cain and Saul, the poet generalizes about the harsh Jewish fate:

> Thus the planetary Jew
> Bears the old law with the new,
> And must suffer Israel
> As stranger nations suffer hell.
>
> (CP, p. 57)

Nemerov comes closest to writing a Christian apology in "Carol," a formal lyric in five line stanzas rhyming a b a c c, and so on; the second line being a refrain repeated in each stanza. The poet indicates that because Christ died for Adam's sin on a cross made from "Eden's Tree," he offers all men hope for salvation. Despite his receptivity toward Christ, Nemerov maintains his vision of humanity founded on his reading of the implacable Jewish will to prevail in the world while still awaiting the Messiah.

Nemerov's prophetic revelation of God is complex, because while he associates God with man's suffering, he also sees the divine inscription upon nature's enduring rhythms and cycles. In effect, the poet provides a second prophetic reading of divinity via the text of nature. God is everywhere the poet looks. In "Moment," the divine spirit is inherent in the timeless present from the mysterious "starflake frozen on the windowpane" to the sea-anemone and beyond:

> And now is quiet in the tomb as now
> Explodes inside the sun, and it is now
> In the saddle of space, where argosies of dust
> Sail outward blazing, and the mind of God,
> The flash across the gap of being, thinks
> In the instant absence of forever: now.
>
> (CP, p. 211)

Although the Lord whom the poet induces to speak in the biblical poems is an ambiguous and haunting figure, in the nature poems and especially in "Runes" His signatures resemble the sacred signs of the God of the prophets and psalmists.

"Runes" is Nemerov's most masterful reading of nature's sacred text and the divine signatures upon it. Julia Bartholomay focuses much of her attention on "Runes" in her book-length study of the poet's works. She believes that "Runes" suggests "the secret and mysterious—the inscription of man's attempt to relate thought and thing. The title also suggests the possibilities and limitations of language as a mirror of nature." According to Bartholomay, "In the mutability of generative substance and form, the poet seeks nature's inscriptions. This is man's timeless search for the secret of life and death in nature's hidden laws."[4]

Along with her sensitive insights into the imagery of the poem, Bartholomay emphasizes the Jewishness of Nemerov's vision: "In his idea of poetry as a doctrine of signatures, in his reflexive turn of mind and proclivity to doubt, and in his refusal to utter the ineffable name of Y-H-W-H, Nemerov is true to his Jewish heritage." Overhearing the prophetic voice in Nemerov's verse and in his other writings, Bartholomay believes that the poet "feels and sees the Divine Presence in the world and responds to It directly" as the psalmist did. She is convinced that in "Runes" and elsewhere the poet "reveals the divine shadow of nature's signature on all things."[5]

Ross Labrie, another outstanding critic of Nemerov's work, provides an overview of the structural and thematic organization of "Runes":

> The principle motifs are given in the opening sections—the stillness in moving things, the movement in still things, the world of generation versus that of thought and art. The principle metaphors are those of water and seed. The sequence, which is composed in blank verse, contains fifteen stanzas of fifteen lines each. The structure is polyphonic and involves complex variations on the central themes of mutability and permanence. The shape of the poem is centrifugal with the eighth stanza being dead center.[6]

It is obvious from Labrie's account, corroborated by the poem, that Nemerov has created a work of complexity and depth with a symphonic richness of imagery and theme. In this meditative and lyric poem, the poet dramatizes the interaction between his own mind and reality as he reveals the divine presence in the universe.

Jewish images and themes are concentrated in the fifth, sixth, seventh, and eleventh runes. As in *Endor* and *Cain* and other poems, Nemerov utilizes Jewish references to render man's suffering, which results from his conflict with an intransigent God. In the fifth rune, for example, he refers to the time of Atonement. He means the Ten Days of Awe, which include the High Holidays: Rosh Hashanah, the Jewish New Year, and Yom Kippur, the Day of Atonement when Jews repent their sins:

> The fat time of the year is also time
> Of the Atonement; birds to the berry bushes,
> Men to the harvest; a time to answer for
> Both present plenty and emptiness to come.
>
> (CP, p. 213)

At the harvest, when the natural world is at its ripest, man is spiritually barren. The poet refers to the shofar or ram's horn, which is blown to awaken those who have forgotten the Law and to announce the coming of the messianic kingdom when men will be one as God will be one:

> When the slain legal deer is salted down,
> When apples smell like goodness, cold in the cellar,
> You hear the ram's horn sounded in the high
> Mount of the Lord, and you lift up your eyes
> As though by this observance you might hide
> The dry husk of an eaten heart which brings
> Nothing to offer up, no sacrifice
> Acceptable but the canceled-out desires
> And satisfactions of another year's
> Abscess, whose zero in His winter's mercy
> Still hides the undecipherable seed.
>
> (CP, p. 213)

With a firm command of his blank verse line and vivid religious imagery and metaphors, Nemerov conveys with subtlety and power the conflict and tension between fertility and barrenness, autumn and winter, life and death. It is a sign of Nemerov's poetic gifts that he is able to both aurally and visually render his arcane reading of man, nature, and God. The essential theme of this rune is depicted in the contrast between the fertility of nature—including its intimate connection with the ancient sacred festival—and man's subsequent estrangement from both God and nature, resulting in emotional and spiritual sterility and the omnipresence of death.

In the sixth rune, Nemerov presents what Labrie calls "a wintry view of God":[7]

> White water now in the snowflake's prison,
> A mad king in a skullcap thinks these thoughts
> In regular hexagons, each one unlike
> Each of the others.
>
> (CP, p. 214)

God is the creator of infinitely various snowflakes, which the poet envisions as moments and seeds, as he watches them falling to earth. Winter is the time of stillness and death but it is part of nature's cyclical rhythms. Nemerov personifies God as a Jewish king, who manifests his meditations in such natural forms as snowflakes. He might also refer ironically to the Jewish poet, who seeks to render his thoughts and perceptions about man, nature, and God.

Despite the poet's imaginative prowess, he knows that in the world existing outside his own mind man is a victim of his limitations and the authority of the Lord. Rune seven begins with Jacob's mixed prophetic blessing to his son Rueben in Genesis 49:4:

> *Unstable as water, thou shalt not excel*
> —Said to the firstborn, the dignity and strength,
> And the defiler of his father's bed.
>
> (CP, p. 214)

According to Bartholomay, this is "the voice of a patriarch, the voice of Israel through whom God speaks—a thundering voice whose repercussions shake the synthetic posture of civilization."[8] In the rest of this rune, Nemerov prophetically condemns modern culture, as if to show that Jacob's rebuke to the generations still holds true in this plastic and "dehydrated age."

In the eleventh rune, the poet discovers evidence of God in the text of human history as noted in Scripture. A holy man asks the poet to break a stick, and when he does, the poet sees signs of divinity wherever he looks. Then he begins to dream. After he beholds the tree of knowledge, he sees Aaron's rod that turned into a writhing serpent before Pharoah's eyes, and then Jesse's rod that flowered in generations of kings. The poet paraphrases Isaiah's announcement of the coming of the Davidic king, who will bring peace to all the world. Finally, the seed becomes Jesus' cross and then Adam's "tainted seed." As in the two poetic dramas, Nemerov renders man's tragic place in the world and his antagonistic relationship with God; however, the poet also responds to the glory and grandeur of nature's ongoing rhythms and cycles. There he sees positive signs of the Lord's presence in the world. The tragic human drama is not the most enduring divine text, because the divine seed grows throughout the universe. Thus, the poet can say he saw "nothing/That was not God" (CP, p. 216).

In "The View from an Attic Window," Nemerov writes simply and passionately about man's mortality and nature's immortality. The poem is in two parts. The first is in tercets rhyming a b b, c d d in a loose iambic tetrameter. The second part is organized into six line stanzas rhyming a b a b c c in iambic pentameter. In part one the poet watches snow falling from his attic window:

> Among the high-branching, leafless boughs
> Above the roof-peaks of the town,
> Snowflakes unnumberably come down.
>
> I watched out of the attic window
> The laced sway of family trees,
> Intricate genealogies
>
> Whose strict, reserved gentility,
> Trembling, impossible to bow,
> Received the appalling fall of snow.
> (CP, p. 225)

With a classic lucidity and grace characteristic of his best verse, the poet describes this wintry scene. As the snow continues to fall, the poet begins to cry and then falls asleep, but he awakens to see snowflakes descending through darkness.

In the second part, the poet develops and deepens his theme. He begins by telling why he cried: "I cried because life is hopeless and beautiful" (CP, p. 226). In many of his poems, the poet creates a persona or mask to speak for him, but in "The View from an Attic Window" it is the poet who speaks openly of the pathos he feels toward life and death. Descending from the attic to the cellar, he sees his appliances, which sustain the domestic life of the house, as by analogy the body's organs sustain human life.

After he describes more of the memorabilia of past generations stored in the attic, in the final three stanzas the poet renders the insight that brought him to tears:

> But what I thought today, that made me cry,
> Is this, that we live in two kinds of thing:
> The powerful trees, thrusting into the sky
> Their black patience, are one, and that branching
> Relation teaches how we endure and grow;
>   The other is the snow,
>   (CP, p. 226–27)

And so there are two forces: the ongoing power and energy of life symbolized by the trees, which is analogous to the changing but enduring seed and water of "Runes," and the snow, which represents the tragic mortality of the human generations, so compellingly rendered in Nemerov's biblical poems.

As he describes the falling snow by means of a series of similes, the poet alludes to the sacred generations of Israel, which God promised Abraham:

> Falling in a white chaos from the sky,
> As many as the sands of all the seas,
> As all the men who died or who will die,
> As stars in heaven, as leaves of all the trees;
> As Abraham was promised of his seed;
> Generations bleed,
>
> Till I, high in the tower of my time
> Among familiar ruins, began to cry
> For accident, sickness, justice, war and crime,
> Because all died, because I had to die.
> The snow fell, the trees stood, the promise kept,
>   And a child I slept.
>   (CP, p. 227)

Although he has probed Christ's alternative to the Jews' tragic wandering in the world, the poet maintains his Jewish vision of sadness and exaltation at the world, as it is, with no supernatural promises. It is a world characterized by man's suffering and mortality, God's complex and menacing words and will, and the majesty of divine signatures evident in nature. Like the psalmist, Nemerov cries out his lament at man's plight and praises God's majesty, and like the prophet he compels God to speak and interprets the divine signatures of creation through his gift of words, which he inscribes upon the Book of Life.

Chapter 11

Muriel Rukeyser

Prophet of Social and Political Justice

Muriel Rukeyser believed that the poetic and spiritual quests are synonymous: "The sources of poetry are in the spirit seeking completeness."[1] And Judaism, which for Rukeyser is crucial to the spirit of life and of poetry, is a heritage of memory and fire exemplified by the martyred Rabbi Akiba and by the Hebrew prophets. She told the critic Louise Kertesz, "We are talking about the endless quarrel between the establishment and the prophets, and I hope to be forever on the side of the prophets."[2] In her poetry she championed social and political justice and invoked a vision of spiritual openness and oneness.

Although Rukeyser's parents were not religious, she did encounter Jewish influences:

> Jewish references have come into some of my poems—the strong cry of the *Shema*, the raw, primitive blast of the *Shofar*, the Friday candles, the tragic migrations, modern tortures and the Warsaw ghetto, Joel and Ezekiel (in terms of John Brown), images started in me by the poetry of the prophets in the English Bible.... On the way out of adolescence, I searched, as others do, for ancestors.[3]

She treasured the Bible because of its "clash and poetry and nakedness, its fiery vision of conflict resolved only in God," which remained true "no matter what I was coming to believe about the reality of the world or power or divinity or death or love."[4] The Bible exemplified for Rukeyser the highest poetry, the poetry of the Prophets, the Psalms, and the Song of Songs, the poetry of what she called "emotional truth." She said that she and Whitman "come from the Bible and from the religious writings where the parallelism enables contradictions to be contained and synthesis to be achieved."[5]

As Rukeyser's reading of the Bible would have shown, and as such modern Jewish theologians as Leo Baeck, Mordecai Kaplan, and Abraham Joshua Heschel have written, the prophetic commitment to moral and ethical responsibility and action is absolutely essential to Judaism. As Rukeyser defines it, the poem's very purpose is prophetic: "The work that a poem does is a transfer of human energy, and I think human energy may be defined as consciousness, the capacity to make change in existing conditions" (LP, Preface). Opposing the myth of the fallen world, she believes that "there is no lost Eden, and God is the future" (LP, p. 221). Deliverance will come if men and women dedicate themselves to spiritual values.

The poet boldly enunciates the value of her Jewishness in section seven of "Letter to the Front," a Petrarchan sonnet:

> To be a Jew in the twentieth century
> Is to be offered a gift. If your refuse,
> Wishing to be invisible, you choose
> Death of the spirit, the stone insanity.
> Accepting, take full life. Full agonies:
> Your evening deep in labyrinthine blood
> Of those who resist, fail, and resist; and God
> Reduced to a hostage among hostages.
>
> (CP, p. 239)

Whether or not one accepts the gift of one's Jewishness, there are overwhelming consequences. Although Rukeyser does not regularly use traditional forms, in this sonnet she skillfully employs metrical variations to heighten impassioned speech rhythms. For example, the third line begins not with the iambic meter that she establishes in the first two lines of the poem but rather with a trochee. The fourth line also begins with a trochee and the fifth line is stressed from "take" through the second "full." The seventh and eighth lines are also irregular and highly accented.

The poet seems to create a dilemma that cannot be solved. Either one rejects his or her Jewishness and becomes spiritually inert, or one chooses an ominous "gift":

> The gift is torment. Not alone the still
> Torture, isolation; or torture of the flesh.
> That may come also. But the accepting wish,
> The whole and fertile spirit as guarantee
> For every human freedom, suffering to be free,
> Daring to live for the impossible.
> (CP, p. 239)

Subtly using rhyme and meter as well as caesuras, repetition of key words, and parallel structure, the poet celebrates her Jewish heritage as necessary to the preservation of the spirit, but she declares that Judaism can only survive against almost impossible odds if the individual Jew is committed to the spiritual quest for freedom and justice in a world where tyranny is rampant.

Rukeyser's imagery and rhythms embody her passionately felt experience. She sings her themes as "Woman, American, and Jew" in the prophetic, life-affirming poem "Bubble of Air":

> Woman, American, and Jew,
> three guardians watch over you,
> three lions of heritage
> resist the evil of your age:
> life, freedom and memory.
> (CP, p. 228)

In its strong denunciation of evil and affirmation of good, this poem resembles the bold prophetic utterance, the apodictic rhetoric, the poet loved, such as these famous lines from Joel 4:10:

> Beat your plowshares into swords,
> And your pruning-hooks into spears;
> Let the weak say: 'I am strong.'

As Rukeyer's "angel of the century" cries out for humankind to fight back against unprecedented evil,

> The angel of the century
> stood on the night and cried the great
> notes Give Create and Fight—
>
> (CP, p. 228)

she suggests the sounding of the Shofar and echoes this declaration from Amos 5:14–15:

> Seek good, and not evil, that ye may live;
> And so the Lord, The God of
> hosts, will be with you, as ye say.
> Hate the evil, and love the good.
> And establish justice in the gate . . .

Inspired by the Prophets, Rukeyser denounces injustice and oppression and defends freedom, justice, and love.

In "Traditional Tune," Rukeyser uses the narrative structure, refrain, and rhythm of spirituals and a demanding rhyme scheme to tell the story of conflict between tyranny and freedom. The Exodus of the Jewish people serves as the poet's emblem of the struggle for freedom from oppression; however, as the refrain (*"Not safe, not free"*) indicates, freedom is not yet at hand:

> Sailing, remembering the rock and the child,
> Sailing remember the sand, the city, the wild
> Holy songs.   Deaths!   Pillar of cloud and sun,
>
> Remember us and remember them all
> *Not safe, not free* sailing again upon
> The sacred dangerous harbor, Jerusalem.
>
> (CP, p. 273)

The poem might well have been partially inspired by the poet's memory of a Seder, the traditional Passover celebration when Jews commemorate their Exodus from Egypt to the Promised Land: "This night was different from all other nights, however. Another song was sung. Among the ritual, it moved everyone, it made tears start, when the singer began the first low notes of 'Let My People Go'" (LP, p. 140).

While Rukeyser remembers the Jews' ancient exodus to freedom and their ensuing struggles, she is drawn to the struggles of oppressed people everywhere. For example, in the long documentary narrative, "The Book of the Dead," which was included in her 1938 volume, *U.S.1*, she strongly identifies with the plight of West Virginia tunnel workers and becomes a passionate firsthand witness to their cause. Utilizing official transcripts and court records, dramatic monologues, photographic and visionary imagery, catalogues, and narration, the poet weaves an imposing poetic sequence, a long poem of enormous social and political significance.

"The Book of the Dead" is based on the Gauley tunnel tragedy, which is outlined in "Statement: Philippa Allen":

> 2,000 men were
>   employed there
>   period, about 2 years
>   drilling, 3.75 miles of tunnel.
>   To divert water (from New River)
>   to a hydroelectric plant (at Gauley Junction).
> The rock through which they were boring was of a high silica content.
> In tunnel No. 1 it ran 97–99% pure silica.
>   (CP, p. 73)

Although the contractors were aware of the extreme work hazards due to the silica dust, they never gave the workers a safety device. Because the company responsible for the tunnel was motivated by profit and cared little about protecting lives, workers died or suffered terrible illness. According to Louise Kertesz, "To the young poet the Gauley tragedy was a striking contradiction: men tapping a vast source of energy and being destroyed in the process."[6] Rukeyser renders a human catastrophe in the midst of nature's power and splendor.

Although the poet never explicitly participates in the action, her presence is always felt, because her consciousness is the focal point of the poem, as manifested in imagery of photographic precision:

> The simple mountains, sheer, dark graded with pine
> in the sudden weather, wet outbreak of spring,
> crosscut by snow, wind at the hill's shoulder.

The point of view of several poems in the sequence is that of a photographer. Emulating the visual dynamism and acuity of film, the poet with her camera-like eye for visual details achieves a documentary accuracy in her description of setting.

Rukeyser also uses court testimony to show what happened during the official investigations of the incident:

> Dr. Goldwater.   First are the factors involving the individual
> Under the heading B, external causes.
> Some of the factors which I have in mind—
> those are the facts upon the blackboard,
> the influencing and controlling factors.
>
> (CP, p. 88)

Selecting and structuring the evidence, the poet skillfully presents the various intonations of the official voices.

In a moving series of dramatic monologues, Rukyeser has the victims speak beyond subtle interpretations of fact and fancy to the heart of the tragedy. Mearl Blankenship's words and the poet's description of him produce a penetrating image of the tunnel worker's oppressed life:

> Dear Sir, my names is Mearl Blankenship
> I have worked for the rhineheart & Dennis Co
> Many days & many nights
> & it was so dusty you couldn't hardly see the lights.
> . . . .
> He stood against the rock
> facing the river
> grey river grey face
> the rock mottled behind him
> like X-ray plate enlarged
> diffuse and stony
> his face against the stone.
>
> (CP, p. 80)

By showing him surrounded by grey and pressed against rock as well as recording his words, Rukeyser renders the bleak drama of Mearl Blankenship's life in a precise and concentrated poetic form.

In "Absalom," a woman laments the death of three sons to silicosis, fibrosis of the lungs caused by excessive inhalation of silica dust that affects breathing. Her husband also has the disease. The poet emphasizes the youngest boy, who is dying from the disease and begs his mother to have the doctors examine his body to "see if the dust killed me," so she can be compensated. Knowing that she can never regain her loved ones, she vows to fight on for human freedom and progress. In her monologues, Rukeyser finds a way to condemn social and economic evil and to advocate justice and compassion through the dramatically realized poetic voices of her characters.

In addition to more monologues and documentary evidence, there are descriptive passages of visionary intensity to suggest the power and energy inherent in nature and the universe, which must be tapped if human society is to progress:

> kinetic and controlled, the sluice
> urging the hollow, the thunder,
> the major climax
>   energy
> total and open watercourse
> praising the spillway, fiery glaze,
> crackle of light, cleanest velocity
> flooding, the moulded force.
>
>   (CP, p. 95)

In this depiction of a dam and of the force of water, which is turned into energy, the poet creates a complex symbol of power. Everything is pictured and intoned syllable by syllable. In this dynamic way, language assumes its own sensuous reality.

The poet's faith in spiritual force and energy balances her renunciation of those who would deny the creative urge toward human progress:

> Nothing is lost, even among the wars,
> imperfect flow, confusion of force.
> It will rise. These are the phases of its face.
> It knows its seasons, the waiting, the sudden.
> It changes. It does not die.
> (CP, pp. 97–98)

Even in the concluding and title section, as the poet catalogues the terrible suffering of the workers and others who have endured and fought against the evil forces of history, she affirms those "many men" who exemplify the courage and fortitude of the human spirit.

Although it has no explicit Jewish references, "The Book of the Dead" reflects the poet's heritage. Her compassion for the suffering workers and their loved ones, her denunciation of the inhumane responses of business and government, and her affirmation of the spiritual energy of humanity in its quest for progress all reflect the prophetic ideals of the Jewish tradition, which, as Ira Eisenstein notes, have been crucial to Western culture:

> Some of these ideas and values—that man is created in the image of the divine, that life is sacred, that man is his brother's keeper, that society must be ruled by law, that justice and compassion are the highest virtues, that moral responsibility is the most authentic form of ethics, that man must serve as a "partner to God" in perfecting this world, etc.—have exerted a tremendous influence upon Western civilization.[7]

Rukeyser envisions her remembrance of this humanitarian Jewish tradition in her prophetic verse. Few poets of any cultural or religious background have been as willing as she to write about social and political subjects with such intense conviction, indeed, with such religious devotion.

Rukeyser was always interested in those who lived according to religious principles, because "these give us the intensity that should be felt in a lifetime of concentration, a lifetime which seems to risk the immortal meanings every day, pure in knowledge that the only way to realize them is to risk them" (LP, p. 34). The life that mattered most to the poet was that of Rabbi Akiba. In her note to her most ambitious poem about Akiba, she says, "The story in my mother's family is that we are descended from Akiba—unverifiable, but a great gift to a child" (CP, p. 474).

Akiba was more than a historical personage to Rukeyser. He was an ancestor, a spiritual father, a man who gave up his life for his faith in God. Akiba was Rukeyser's crucial link to her ancient heritage:

> A silver goblet, hearsay of a cantor's songs, is all you know; then a gap of two thousand years until the Ancestor, Akiba, who fought to include the Song of Songs in the Bible, who was smuggled out of Jerusalem in a coffin by his disciples, who believed in Bar Cochba's revolution, who was tortured to death by his Roman friend, the general Rufus, until he said smiling: "The commandant says: Thou shalt love the Lord thy God with all thy heart, with all thy soul, and with all thy might. I have always loved Him with all my heart and with all my soul; now I know that I love Him with all my life." And he died.
> (LP, p. 207)

In *Aboth: Sayings of the Fathers* (III, 19), Akiba says, "Everything is foreseen, yet freedom of choice is given; and the world is judged by grace, yet all is according to the amount of work." He means that although God is merciful, His rewards and punishments are based on man's deeds, because man has free choice despite divine foreknowledge.[8] It is up to man to live in God's image. As we have seen, in her Petrarchan sonnet in "Letter to the Front," Rukeyser believes that the very act of being a Jew involves choosing the courageous way toward the "whole and fertile spirit."

In "Akiba," the poet commemorates her ancestor's exemplary life but also the heroic struggle of the Jewish people, of Israel, to create a great "song of the way in," a way not only to survive but to find spiritual meaning in the world. As the poem begins, the poet uses long flowing lines and symbolic images to render the movement, conflict, and clash of elements in the universe. Then she depicts the way of the Jews, the music of Moses and the Exodus:

> Music of one child carried into the desert;
> firstborn forbidden by law of the pyramid.
> Drawn through the water with the water-drawn people
> led by the water-drawn man to the smoke mountain.
>
> (CP, p. 474)

Because of their love for freedom and liberty, the Jews are in touch with the divine force and unity of the world, and they embody the "Music of those who have walked out of slavery":

> This is not the past walking into the future,
> the walk is painful, into the present, the dance
> not visible as dance until much later.
> These dancers are discoverers of God.
>
> (CP, p. 474)

Moved by the spiritual journey of her people, the poet composes an incantatory and meditative music. As one phrase and clause flows into another, the cadence and structure seem natural and right. The poet's considerable gift for a music of visionary intensity is complemented by the symbolic and mythic dimensions of her subject.

After comparing Israel's fight for freedom with subsequent revolutionary movements, the poet refers to the rescue of Akiba's body after his death by his disciples:

> The wilderness journey through which we move
> under the whirlwind truth into the new,
> the only accurate. A cluster of lights at night:
> faces before the pillar of fire. A child watching
> while the sea breaks open. This night. The way in.
>
> (CP, p. 475)

Evoking images of Israel's Exodus, the poet believes that the "Energies, rhythms, journey," which the Jews experienced thousands of years ago, can still be the source of great songs and holy poems.

Like Akiba, Rukeyser defends the Song of Songs, the poetry of sexual desire and creation:

> I defend the desire
> Lightning and poetry
> Alone in the dark city
> Or breast to breast.
>
>   (CP, pp. 475–76)

Emulating the sensuous poetry of the ancient Song of Songs, Rukeyser praises the holiness of human desire. Like the poet of Song of Songs and like Blake, Whitman, and others, Rukeyser believes sexual desire and energy emanate from spiritual and creative forces.

In her tribute to Akiba's search for the Word, the poet implies that she, as well as her ancestor, wants to unify the clashing dissonance in the world, which prevents humanity from realizing its promise:

> We are the rock acknowledging water, and water
> Fire, and woman man, all brought through wilderness;
> And Rachel finding in the wordless shepherd
> Akiba who can now come to his power and speak:
> The need to give having found the need to become . . .
>
>   (CP, p. 477)

Rukeyser indicates that humanity must engage in a constant process of discovery trying to learn to speak and sing the burning Word.

"Akiba Martyr" depicts the last act of the great rabbi as he "flowers into spiritual fire." In martyrdom, Akiba has found a way to unify the disparate forces in his life:

> The look of delight of the martyr
> Among the colors of pain, at last knowing his own response
> Total and unified.
> To love God with all the heart, all passion,
> Every desire called evil, turned toward unity,
> All the opposites, all in the dialogue.
> All the dark and light of the heart, of life made whole.
>
>   (CP, p. 478)

As he dies, Akiba recites the Shema, the affirmation of Israel's one God. The late Rabbi Joseph Hertz described the Shema as "Israel's Confession of Faith," because it represents the worshipper's "allegiance to the Kingdom of Heaven, and his joyful submission to God's laws and commandments."[9] It was the Word of this immortal declaration that Akiba was willing to die for and it is his memory that burns with prophetic fire in Rukeyser's elegy to her ancestor.

Having served as witness to Akiba's martyrdom and to the courage and faith of the Jewish people, Rukeyser becomes her own example as well as witness to the twentieth century life devoted to freedom, equality, peace, and justice. These principles come in large part from the prophetic commitment to social and political justice, which is exemplified by the role that Jews have played in humane causes throughout the world, and by the spirit as well as the letter of Mosaic Law, which emphasizes a just response to human problems and concerns. Motivated by Akiba, the prophets, and the principles of Jewish life and law, Rukeyser acts as the protagonist of some of her most moving and religious poems in which she, too, "flowers into spiritual fire."

In "Don Baty, the Draft Resister," the poet and other anti-Vietnam War protestors are joined at the altar-table by Don Baty, who engenders such strong feelings in Muriel that she declares, "I am Don Baty," knowing the police will soon come to take him to jail. Then all the protestors speak as one:

> I am Don Baty, say we all
> we eat our bread, we drink our wine.
> Our heritance has come, we know,
> your arrest is mine.
>
> (CP, p. 512)

As the political commitment becomes a religious communion, a sharing of the ritual bread and wine, the poet uses incantatory rhythms to indicate a feeling of oneness in the act of resolution.

In "Breaking Open," the poet employs the methodology of journals and diaries to create a sense of immediacy. Some of the poems describe political protest during the Vietnam war:

> And then we go to Washington as if it were
> Jerusalem . . .
> and some of us lie gravely down
> on that cool mosaic floor,
> the Senate.
> Washington! Your bombs rain down!
> I mourn, I lie down, I grieve.
>
> (CP, p. 528)

This and other segments consist of simple, direct statements and images, notations of personal experience, but, as Louise Kertesz suggests, the poet expresses a religious concern here: "Like Akiba she struggles to speak the burning words needed in this time when 'we are Asia and New York/bombs, roaches, mutilation.'"[10] As the poet breaks open her life to find holy light, she lives out the poetry of her tradition.

Rukeyser meditates about the meaning of what she experiences in journal-like entries interspersed throughout the sequence. She is most concerned with the present, but in a personal way she is interested in history, "In facing history, we look at each other, and in facing our entire personal life, we look at each other" (CP, p. 529). Although she says she wants to see images of divine light, some of the most effective sections show the poet's personal experience of prison darkness. In one of the most memorable of these poems, a young black woman prisoner, who has murdered her child, keeps asking what freedom means. In another, the poet creates the feeling of the prison environment through a catalogue of items she keeps in a paper bag. In "Rational Man," Rukeyser refers to another kind of prison:

> The marker at Auschwitz
> The scientists torturing male genitals
> The learned scientists, they torture female genitals . . .
>
> (CP, p. 533)

Then she catalogues some of the horrors of the war in Vietnam and asks for mercy on all beings. For Rukeyser protest is not an end in itself, because she realizes that the end of protest must be love and mercy for all of life.

The poet concludes the sequence by offering a small but significant glimpse of what all these experiences have led her to:

> Then came I entire to this moment
> process and light
>   to discover the country of our waking
> breaking open
>   (CP. p. 535)

The poet wants to open out to the music, the light, the burning Word of her ancestors. To accomplish this she must live and experience the ideals of her tradition. It is in the prophetic moment of total consciousness that the poet believes we touch life and reach a "further humanity."

Knowing that she is a Jew and that her spirit must remain open, the poet intuitively expresses her heritage. As she speaks to her mother in "Trinity Churchyard," the poet refers to Rabbi Akiba. The main point of the poem is that, unlike her mother, who became "shut in" and seemingly victimized by wealth, Rukeyser, moved by Akiba's example, finds a free and open way as a poet:

> Mother I walk, going even here in green Galilee
> Where our ancestor, Akiba, resisted Rome,
> Singing forever for the Song of Songs
> Even in torture knowing. Mother, I walk, this blue,
> The sea, Mother, this hillside, to his great white stone.
> And again here in New York later I come alone
> To you, Mother, I walk, making our poems.
>   (CP, p. 560)

She writes of Akiba once more in the seventh section of the long and powerful sequence "The Gates," the final work in *The Collected Poems*. "The Gates" describes the poet's courageous odyssey to Korea to try and help free from prison the Korean poet Kim Chi Ha, who has been placed in solitary confinement for criticizing his repressive government.

In her preface to the poem, Rukeyser describes her vigil at the prison gates: "She stands in the mud and rain at the prison gates—also the gates of perception, the gates of the body. She is before the house of the poet. He is in solitary" (CP, p. 564–65). In the spirit of the ancient Prophet, Rukeyser wants to "bring out the prisoners from the dungeon,/and them that sit in darkness out of the prison-house" (Isaiah 42: 7). Surrounded by the paranoia and terror of tyranny, she reminds herself of Akiba's life and takes courage from it:

> Grave of my ancestor
> Akiba at rest over Kinneret.
> The holy poem, he said to me,
> the Song of Songs always;
> and know what I know, to love
> your belief with all your life,
> and resist the Romans, as I did
> even to the torture and beyond.
> (CP, p. 568)

Much of the spirit of Rukeyser's life and her art is contained in this tribute to Akiba's absolute commitment to his faith. The result of the holy life, the life of spiritual commitment, is the holy poem, the poem of full prophetic consciousness.

With the skills she used so well in "The Book of the Dead" and in "Breaking Open," Rukeyser documents the occasion of her courageous presence in a series of dramatic scenes depicting life under a tyrannical regime:

> The harsh police are everywhere,
> they have hunted this fellowship away before
> and they are everywhere, at the street-corner,
> listening to all hymns,
> standing before all doors,
> hearing over all wires.
> (CP, p. 567)

As she pictures the poet's family, friends, and sympathizers, the police, the bureaucrats, lawyers, and politicians, the poet opens to the life around her, and, like Akiba, she breaks through silence to song:

> Speak for   sing for   pray for
> everyone in solitary
> every living life.
>   (CP, p. 571)

Suddenly the prison gates open but only to allow in new prisoners of the regime. The Korean poet must stay in solitary. Rukeyser ends what she calls "a film strip of a life in poetry" still searching for answers to burning questions.

How to free the poet? How to fight for freedom for those just coming into the world? In acting as witness and example of her people's heritage and pointing toward the future, Rukeyser's words and deeds point toward a more humane way of life, a life of liberty, freedom, love, and full creative expression. Breathing in the memory of Exodus, Akiba, and the Hebrew prophets, she breathes out the fire of prophecy, this dynamic American Jewish poet whose great theme is "the spirit seeking completeness."

Chapter 12

Conclusion

Critics and scholars have tried to isolate the essential factors of American Jewish writing. Irving Malin speaks of the attempt by the writers to discover "new images of divinity in the absence of Orthodox belief." Allen Guttman concentrates on marginality, assimilation, and crisis of identity in his book devoted mostly to Jewish fiction writers in the United States. The formidable critic and scholar David Daiches stresses the Jewish writers' "inwardness with suffering" as the crucial attribute which enables them to be at the center of modern letters. Most of these observations as well as others have been based on the critics' reading of Jewish fiction writers. The poets have been largely disregarded, but that in no way diminishes their achievement.[1]

The ten poets I have chosen for this study often use their artistic gifts to express a personal identification with the Jewish heritage through a rich and complex dynamic of memory and prophecy. The five poets of memory revivify their ancestral Jewish past. While he is primarily known for his brief imagistic poems, Charles Reznikoff spent the better part of a long career writing about his personal remembrance of immigrant life in this country and also documenting Jewish exile, suffering, and survival through the legal testimony of witnesses and the glossing of biblical texts and other traditional sources. Much of his work can be seen as a tribute to the Jewish people.

While the form and structure of Louis Zukofsky's art differs considerably from that of Reznikoff, his fellow Objectivist, he, too, remembers Zion in his poetry inspired by his father, Reb Pinchos, and articulated in the venerable forms of rabbinic sayings, proverbs, psalms, and prophecies. For decades Zukofsky worked quietly and diligently on "A," his masterpiece, which contains his

Jewish poetry celebrating the bond of the generations and the ancient religious tradition. A number of passages in "A" are resplendent with echoes of psalmists, prophets, and sages.

In *Poland/1931* Jerome Rothenberg creates a vibrant collage of his ancestral Poland and evokes the tradition of mystics, madmen, and messiahs that he loves. His central characters, the Shekinah, the Baal Shem, and their counterparts Esther K. and Leo Levy, enact the poet's central myth of Jewish exile and unification. Rothenberg often tries to merge Jewish and American Indian mythology in order to render an American prophecy of intertribal unity.

Only after leaving Jamaica and coming to live in New York as a young man did Louis Simpson discover that he was a Jew. Since that time he has expressed a deep and abiding bond with Jewish suffering, laughter, pathos, and moral rectitude as evidenced in his poem "A Story About Chicken Soup" and his poems that depict the lives of his Russian Jewish maternal ancestors. In his *Poems of a Jew*, Karl Shapiro dramatizes the American Jew's marginality and crisis of identity, but he also writes passionately about the Jewish God and Israel and retells the ancient story of human creation and sin in his masterful poem "Adam and Eve."

In their distinctive ways the poets of memory all strive to re-create their Jewish past. While the poets of fire, as I have designated them, reassert the ancient prophetic voice of condemnation and praise, their catalyst is often personal memory of Jewish exile, suffering, and faith. Although he was deeply influenced by Blake and Whitman, Allen Ginsberg's seminal experience was his relationship with his mother Naomi. Her tormented and visionary Jewish response to exile and suffering is the essential source of "Kaddish," and also a crucial factor in the writing of "Howl." "Howl" is an apocalyptic vision of a country that will not tolerate its mad saints, including the poet's mother, whose memory he wished to honor.

Although David Ignatow might appear to be Ginsberg's antithesis, his incisive images of New York City life have a dimension of moral judgment and religious compassion, and Ignatow, too, has denounced the immorality of the modern Babylon. His poetry is often distinguished by his sensitivity to suffering and, in particular, the tragic relationships between fathers and sons. In his more recent work, he searches through the darkness and terror of his own life for a source of light and truth. Subtly shifting between comic, surreal, and tragic inflections of voice and tone, Ignatow, like a prophet in a terrible wilderness, looks for a way toward redemption.

While Howard Nemerov has not seriously challenged the influence of Yeats, Auden, and Eliot and makes no claims to be a visionary or Romantic poet, he has imagined the nightmare of human life devoid of spiritual values, and he has dramatized the divine role in the stories of Lot's wife, Saul, Cain, and other biblical characters. In his "Runes," he shows the divine signatures upon the sacred texts of nature and human history. The spirit of the Jewish people is at the core of Nemerov's tragic human vision, and he has devoted his considerable poetic gifts "to compel God into speaking."

Philip Levine is ostensibly a poet of exile and suffering, who identifies with all those who are lost and nameless, but he also searches for a visionary country where justice and oneness will prevail. Muriel Rukeyser constantly expressed passionate concern for social and political justice and tried to break through all barriers to a more free, creative, and spiritual life. For Rukeyser, the human spirit and poetry were synonymous and the prophetic tradition of her people was a primary source of inspiration both in life and poetry. Her great example was her spiritual ancestor Rabbi Akiba, who was willing to die for his Jewish faith.

Although these ten American Jewish poets have created striking Jewish poems of memory and fire, they are devoted to their personal experience of the world and are as alienated from traditional Judaism as they are from much of American culture. It is important to note that there are theological arguments both for and against the religious independence of these poets. According to Will Herberg, the faithful Jew identifies with Israel's past and meets "God as a son of the Covenant, within the framework of the divine election."[2] This was the prevailing view of the committed Jewish life for centuries.

A man of great magnitude and courage, the rabbi and theologian Leo Baeck described the poetry that has emanated from the covenant between God and the Jewish people:

> In its Book, this people constantly rediscovered itself. In it, Israel could learn how the history into which it was sent was also like a great poem: the commandment of the One Eternal God to one people on earth and, at the same time, the poetry of the One Eternal God through one people on earth.[3]

For this man who lived such an exemplary life poetry was the highest form of religious expression—a poetry that rendered the unique relationship between God and the Jewish people.

For centuries Jews survived the Diaspora by living according to a strict Orthodox code; however, since the Emancipation Halakic Judaism has been challenged by voices advocating a humanistic as opposed to a theocentric Judaism. Mordecai Kaplan captures much of the spirit of modern and liberal Jewish life when he says, "The *meaning* of Jewish existence is to foster in ourselves as Jews, and to awaken in the rest of the world, a sense of moral responsibility in action."[4] Kaplan believes the Jew must have "a conception of God that is compatible with what has come to be regarded as the most helpful and creative approach to the philosophic problem of what is authentic in human experience."[5]

The poets' humanistic faith is reflected in Martin Buber's Hasidic maxim: "Man cannot approach the divine by reaching beyond the human; he can approach Him through becoming human."[6] Buber comes very close to the spirit of these ten American Jewish poets:

> Thus, the way by which a man can reach God is revealed to him only through the knowledge of his own being, the knowledge of his essential quality and inclination. . . . But this precious something in a man is revealed to him if he truly perceives his strongest feeling, his central wish, that in him which stirs his inmost being.[7]

Above and beyond theological perspectives, we are dealing with poets, who must respond to religion and culture through their personal experience. The moment the poet ceases to be moved by his or her deepest intuitions and feelings is the moment he or she ceases to write genuine poems.

True to their feelings and beliefs, the ten Jewish poets will not defer to the strictures of traditional Judaism; however, as the Rabbi of Kotzk said, "God dwells wherever man lets Him in," and these American Jewish poets have let God in.[8] God is present in Reznikoff's celebration of the traditional fall and winter holidays, in the lyric voices of "In Memoriam: 1933," and, at least implicitly, in the entire range of his poems commemorating Israel's past. In "A," Zukofsky sings his own versions of sacred psalms in his search for divine light and remembrance of ancient grandeur. Along with his celebration of the ebullient Jews of *Poland/1931*, Jerome Rothenberg aspires toward a prophetic unification of the Shekinah and God, inspired by his readings of the Kabbalah and other mystical and esoteric Jewish sources. God may be behind some of the magical transformations that occur in Louis Simpson's story poems of his mother's Russia. In several of his poems, Karl Shapiro speaks forcefully to the God who has brought suffering and exile to the Jews and evil to the world.

In "Kaddish," "Magic Psalm," "The Reply," "The End," and in other prophecies and psalms, Allen Ginsberg encounters the Lord and does indeed "sing toward God in the wilderness." In great distress because of his son's mental illness, David Ignatow meets a God who can be compassionate one moment and menacing the next. Philip Levine identifies God with the spiritual world of his ancestors, but there is also a divine force that sings its terrifying and beautiful song through all living beings upon the earth. The stern Jewish God enters into Howard Nemerov's depiction of the tragic human drama of the Jews, but the poet also shows God's signatures in nature. Muriel Rukeyser sees divine light and signatures in her prophetic encounters with the forces of good and evil.

And so these highly independent poets question and celebrate their bond and/or their empathy with the Jewish tradition by depicting the lives of their ancestors and by creating prophetic poems of condemnation and praise. In their deeply human stories, myths, visions, and prophecies, these poets reveal the suffering, exile, and alienation of past and present Jewish life; however, through their art of memory and fire they also remember Zion and chant their versions of "the Lord's song" in a strange new land.

Biographies

Allen Ginsberg

Because Allen Ginsberg has written so consumingly and candidly about himself and has become a public figure as well as a poet, the facts of his life are almost legendary. He was born on June 3, 1926 in Newark, New Jersey, the son of Naomi, a Russian immigrant, and Louis, a high school teacher and published poet. Ginsberg describes his agonizing early years in "Kaddish," his elegy for Naomi.

As a young poet, Ginsberg came to know William Carlos Williams, the famous doctor-poet of Paterson, New Jersey. Williams criticized Ginsberg's youthful attempts at metrical poetry and advised him to experiment with personal speech rhythms and diction, breath units, and graphic visual images. Although Ginsberg never became an imitator of Williams, it was the latter, destined to be recognized as one of America's greatest poets, who gave the much younger poet the courage to find his own way and to trust his own extreme instincts. It is also noteworthy that Williams wrote introductions for both *Empty Mirror* and *Howl*.

While attending Columbia University, Ginsberg met the writers with whom he was to inaugurate the Beat Generation: Jack Kerouac, William Burroughs, and Gregory Corso. His association with these writers together with Neal Cassady and an assortment of other counterculture figures is noted in *Howl*, published by Lawrence Ferlinghetti's City Lights Books in 1956. *Howl* became the target of a censorship trial, which helped to make Ginsberg and the Beats the objects of national attention. Ginsberg was strongly influenced by Kerouac's spontaneous approach to life and to writing and has always claimed the latter was a great and original writer and poet.

While Williams was instrumental in teaching Ginsberg an approach to the craft of poetry, the latter was also influenced by the Hebrew prophets and by the prophetic poetry of William Blake and Walt Whitman. Like most twentieth century poets, Ginsberg has learned from Ezra Pound's poetry and poetics. He has also learned from the Black Mountain poets: Charles Olson, Robert Duncan, Robert Creeley, and others. These poets experimented with the breath unit, field composition, and other approaches to what they called projective verse, and, like Ginsberg, they were attracted to the principles and practices of Ezra Pound and William Carlos Williams.

While continuing his poetry writing and his political activities, Ginsberg has served as director of the Committee on Poetry Foundation and the Kerouac School of Poetics, Naropa Institute in Boulder, Colorado. He received a Guggenheim Fellowship in 1965 and in 1974 the National Book Award for poetry. Among his noteworthy poetry collections besides *Howl* (1956) and *Kaddish* (1961) are *Empty Mirror: Early Poems* (1961); *Reality Sandwiches 1953–1960* (1963); *Planet News, 1961–1967* (1968); *The Fall of America: Poems of These States 1965–71* (1972); *Mind Breaths: Poems 1972–77* (1978); *Collected Poems: 1947–1980* (1984); and *White Shroud, 1980–1985* (1986).

David Ignatow

David Ignatow was born to immigrant Jewish parents in Brooklyn on February 7, 1914. His mother was from Austro-Hungary and his father was from Russia. While Ignatow had a warm relationship with his mother, he and his father were hostile. The same father who introduced his son to the great Russian writers later discouraged his literary efforts and demanded that he work in the family bindery business. Although he studied briefly at Brooklyn College, Ignatow never received his degree and instead worked off and on in his father's business and at other jobs while writing poetry. After many years, he began to gain notice as a poet, but the long struggle for literary recognition took its toll on the poet, his wife Rose, an artist and writer, and his son David.

Through a curious twist of literary fate, while Ignatow was never recognized by his own generation, he began to gain the respect of the younger generation of poets born in the 1920s, such as Robert Bly and James Wright. During the 1960s, while Wesleyan University Press was publishing Ignatow's poetry books, Bly, Wright, and other younger poets began to praise his work and serve as its advocates. Finally, recognition came in the form of fellowships, prizes, teaching positions, anthologized poems, and new books, including *Poems: 1934–1969*, Guggenheim Fellowships in 1965 and 1973, and the 1977 Bollingen Prize. Ignatow has survived his agony to enjoy literary success and some happy years with his wife and his daughter Yaedi, born in 1956. Ignatow's poetry volumes include *The Gentle Weight Lifter* (1955); *Say Pardon* (1961); *Figures of the Human* (1964); *Rescue the Dead* (1968); *Facing the Tree* (1975); *Tread the Dark* (1978); *Whisper to the Earth* (1981); *Leaving the Door Open* (1984); and *New and Collected Poems, 1970–1985* (1986). His prose has been collected in *The Notebooks of David Ignatow* (1973) and *Open Between Us* (1979).

Philip Levine

Born in Detroit, Michigan on January 10, 1928, Philip Levine was educated at Wayne State University, The University of Iowa, and Stanford University. During the 1950s when he was in his early twenties, he was a factory worker in Detroit. In 1954 he married Frances Artley and they have three sons. Since 1958 he has been a member of the English Department of California State University at Fresno, but he has taught at other schools around the country. Levine's first book of poems *On the Edge* was published by Stone Wall Press of Iowa City in 1963. Since then he has published many poetry collections and won prizes and fellowships for his work, including the 1976 Lenore Marshall Prize and the National Book Critics Circle Award and the American Book Award for *7 Years from Somewhere* and *Ashes: Poems New and Old* (1979). Levine's other poetry volumes include *Not This Pig* (1968); *Pili's Wall* (1971); *Red Dust* (1971); *They Feed They Lion* (1972); *1933* (1974); *The Names of the Lost* (1976); *One for the Rose*(1981); *Sweet Will* (1985); and *Selected Poems* (1984). *Don't Ask* (1981) is a collection of Levine's interviews.

Howard Nemerov

Howard Nemerov was born on March 1, 1920 in New York City, the son of a wealthy merchant, who sent him to private schools and expected him to enter the family business; however, the poet was a rebellious son. After graduating from Harvard with a B.A. in 1941, he enlisted as a pilot in the Canadian Air Force and in American uniform flew combat missions with a Royal Air Force squadron against German shipping in the North Sea. For the last two years of the war, he joined the U.S. Army Air Corps. Married to Margaret Russell in 1944, he began a distinguished career in teaching and writing.

While living the sedentary life of the college professor at Bennington, Brandeis, and Washington University, Nemerov has not been idle. From 1949 to 1957, he published three novels, one of which, *The Homecoming Game*, was turned into a Hollywood movie and a Broadway play and made Nemerov as rich as he cared to be. Although he has also published two collections of short fiction and three books of critical essays to date, his most sustained and significant achievement is in poetry. Beginning with *The Image and the Law* in 1947, he has published such collections of his verse as *Mirrors and Windows* (1958); *New and Selected Poems* (1960); *The Next Room of the Dream: Poems and Two Plays* (1962); *The Blue Swallows* (1967); *Gnomes and Occasions* (1972); *The Western Approaches* (1975); *Sentences* (1980); *Inside the Onion* (1984); and *War Stories: Poems About Long Ago & Now* (1987). He received both the Pulitzer Prize and the National Book Award for his *Collected Poems* (1977). Nemerov and his wife have three children. On May 16, 1988 Nemerov was named Poet Laureate of the United States, following Robert Penn Warren and Richard Wilbur in that honorary post.

Charles Reznikoff

Born in Brooklyn on August 30, 1894, Charles Reznikoff was the son of Russian Jewish immigrant parents. He studied journalism for a year at The University of Missouri and entered the law school of New York University in 1912. Although he was admitted to the New York bar in 1916, Reznikoff made writing, not law, his life's work. He translated I.J. Benjamin's *My Three Years in the United States: 1859–1862* from the German, wrote a history of the Jews of Charleston, edited the public papers of Louis Marshall, the prominent Jewish attorney, and worked for the firm that published *Corpus Juris*, an encyclopedia for lawyers.

In 1930 Reznikoff married Marie Syrkin, a writer and for many years a professor at Brandeis. He seldom left New York City and loved to walk through the city's streets and parks. Despite his prolific literary output, as poet, playwright, and novelist, his work was not widely known until New Directions published *By the Waters of Manhattan: Selected Verse* in 1962. Among Reznikoff's many literary works, some of which were privately published, are *Poems* (1920); *Five Groups of Verse* (1927); *Jerusalem the Golden* (1934); *In Memoriam: 1933* (1934); *Inscriptions: 1944–1956* (1959); *Testimony, the United States 1885–1890 Recitative* (1965); *By the Well of Living and Seeing: New and Selected Poems 1918–1973* (1974); and *Holocaust* (1975). He died on January 22, 1976 before Black Sparrow Press published the first of his two volume *Complete Poems*.

Jerome Rothenberg

Born in New York City on December 11, 1931, Jerome Rothenberg has deep Jewish roots in Poland. His paternal grandfather, who spent several years in the U.S. and then returned to Poland, had been connected with the rebbe of Radzymin. The poet's father and mother both came to this country from Poland. Although the poet's father studied at the Slabodka Yeshiva in Lithuania, he later rejected Judaism and seldom, if ever, attended the synagogue. Jerome Rothenberg read and wrote poetry during his boyhood and by his fifteenth year knew he was a poet. By the time he was seventeen, he was an avid reader of such modern writers and poets as Gertrude Stein and E.E. Cummings, and before long he was reading or listening to Williams, Pound, the French Surrealists, the Dada poets, Shakespeare, the Bible, Jewish liturgy, and so on. Although he was twenty six or seven before his first publication, he always knew that poetry was the art whereby he would define himself and his life.

As poet, editor, anthologist, and translator, Rothenberg, has been prolific. Among his many poetry books are *Poems for the Game of Silence 1960–1970* (1971); *Poland/1933* (1974); *A Seneca Journal* (1978); *Vienna Blood and Other Poems* (1980); and *New Selected Poems 1970 to 1985* (1986). In addition to his original poetry, Rothenberg has translated extensively, and he has edited such innovative anthologies as *Technicians of the Sacred* (1968); *Shaking the Pumpkin* (1972); *America a Prophecy* (1973); and *A Big Jewish Book* (1978). He has also been active in poetry performance and in his pioneering efforts in the field of ethnopoetics.

Rothenberg has taught at such schools as The University of Wisconsin, Milwaukee, San Diego State University, University of California, San Diego, and State University of New York at Binghamton. For many years he was the publisher of Hawk's Well Press. He has also edited several magazines, including *Alcheringa: A First Magazine of Ethnopoetics*. The poet was educated in the New York Public schools and received a B.A. in 1952 from City College of New York and an M.A. from The University of Michigan in 1953. Married to Diane Brodatz in 1952, he has one son Matthew.

Muriel Rukeyser

Muriel Rukeyser was born in New York City on December 19, 1913. Her father, a wealthy builder, lost most of his fortune during the Depression. She was educated at Fieldston Schools, Vassar College, and Columbia University. In 1935 her first book of poems *Theory of Flight* won the Yale Series of Younger Poets Award. Subsequent poetry volumes included *Wake Island* (1942); *The Green Wave* (1948); *Elegies* (1949); *Body of Waking* (1958); *Waterlily Fire: Poems 1932–1962* (1962); *Breaking Open* (1973); and *The Gates* (1976). Her *Collected Poems* was published in 1979. She also wrote biographies, such as *Willard Gibbs* (1942) and *One Life* (1957) about Wendell Willkie as well as *The Life of Poetry* (1949), her poetics. Besides winning such fellowships and prizes as The National Institute of Arts and Letters Award in 1942 and a Guggenheim Fellowship in 1943, she was president of P.E.N., the international writers organization from 1975 to 1976. In 1945 she was married briefly to Glynn Collins in San Francisco. She had one son. Muriel Rukeyser died on February 12, 1980.

Karl Shapiro

Born in Baltimore, Maryland on November 10, 1913, Karl Shapiro was educated at The University of Virginia and Johns Hopkins University. The private printing of his first poetry collection in 1935 was hardly a literary event; however, literary fame did come soon thereafter. In 1942, while the poet was still serving in the South Pacific with the U.S. Army, his volume *Person, Place and Thing* was published. When he returned to civilian life, he was already known in literary circles. In 1945 his collection *V-Letter and Other Poems* won the Pulitzer Prize and Shapiro became eminent at a remarkably young age.

Because of national literary recognition, Shapiro was able to secure appointments as consultant, editor, and teacher. For example, in 1946 he was named Consultant in Poetry at the Library of Congress, and in 1947 he began to teach at Johns Hopkins. In 1950 he left Johns Hopkins to become editor of the prestigious *Poetry* magazine in Chicago, and he remained there as editor until 1956. From 1956 to 1966 he was Professor of English at University of Nebraska and edited *Prairie Schooner*. From 1968 until retirement he was Professor of English at The University of California, Davis.

Shapiro received a National Institute of Arts and Letters grant in 1944, Guggenheim Fellowships in 1944 and 1953, and the 1969 Bollingen Prize. His poetry books include *Poems 1940–1953* (1953); *Poems of a Jew* (1958); *The Bourgeois Poet* (1964); *White Haired Lover* (1968); *Adult Bookstore* (1976); *Collected Poems 1940–1977* (1978); and *New Selected Poems* (1987). His criticism is collected in such volumes as *In Defense of Ignorance* (1960); and *The Poetry Wreck: Selected Essays 1950–1970* (1975). Shapiro's first marriage ended in divorce, and he remarried in 1969. He has three children.

Louis Simpson

Louis Simpson was born on March 27, 1923 in Jamaica, West Indies, the son of a wealthy Kingston lawyer of Scots Presbyterian ancestry and a Russian Jewess, who came to the United States prior to World War I and became an actress. After his father and mother divorced, Louis Simpson emigrated from Jamaica to the U.S. at the age of seventeen, became an American citizen, and enrolled at Columbia University. In 1943 he joined the U.S. Army and served in Europe, winning the Purple Heart and the Bronze Star. At the war's end he suffered a nervous breakdown, but recovered and returned to Columbia where he earned a doctorate with a dissertation on the Scottish writer James Hogg.

After a short career in publishing, he began to teach at Berkeley and then took a position at The State University of New York at Stony Brook where he has remained since 1967 and is Professor of English. Among Simpson's many poetry books are *Good News of Death and Other Poems* (1955); *A Dream of Governors* (1959); *At the End of the Open Road* (1963), which was awarded the 1964 Pulitzer Prize; *Selected Poems* (1965); *Adventures of the Letter I* (1972); *Searching for the Ox* (1976); *Caviare at the Funeral* (1980), which received The Jewish Book Council's Award for poetry; and *People Live Here: Selected Poems 1948–1983* (1983). Simpson has also published critical studies: *James Hogg: A Critical Study* (1963); *Three on a Tower: The Lives and Works of Ezra Pound, T.S. Eliot, and William Carlos Williams* (1975); and *A Revolution in Taste: Studies of Dylan Thomas, Allen Ginsberg, Sylvia Plath, and Robert Lowell* (1978). In addition, the poet has written a novel *Riverside Drive* (1962) and an autobiography *North of Jamaica* (1972).

Louis Zukofsky

Louis Zukofsky was born on January 23, 1904 in New York City. The poet grew up speaking Yiddish at home with his Russian Jewish immigrant parents. His father Reb Pinchos, an Orthodox Jew, is the subject of some of Zukofsky's most moving poetry. The poet attended Columbia University and received an M.A. in 1924. In 1939 he married Celia Thaew. Their son Paul is a talented musician and composer.

Zukofsky edited the now famous February 1931 issue of *Poetry* in which he selected poems by a group of Objectivist poets and defined his standards for an Objectivist poetics. Along with Charles Reznikoff and George Oppen, he helped to establish To Publishers and the Objectivist Press. He maintained friendships with William Carlos Williams and Ezra Pound and became a source of inspiration to such younger poets as Robert Creeley, Robert Duncan, and Allen Ginsberg, who particularly admired Zukofsky's devotion to poetic craft.

Zukofsky taught at The University of Wisconsin, Colgate University, and from 1947 to 1966 at Polytechnic Institute of Brooklyn. One of his students was the poet Hugh Seidman. Many of Zukofsky's books were privately printed. It wasn't until 1966, when Norton published *All: the Collected Short Poems 1923–1964*, that the poet had a book that was generally available to American poetry readers. "A" was published in installments by small presses until Doubleday brought out "A" 13–21 in 1969. In 1978, the year of Zukofsky's death, University of California Press printed the complete version of "A" in 24 sections. In addition to poetry, Zukofsky published a play *Arise, Arise* (1973); short fiction *It Was* (1961), *Little: A Fragment for Careenagers* (1970), and *Ferdinand, Including It Was* (1968); and criticism *Bottom: On Shakespeare* (1963) and *Prepositions: The Collected Critical Essays of Louis Zukofsky* (1968). The poet died on May 12, 1978.

Notes

Chapter 1

1. See Robert Alter, *After the Tradition*, pp. 9–13, 35–60; and Harold Bloom, *Figures of Capable Imagination*, pp. 247–62 and "The Heavy Burden of the Past," *New York Times Book Review*, January 4, 1981, pp. 5, 24.
2. The Jews have certainly had a remarkable poetic tradition, concentrated in the Hebrew Bible but including, besides liturgical verse, the medieval Spanish poets Solomon ibn Gabirol, Moses ibn Ezra, and Judah Halevi as well as the modern Hebrew poets Hayim Nachman Bialik and Shaul Tchernichovsky and such important Yiddish poets as Jacob Glatstein, Moshe Leib Halpern, and H. Leivick. For the most generous gathering of twentieth century Jewish poets to date, see Anthony Rudolf and Howard Schwartz, eds., *Voices Within the Ark: the Modern Jewish Poets* (New York: Avon Books, 1980).
3. Karl Shapiro, *The Poetry Wreck*, pp. 210–11.
4. Quoted in *Jewish-American Literature*, ed. Abraham Chapman, p. 325.
5. Will Herberg, *Judaism and Modern Man*, p. 287.
6. Mordecai Kaplan, *The Purpose and Meaning of Jewish Existence*, p. 294.
7. Abraham Joshua Heschel, *The Prophets*, pp. 367–68.
8. Abraham Joshua Heschel, *God in Search of Man*, p. 26.
9. Kaplan, *The Purpose and Meaning of Jewish Existence*, pp. 311, 313.
10. Ibid., pp. 294–94.
11. Martin Buber, *Hasidism and Modern Man*, pp. 42–43.

Chapter 2

1. Charles Reznikoff, *Poems 1937–1975 Volume II of the Complete Poems of Charles Reznikoff*, p. 91. All further references to Charles Reznikoff's poetry will be identified within the body of the text by the following abbreviations: *Complete Poems, vol. I* (CP I); *Complete Poems, vol. II* (CP II); *Holocaust* (H).
2. Carl Rakosi, "An Interview by Martin Rosenblum," *Margins* 17 (February 1975): 23.
3. Robert Alter, *Defenses of the Imagination*, p. 132.
4. Ibid., p. 128.
5. Ibid., p. 104.

6. Milton Hindus, *Charles Reznikoff*, p. 58.
7. Ibid.
8. Ibid., p. 46.
9. Ibid., p. 57.
10. Ibid., p. 46.
11. Shirley Kaufman, "Charles Reznikoff, 1894–1976," pp. 55–56.
12. David Lehman, "Holocaust," p. 39.
13. Hindus, *Charles Reznikoff*, p. 54.
14. Ibid., p. 59–60.

Chapter 3

1. Jerome Rothenberg, *Pre-Faces and Other Writings*, p. 229. All further references to Jerome Rothenberg's poetry and prose will be identified within the body of the text by the following abbreviations: *A Big Jewish Book* (BJB); *Poland/1931* (P); *Pre-Faces* (PF); *A Seneca Journal* (SJ); *Vienna Blood* (VB).
2. Kevin Power, "Poland/1931," p. 688.
3. Jerome Rothenberg, "Craft Interview with Jerome Rothenberg," pp. 44–45.
4. Ibid., p. 45.
5. Ibid., pp. 47, 48.
6. Gershom Scholem, *On the Kabbalah and Its Symbolism*, p. 108.
7. Scholem, *Kabbalah*, pp. 310–11.
8. Unpublished letter from Jerome Rothenberg to Gary Pacernick (December 14, 1981). I am indebted to the poet for a great deal of information about his work conveyed in personal correspondence.
9. Harris Lenowitz, "Rothenberg: The Blood," pp. 181, 184.
10. Ibid., p. 182.
11. Ibid., p. 180.
12. Unpublished letter from Jerome Rothenberg to Gary Pacernick (December 14, 1981).
13. Power, "Poland/1931," pp. 691–93.
14. Scholem, *Kabbalah*, pp. 23–24.
15. Eric Mottram, "Where the Real Song Begins," p. 178.

Chapter 4

1. Karl Shapiro, *The Poetry Wreck*, p. 208. All further references to Karl Shapiro's poetry and prose will be identified within the body of the text by the following abbreviations: *Collected Poems 1940–1978* (CP); *Poems of a Jew* (PJ); *The Poetry Wreck* (PW).
2. Richard Rubenstein, *The Religious Imagination*, p. 47.
3. Ibid., p. 55.

Chapter 5

1. Louis Simpson, *North of Jamaica*, p. 283. All further references to Louis Simpson's poetry and prose will be identified within the body of the text by the following abbreviations: *Adventures of the Letter I* (ALI); *A Dream of Governors* (DG); *At the End of the Open Road* (OR); *Caviare at the Funeral* (CAF); *North of Jamaica* (NJ); *Riverside Drive* (RD); *Searching for the Ox* (SO).
2. Louis Simpson, "A Response to the Jewish Book Council" (unpublished address, May 3, 1981).
3. Ibid.
4. Ibid.
5. Ibid.
6. Unpublished letter from Louis Simpson to Gary Pacernick (October 16, 1981).
7. Ronald Moran, *Louis Simpson*, p. 131.

Chapter 6

1. Louis Zukofsky, "A," p. 193. All further references to Louis Zukofsky's poetry and prose will be identified within the body of the text by the following abbreviations: "A" (A); *All: The Collected Short Poems 1923–1964* (CSP); *Autobiography* (Au).
2. Celia Zukofsky, "A Commemorative Evening for Louis Zukofsky," *American Poetry Review* 9, no. 1 (January-February 1980): 27 (hereafter cited as "Commemorative Evening").
3. Louis Zukofsky, Interview, in L.S. Dembo and Cyrina Pondrom, eds., *The Contemporary Writer: Interviews with Sixteen Novelists and Poets* (Madison, Wis.: University of Wisconsin Press, 1972), p. 218.
4. Allen Ginsberg, "Commemorative Evening," p. 22.
5. Guy Davenport, "Zukofsky's 'A-24,'" *Parnassus: Poetry in Review* (Spring/Summer 1974): 23.

6. Hugh Kenner, *New York Times Book Review*, March 14, 1976, p. 7.
7. L.S. Dembo, "Louis Zukofsky: Objectivist Poetics and the Quest for Form," p. 91.
8. According to Harold Schimmel, "For Zukofsky Hebrew was 'speech' and made possible such elements of a historical past as 'Temple,' 'Wall,' 'Psalms' and 'The Land Itself' .... The accepted epithet for Yiddish was 'jargon' (miniscule), that is, not 'Speech' with its national 'historical' implications but a bastard lingua franca.... Ideally Zukofsky would like to tie himself as Jew and poet to the Hebrew past. Realistically he accepts 'roots' as Yiddish and unabashedly transliterates bits and pieces of jargon throughout 'A', as he feels inclined. His Hebrew has undergone a long exile and, shored on New York's East Side, is rendered as the lion beneath the mangy pelt." See Harold Schimmel, "Zuk. Yehoash David Rex," in *Louis Zukofsky: Man and Poet*, ed. Carroll F. Terrell (Orono, Maine: National Poetry Foundation, 1979), pp. 235–46.
9. Hugh Seidman, "Commemorative Evening," p. 23.

Chapter 7

1. Allen Ginsberg, "How *Kaddish* Happened," in *The Poetics of the New American Poetry*, eds. Donald Allen and Warren Tallman, pp. 345–46. All further references to Allen Ginsberg's poetry will be identified within the body of the text by the following abbreviations: *The Fall of America* (FA); *Howl* (H); *Kaddish* (K); *Mind Breaths* (MB); *Planet News* (PN); *Reality Sandwiches* (RS).
2. Ginsberg, "How *Kaddish* Happened," pp. 345–47.
3. Quoted in Jane Kramer, *Allen Ginsberg in America* (New York: Random House, 1969), p. 174.
4. Ginsberg, *To Eberhart from Ginsberg*, pp. 11–12.
5. Ibid., p. 43.
6. Paul Portuges, *The Visionary Poetics of Allen Ginsberg*, p. 88.
7. Ginsberg, "Notes for *Howl and Other Poems*," in *Poetics of the New American Poetry*, p. 320.
8. Ginsberg, Interview, in *Writers at Work*, p. 295.
9. Ginsberg, *To E from G*, p. 19.
10. Ginsberg, "Notes for *Howl and Other Poems*," p. 319.

Chapter 8

1. David Ignatow, *The Notebooks of David Ignatow*, ed. Ralph J. Mills, Jr., p. 4. All further references to David Ignatow's poetry and prose will be identified within the body of the text by the following abbreviations: *Facing the Tree* (FT); *Notebooks* (N); *Poems 1934–1969* (P); *Tread the Dark* (TD); *Whisper to the Earth* (WTE).
2. William Carlos Williams, Preface to *Empty Mirror: Early Poems*, by Allen Ginsberg, p. xiii.
3. Denise Levertov, "An Order that Will Sing," p. 417.
4. Unpublished letter from David Ignatow to Gary Pacernick (January 20, 1981).
5. Ralph J. Mills, Jr., *Cry of the Human*, p. 73.
6. Quoted in *Contemporary Poets*, ed. James Vinson, p. 774.
7. David Daiches, "Breakthrough," in Irving Malin, ed. *Contemporary American-Jewish Literature*, p. 31.
8. Quoted in *Contemporary Poets*, ed. James Vinson, p. 775.
9. James Dickey, *Babel to Byzantium*, p. 27.
10. Ibid.
11. Mills, *Cry of the Human*, p. 107.
12. Richard Rubenstein, *After Auschwitz*, p. 128.
13. Ibid., p. 154.
14. Unpublished letter from David Ignatow to Gary Pacernick (January 20, 1981).

Chapter 9

1. Philip Levine, *On the Edge and Over: Poems Old, Lost, and New*, p. 13. All further references to Philip Levine's poetry and prose will be identified within the body of the text by the following abbreviations: *Ashes* (A); *The Name of the Lost* (NL); *1933* (1933); *Not this Pig* (NTP); *7 Years from Somewhere* (7); *They Feed They Lion* (L).
2. Quoted in *Contemporary Poets*, ed. James Vinson, p. 910.
3. Ibid.
4. Paul Zweig, "One + One + One + One," *Parnassus: Poetry in Review* (Fall/Winter 1972): 173 (hereafter cited as Zweig).
5. Herberg, *Judaism and Modern Man*, p. 158.
6. Zweig, p. 171.
7. Phoebe Pettingell, "The Politics of Philip Levine," *The New Leader* 62, no 16 (August 13, 1979): 17.

Chapter 10

1. Howard Nemerov, *The Collected Poems of Howard Nemerov*, p. 271. All further references to Howard Nemerov's poetry and prose will be identified within the body of the text by the following abbreviations: *Collected Poems* (CP); *Journal of the Fictive Life* (JFL).
2. Quoted in Robert D. Harvey, "A Prophet Armed: An Introduction to the Poetry of Howard Nemerov," p. 125.
3. Ibid., p. 126.
4. Julia Bartholomay, *The Shield of Perseus*, pp. 112–13.
5. Ibid., pp. 147, 145.
6. Ross Labrie, *Howard Nemerov*, p. 105.
7. Ibid., p. 108.
8. Bartholomay, *Shield of Perseus*, p. 129.

Chapter 11

1. Muriel Rukeyser, *The Life of Poetry*, p. 224. All further references to Muriel Rukeyser's poetry and prose will be identified within the body of the text by the following abbreviations: *The Collected Poems* (CP); *The Life of Poetry* (LP).
2. Quoted in Louise Kertesz, *The Poetic Vision of Muriel Rukeyser*, p. 366.
3. Muriel Rukeyser, "Under Forty," in *The Literature of American Jews*, ed. Theodore L. Gross, pp. 367–68.
4. Ibid., pp. 366–67.
5. Quoted in Louise Kertesz, *The Poetic Vision of Muriel Rukeyser*, p. 366.
6. Ibid., p. 99.
7. Ira Einsenstein, Interview, in *The Condition of Jewish Belief: A Symposium Compiled by the Editors of Commentary Magazine* (New York: MacMillan, 1966), p. 46.
8. Dr. Joseph Hertz, *The Authorized Jewish Prayer Book*, p. 661.
9. Ibid., p. 108.
10. Kertesz, *The Poetic Vision of Muriel Rukeyser*, p. 328.

Chapter 12

1. Irving Malin, *Jews and Americans*, p. 4; Allen Guttman, *The Jewish Writer in America*; David Daiches, "Breakthrough?" in *Contemporary American-Jewish Literature*, ed. Irving Malin, p. 31. R. Barbara Gitenstein's book-length study, *Apocalyptic Messianism and Contemporary Jewish-American Poetry*, should help to begin a serious discussion of the mystical roots of the poets' achievement.
2. Herberg, *Judaism and Modern Man*, p. 287.
3. Leo Baeck, *This People Israel*, p. 60.
4. Kaplan, *The Purpose and Meaning of Jewish Existence*, p. 318.
5. Ibid., p. 294.
6. Buber, *Hasidism and Modern Man*, pp. 42–43.
7. Ibid., p. 142.
8. Ibid., p. 176.

Bibliography

Alter, Robert. *After the Tradition: Essays on Modern Jewish Writing.* New York: Dutton, 1971.

———. *Defenses of the Imagination: Jewish Writers and Modern Historical Crisis.* Philadelphia: Jewish Publication Society, 1977.

Agus, Joseph. *Jewish Identity in an Age of Ideologies.* New York: Frederic Unger, 1978.

Baeck, Leo. *The Essence of Judaism.* New York: Schocken Books, 1948.

———. *This People Israel: The Meaning of Jewish Experience.* New York: Holt, Rinehart & Winston, 1964.

Bloom, Harold. *Figures of Capable Imagination.* New York: Seabury Press, 1976.

Borowitz, Eugene. *A New Jewish Theology in the Making.* Philadelphia: Westminster Press, 1968.

Buber, Martin. *Hasidism and Modern Man.* Translated and edited by Maurice Friedman. New York: Harper & Row, 1958.

———. *I and Thou.* Translated by Ronald Gregor Smith. New York: Scribners, 1958.

Chapman, Abraham, ed. *Jewish-American Literature.* New York: New American Library, 1974.

Daiches, David. "Breakthrough?" In *Contemporary American-Jewish Literature: Critical Essays,* edited by Irving Malin, pp. 30–38. Carbondale, Ill.: Southern Illinois University Press, 1973.

Dawidowicz, Lucy. *The Jewish Presence: Essays on Identity and History.* New York: Holt, Rinehart & Winston, 1977.

Dembo, L.S. "Louis Zukofsky: Objectivist Poetics and the Quest for Form." *American Literature* 44 (1972): 74–96.

Dickey, James. *Babel to Byzantium: Poets and Poetry Now.* New York: Farrar, Straus & Giroux, 1968.

Ginsberg, Allen. *Airplane Dreams.* San Francisco: City Lights, 1968.

———. *Allen Verbatim: Lectures on Poetry, Politics, Consciousness.* Edited by Gordon Ball. New York: McGraw Hill, 1974.

———. *Collected Poems: 1947–1980.* New York: Harper & Row, 1984.

———. *Empty Mirror: Early Poems.* New York: Totem-Corinth, 1961.

———. *The Fall of America: Poems of These States 1965–1971.* San Francisco: City Lights, 1972.

———. *First Blues: Rags, Ballads, and Harmonium Songs 1971–74.* New York: Full Court Press, 1975.

———. *The Gates of Wrath: Rhymed Poems 1948–1952.* Bolinas, Ca.: Grey Fox Press, 1972.

___. "How *Kaddish* Happened." In *Poetics of the New American Poetry*, edited by Donald Allen and Warren Tallman, pp. 344–47. New York: Grove Press, 1973.
___. *Howl and Other Poems*. San Francisco: City Lights, 1956.
___. Interview. In *Writers at Work: The Paris Review Interviews: Third Series*, edited by George Plimpton, pp. 279–320. New York: Penguin Books, 1979.
___. *Iron Horse*. San Francisco: City Lights, 1974.
___. *Journals: Early Fifties-Early Sixties*. Edited by Gordon Ball. New York: Grove Press, 1977.
___. *Kaddish and Other Poems 1958–1960*. San Francisco: City Lights, 1961.
___. *Mind Breaths: Poems 1972–1977*. San Francisco: City Lights, 1978.
___. "Notes for *Howl and Other Poems*." In *Poetics of the New American Poetry*, edited by Donald Allen and Warren Tallman, pp. 318–21. New York: Grove Press, 1973.
___. *Planet News 1961–1967*. San Francisco: City Lights, 1968.
___. *Plutonium Ode and Other Poems 1977–1980*. San Francisco: City Lights, 1982.
___. *Poems All over the Place: Mostly Seventies*. Cherry Valley, N.Y.: Cherry Valley Editions, 1978.
___. *Reality Sandwiches 1953–60*. San Francisco: City Lights, 1963.
___. *To Eberhart from Ginsberg*. Lincoln, Mass.: Penmaen Press, 1976.
___. *T.V. Baby Poems*. New York: Grossman, 1968.
___. *White Shroud, Poems. 1980–1985*. New York: Harper & Row, 1986.
Gitenstein, R. Barbara. *Apocalyptic Messianism and Contemporary Jewish-American Poetry*. Albany: State University of New York Press, 1986.
Glatzer, Nahum, ed. *Modern Jewish Thought: A Source Reader*. New York: Schocken Books, 1977.
Gross, Theodore L., ed. *The Literature of American Jews*. New York: The Free Press, 1973.
Grunfeld, Frederic. *Prophets Without Honor: A Background to Freud, Kafka, Einstein and Their World*. New York: Holt, Rinehart & Winston, 1979.
Guttman, Allen. *The Jewish Writer in America*. New York: Oxford University Press, 1971.
Halkin, Simon. *Modern Hebrew Literature*. New York: Schocken Books, 1970.
Harvey, Robert D. "A Prophet Armed: An Introduction to the Poetry of Howard Nemerov." Reprinted in *Poets in Progress: Critical Prefaces to Thirteen Modern American Poets*, edited by Edward Hungerford, pp. 116–33. Evanston, Ill.: Northwestern University Press, 1967.
Herberg, Will. *Judaism and Modern Man: An Interpretation of Jewish Religion*. New York: Harper & Row, 1951.
Hertz, Joseph. *The Authorized Jewish Prayer Book*. New York: Bloch, 1974.
Heschel, Abraham J. *God in Search of Man: A Philosophy of Judaism*. New York: Farrar, Straus, & Giroux, 1955.
___. *Man's Quest for God*. New York: Scribners, 1954.
___. *The Prophets*. New York: Harper & Row, 1962.

Hindus, Milton. *Charles Reznikoff: A Critical Essay*. Santa Barbara, Ca.: Black Sparrow Press, 1977.
Ignatow, David. *Facing the Tree: New Poems*. Boston: Little Brown, 1975.
___. *Figures of the Human*. Middletown, Conn.: Wesleyan University Press, 1964.
___. *The Gentle Weight Lifter*. New York: Morris Gallery, 1955.
___. *Leaving the Door Open*. New York: Sheep Meadow, 1984.
___. *New and Collected Poems, 1970–1985*. Middletown, Conn.: Wesleyan Press, 1986.
___. *The Notebooks of David Ignatow*. Edited by Ralph J. Mills, Jr. Chicago: Swallow Press, 1973.
___. *Open Between Us*. Edited by Ralph J. Mills, Jr. Ann Arbor: University of Michigan Press, 1979.
___. *Poems*. Prairie City, Ill.: Decker Press, 1948.
___. *Poems 1934–1969*. Middletown, Conn.: Wesleyan University Press, 1970.
___. *Rescue the Dead*. Middletown, Conn.: Wesleyan University Press, 1968.
___. *Say Pardon*. Middletown, Conn.: Wesleyan University Press, 1961.
___. *Selected Poems*. Edited by Robert Bly. Middletown, Conn.: Wesleyan University Press, 1975.
___. *Tread the Dark: New Poems*. Boston: Little Brown, 1978.
___. *Whisper to the Earth*. Boston: Little Brown, 1981.
Kaplan, Mordecai. *The Purpose and Meaning of Jewish Existence: A People in the Image of God*. Philadelphia: Jewish Publication Society, 1971.
Kaufman, Shirley. "Charles Reznikoff, 1894–1976: An Appreciation." *Midstream* 22 (1976): 51–56.
Kertesz, Louise. *The Poetic Vision of Muriel Rukeyser*. Baton Rouge, La.: Louisiana State University Press, 1980.
Labrie, Ross. *Howard Nemerov*. Boston: Twayne, 1980.
Lehman, David. "Holocaust." *Poetry* 128 (April 1976): 37–45.
Lenowitz, Harris. "Rothenberg: The Blood." *Vort* 3 (1975): 179–84.
Levertov, Denise. "An Order that Will Sing." *Nation* 192 (may 13, 1961): 417–418.
Levine, Philip. *Ashes: Poems New and Old*. New York: Atheneum, 1979.
___. *Don't Ask*. Ann Arbor: University of Michigan Press, 1981.
___. *1933*. New York: Atheneum, 1974.
___. *Not This Pig*. Middletown, Conn.: Wesleyan University Press, 1968.
___. *On the Edge*. Iowa City: Stone Wall Press, 1963.
___. *On the Edge and Over: Poems Old, Lost, and New*. Oakland, Ca.: Cloud Marauder Press, 1976.
___. *One for the Rose*. New York: Atheneum, 1981.
___. *Pili's Wall*. Santa Barbara, Ca,: Unicorn Press, 1971.
___. *Red Dust*. Santa Cruz, Ca.: Kayak, 1971.
___. *Selected Poems*. New York: Atheneum, 1984.
___. *7 Years from Somewhere*. New York: Atheneum, 1979.
___. *Sweet Will*. New York: Atheneum, 1985.
___. *They Feed They Lion*. New York: Atheneum, 1972.

Malin, Irving. *Jews and Americans*. Carbondale, Ill.: Southern Illinois University Press, 1965.

___, ed. *Contemporary American-Jewish Literature: Critical Essays*. Carbondale, Ill.: Southern Illinois University Press, 1973.

Mazzaro, Jerome. *Post Modern American Poetry*. Urbana, Ill.: University of Illinois Press, 1980.

Meinke, Peter. *Howard Nemerov*. Minneapolis: University of Minnesota Press, 1968.

Mills, Ralph J., Jr. *Cry of the Human: Essays on Contemporary American Poetry*. Urbana, Ill.: University of Illinois Press, 1975.

Moran, Ronald. *Louis Simpson*. New York: Twayne, 1972.

Mottram, Eric. "Where the Real Song Begins: The Poetry of Jerome Rothenberg." *Vort* 3 (1975): 163–79.

Nemerov, Howard. *The Blue Swallows*. Chicago: University of Chicago Press, 1967.

___. *The Collected Poems of Howard Nemerov*. Chicago: University of Chicago Press, 1977.

___. *A Commodity of Dreams and Other Stories*. New York: Simon & Schuster, 1960.

___. *Federigo; or, The Power of Love*. Boston: Little Brown, 1954.

___. *Figures of Thought: Speculations on the Meaning of Poetry and Other Essays*. Boston: Godine, 1978.

___. *Guide to the Ruins*. New York: Random House, 1950.

___. *Gnomes and Occasions*. Chicago: University of Chicago Press, 1972.

___. *The Homecoming Game*. New York: Simon and Schuster, 1957.

___. *The Image and the Law*. New York: Holt, Rinehart & Winston, 1947.

___. *Inside the Onion*. Chicago: University of Chicago Press, 1984.

___. *Journal of the Fictive Life*. New Brunswick, N.J.: Rutgers University Press, 1965.

___. *The Melodramatists*. New York: Random House, 1949.

___. *Mirrors and Windows*. Chicago: University of Chicago Press, 1958.

___. *New and Selected Poems*. Chicago: University of Chicago Press, 1960.

___. *The Next Room of the Dream: Poems and Two Plays*. Chicago: University of Chicago Press, 1962.

___, ed. *Poets on Poetry*. New York: Basic Books, 1966.

___. *Poetry and Fiction: Essays*. New Brunswick, N.J.: Rutgers University Press, 1963.

___. *Reflexions on Poetry and Poetics*. New Brunswick, N.J.: Rutgers University Press, 1972.

___. *The Salt Garden*. Boston: Little Brown, 1955.

___. *Sentences*. Chicago: University of Chicago Press, 1980.

___. *Stories, Fables and Other Diversions*. Boston: Godine, 1971.

___. *War Stories: Poems About Long Ago & Now*. Chicago: University of Chicago Press, 1987.

___. *The Western Approaches: Poems 1973–1975*. Chicago: University of Chicago Press, 1975.
Neusner, Jacob. *Judaism in the Secular Age*. New York: KTAV, 1970.
Patai, Raphael. *The Jewish Mind*. New York: Scribners, 1977.
Portuges, Paul. *The Visionary Poetics of Allen Ginsberg*. Santa Barbara, Ca.: Ross-Erikson Publishing, 1978.
Power, Kevin. "*Poland/1931*: Pack up Your Troubles in Your Old Kit Bag & Smile, Smile, Smile from Diaspora to Galut." *Boundary II* 3 (Spring 1975): 683–705.
Reznikoff, Charles. *By the Well of Living and Seeing: New and Selected Poems 1918–1973*. Edited by Seamus Cooney. Santa Barbara, Ca.: Black Sparrow Press, 1974.
___. *Holocaust*. Santa Barbara, Ca.: Black Sparrow Press, 1975.
___. *The Manner Music*. Santa Barbara, Ca.: Black Sparrow Press, 1977.
___. *Poems 1918–1936. Volume I of the Complete Poems of Charles Reznikoff*. Edited by Seamus Cooney. Santa Barbara, Ca.: Black Sparrow Press, 1977.
___. *Poems 1937–1975. Volume II of the Complete Poems of Charles Reznikoff*. Edited by Seamus Cooney. Santa Barbara, Ca.: Black Sparrow Press, 1977.
___. *Testimony, The United States 1885–1890 Recitative*. Berkeley, Ca.: Small Press Distribution, 1965.
___. *Testimony: The United States 1885–1915 Recitative, vol. 1*. Edited by Seamus Cooney. Santa Barbara, Ca.: Black Sparrow Press, 1978.
___. *Testimony: The United States, 1885–1915 Recitative, vol. 2*. Edited by Seamus Cooney, Santa Barbara, Ca.: Black Sparrow Press, 1979.
Rothenberg, Jerome, ed. *A Big Jewish Book: Poems and Other Visions of the Jews from Tribal Times to the Present*. New York: Doubleday, 1978.
___. "Craft Interview with Jerome Rothenberg." In *Interviews from the New York Quarterly*, edited by William Packard, pp. 37–51. Garden City, N.Y.: Doubleday, 1974.
___. *New Selected Poems 1970 to 1985*. New York: New Directions, 1986.
___. *Poems for the Game of Silence 1960–1970*. New York: Dial Press, 1971.
___. *Poland/1931*. New York: New Directions, 1974.
___. *Pre-Faces and Other Writings*. New York: New Directions, 1981.
___, ed. *Revolution of the Word: A New Gathering of American Avant Garde Poetry 1914–1945*. New York: Seabury Press, 1974.
___. *A Seneca Journal*. New York: New Directions, 1978.
___, ed. *Shaking the Pumpkin: Traditional Poetry of the Indian North Americas*. New York: Doubleday, 1972.
___, ed. *Technicians of the Sacred: A Range of Poetries from Africa, America, Asia, and Oceania*. New York: Doubleday, 1968.
___. *That Dada Strain*. New York: New Directions, 1983.
___. *Vienna Blood and Other Poems*. New York: New Directions, 1980.
Rubenstein, Richard L. *After Auschwitz*. Indianapolis: Bobbs-Merrill, 1966.
___. *The Religious Imagination: A Study in Psychoanalysis and Jewish Theology*. Indianapolis: Bobbs-Merrill, 1968.

Rukeyser, Muriel. *Beast in View*. New York: Doubleday, 1942.
___. *Body of Waking*. New York: Harper & Row, 1958.
___. *Breaking Open*. New York: Random House, 1973.
___. *The Collected Poems*. New York: McGraw Hill, 1979.
___. *Elegies*. New York: New Directions, 1949.
___. *The Green Wave*. New York: Doubleday, 1948.
___. *The Life of Poetry*. New York: Current, 1949.
___. *The Outer Banks*. Santa Barbara, Ca.: Unicorn Press, 1967.
___. *Selected Poems*. New York: New Directions, 1951.
___. *Theory of Flight*. New Haven, Conn.: Yale University Press, 1935.
___. *A Turning Wind*. New York: Viking Press, 1939.
___. "Under Forty." In *The Literature of American Jews*, edited by Theodore L. Gross, pp. 364–69. New York: The Free Press, 1973.
___. *Wake Island*. New York: Doubleday, 1942.
___. *Waterlily Fire: Poems 1932–1962*. New York: MacMillan, 1962.
Scholem, Gershom. *Kabbalah*. New York: Quadrangle, 1974.
___. *On the Kabbalah and Its Symbolism*. New York: Schocken Books, 1960.
___. *The Messianic Idea in Judaism*. New York: Schocken Books, 1971.
Schulz, Max. *Radical Sophistication: Studies in Contemporary Jewish-American Novelists*. Athens, Ohio: Ohio University Press, 1969.
Scott, Nathan, Jr. *The Wild Prayer of Longing: Poetry and the Sacred*. New Haven, Conn.: Yale University Press, 1971.
Shapiro, Harvey. *Battle Report: Selected Poems*. Middletown, Conn.: Wesleyan University Press, 1966.
___. *Lauds and Nightsounds*. New York: Sun, 1978.
___. *This World*. Middletown Conn.: Wesleyan University Press, 1972.
Shapiro, Karl. *Adult Bookstore*. New York: Random House, 1976.
___. *Beyond Criticism*. Lincoln: University of Nebraska Press, 1953.
___. *The Bourgeois Poet*. New York: Random House, 1964.
___. *Collected Poems 1940–1977*. New York: Random House, 1978.
___. *In Defense of Ignorance: Essays*. New York: Random House, 1960.
___. *Edsel*. New York: Geis, 1971.
___. *Essay on Rime*. New York: Reynal, 1945.
___. *New Selected Poems*. Chicago: University of Chicago Press, 1987.
___. *Person, Place and Thing*. New York: Reynal, 1942.
___. *Poems*. Baltimore: Waverly Press, 1935.
___. *Poems: 1940–1953*. New York: Random House, 1953.
___. *Poems of a Jew*. New York: Random House, 1958.
___. *The Poetry Wreck: Selected Essays 1950–1970*. New York: Random House, 1975.
___. *Selected Poems*. New York: Random House, 1968.
___. *Trial of a Poet and Other Poems*. New York: Reynal, 1947.
___. *V-Letter and Other Poems*. New York: Reynal, 1944.
___. *White-Haired Lover*. New York: Random House, 1968.

Simpson, Louis. *Adventures of the Letter I*. New York: Harper & Row, 1972.
___. *The Arrivistes: Poems 1940–1949*. New York: Fine Editions Press, n.d.
___. *At the End of the Open Road*. Middletown, Conn.: Wesleyan University Press, 1963.
___. *Caviare at the Funeral*. New York: Franklin Watts, 1980.
___. *A Dream of Governors*. Middletown, Conn.: Wesleyan University Press, 1959.
___. *Good News of Death and Other Poems*. New York: Scribners, 1955.
___. *North of Jamaica*. New York: Harper & Row, 1972.
___. *People Live Here: Selected Poems 1948–1983*. Brockport, N.Y.: BOA Editions, 1983.
___. "A Response to the Jewish Book Council." Unpublished Address: May 3, 1981.
___. *Riverside Drive*. New York: Atheneum, 1962.
___. *Searching for the Ox: New Poems and a Preface*. New York: Morrow, 1976.
___. *Selected Poems*. New York: Harcourt Brace, 1965.
Sklare, Marshall. *America's Jews*. New York: Random House, 1971.
Tytell, John. *Naked Angels: The Lives and Literature of the Beat Generation*. New York: McGraw Hill, 1976.
Vinson, James, ed. *Contemporary Poets*. 3d ed. New York: St. Martins Press, 1980.
Wiesel, Eli. Forward to *The Literature of American Jews*, edited by Theodore L. Gross, pp. xiii–xiv. New York: The Free Press, 1973.
Williams, Williams Carlos. Preface to *Empty Mirror: Early Poems*, by Allen Ginsberg. New York: Totem-Corinth, 1961.
Zukofsky, Louis. "A". Berkeley: University of California Press, 1978.
___. *All: The Collected Short Poems 1923–1964*. New York: Norton, 1971.
___. *Anew*. Prairie City, Ill.: Decker Press, 1946.
___. *Arise, Arise*. New York: Grossman, 1973.
___. *Autobiography*. New York: Grossman, 1970.
___. *Barely and Widely*. New York: Celia Zukofsky, 1958.
___. *Bottom: On Shakespeare*. Austin: Ark Press, 1963.
___. *Ferdinand, Including It Was*. New York: Grossman, 1968.
___. *55 Poems*. Prairie City, Ill.: Decker Press, 1941.
___. *Found Objects 1926–1962*. Georgetown, Ky.: H.B. Chapin, 1964.
___. *Little: A Fragment for Careenagers*. New York: Grossman, 1970.
___, ed. *An "Objectivists" Anthology*. Folcroft, Pa.: Folcroft Editions, 1975.
___. *Prepositions: The Collected Critical Essays of Louis Zukofsky*. New York: Horizon Press, 1968.

Index

Alter, Robert, 1, 13, 14
Auden, W.H., 61, 187, 190, 227
Baeck, Leo, 210, 228
Bartholomay, Julia, 201–202, 204
Blake, William, 4, 119, 126, 135, 138, 173, 178, 181, 187, 219, 226
Bloom, Harold, 1
Buber, Martin, 8, 31, 42, 228
Chapman, Abraham, 169
Daiches, David, 151, 225
Davenport, Guy, 101
Dembo, L.S., 103
Dickey, James, 154
Einsenstein, Ira, 216
Eliot, T.S, 4, 89, 131, 152, 153, 187, 189, 227
Ginsberg, Allen, 4, 5, 6, 7, 35, 38, 45, 59, 75, 87, 100–101, 102, **119–142**, 162, 168, 187, 226, 229, 231–32
Guttman, Allen, 225
Herberg, Will, 6, 168, 227
Hertz, Joseph , 220
Heschel, Abraham J., 7, 8, 210
Hindus, Milton, 18–19, 20, 23
Ignatow, David, 5, 7, 35, 59, **143–163**, 178, 187, 226, 227, 229, 233
Kaplan, Mordecai, 7, 8, 210, 228
Kaufman, Shirley, 21
Kenner, Hugh, 101
Kertesz, Louise, 209, 213, 221
Labrie, Ross, 202, 203
Lehman, David, 22
Lenowitz, Harris, 38–39, 41
Levertov, Denise, 144
Levine, Philip, 7, 59, **165–186**, 187, 227, 229, 234

Malin, Irving, 225
Mills, Ralph J., 148, 149, 158
Moran, Ronald, 90
Mottram, Eric, 45
Nemerov, Howard, 7, 24, 35, 59, **187–207**, 227, 229, 235
Oppen, George, 11, 12
Pettingell, Phoebe, 184
Portuges, Paul, 130
Pound, Ezra, 4, 11, 12, 14, 36, 99, 100, 105, 106, 119, 139
Power, Kevin, 44
Rakosi, Carl, 11, 12
Reznikoff, Charles, 5, 6, **11–29**, 59, 84, 100, 145, 225, 229, 236
Rothenberg, Jerome, 6, **31–58**, 59, 226, 229, 237–38
Rubenstein, Richard, 70, 72, 160, 161
Rukeyser, Muriel, 5, 7, 59, 168, 187, **209–24**, 227, 229, 239
Scholem, Gershom, 33
Seidman, Hugh, 107
Shapiro, Karl, 3, 5, 6, 35, **59–78**, 226, 229, 240
Simpson, Louis, 6, 59, **79–98**, 226, 229, 241
Smart, Christopher, 126, 175, 178
Stein, Gertrude, 36, 37
Whitman, Walt, 4, 36, 83, 85, 86, 101, 102, 116, 119, 123, 126, 137, 152, 153, 178, 187, 209–10, 219, 226
Williams, William Carlos, 4, 12, 100, 106, 119, 139, 143, 144, 178, 187
Yeats, William Butler, 187, 188, 227
Zukofsky, Louis, 5, 6, 11, 12, 59, 84, **99–117**, 225–26, 229, 242–43
Zweig, Paul, 167–68, 175

The **Twentieth Century American Jewish Writers** Series will present the very best, up-to-date, imaginative scholarship. Studies on novelists, writers, poets, essayists, and critics are needed and will be carefully read. New interpretations will be especially welcomed.

All manuscripts should be sent to:

> Dr. Daniel Walden, Editor
> Twentieth Century American Jewish Writers Series
> English Department
> Penn State University
> University Park, PA 16802

Rachel Feldhay Brenner

ASSIMILATION AND ASSERTION
The Response to the Holocaust in Mordecai Richler's Writing

American University Studies: Series 19 (General Literature). Vol. 19
ISBN 0-8204-0811-5 232 pages, hardback approx. US $ 32.50/ca. sFr. 45.50

Recommended prices – alterations reserved

The book explores the consciousness of the Holocaust in Canadian Jewish literature. Drawing upon Mordecai Richler's work, it examines the predicament of the North American Jew responding to the national catastrophe he did not experience directly. Richler's writing demonstrates Jewish powerlessness intensified through the direct experience of anti-Semitism in Canada in the 1930s and the 1940s and the loss of faith in humanist liberal values emerging from the consciousness of the European tragedy. The study focuses on the literary representations of the post-Holocaust Jewish identity crisis manifested in ideological and emotional vacillations between assimilation and self-assertion.

Contents: The response to the Holocaust in Canadian Jewish literature. Mordecai Richler's view of the break-up of the liberal humanist ideal. Vacillations of the North American Jew between self-assertion and assimilation.

The study explores the hitherto unexamined impact of anti-Jewish climate in Canada and the concurrent Holocaust in Europe on the consciousness of the Canadian Jewish writer.

PETER LANG PUBLISHING, INC.
62 West 45th Street
USA – New York, NY 10036

Rose Yalow Kamel

AGGRAVATING THE CONSCIENCE
Jewish-American Literary Mothers in the Promised Land

American University Studies: Series 4 (English Language and Literature).
Vol. 64
ISBN 0-8204-0554-X   202 pages   hardback US $ 30.50/sFr. 42.40

Recommended prices – alterations reserved

Jewish-American women writers have struggled with a patriarchal tradition in the old country and the new that silences creativity. This study focuses on five writers who have defined themselves as secular and feminist. Generationally and experientally diverse, they transform mothering into literary enactment that engenders a stronger sense of selfhood and fosters the writing of sustained narratives.

Contents: The only extensive analysis of women writers whose collective sensibility has enriched American literature. «A study which reshapes the tradition and breaks the ‹silences›, this book alters our evaluation of 20th century writing in substantive ways.» (Angela G. Dorenkamp, Associate Professor of English, Assumption College, Co-Editor, *Images of Women in American Popular Culture*, [Harcourt Brace, 1985])

«With this important analysis of five twentieth-century Jewish American women writers, Rose Kamel illuminates both the process and the significance to women's lives of literary mothering. Her study explores how women have used the genres of writing – letters, autobiography, fiction – to come to terms with themselves inside a larger and often hostile culture.» (Virginia Walcott Beauchamp, Editor, *A Private War: Letters and Diaries of Madge Preston, 1862–1865*)

PETER LANG PUBLISHING, INC.
62 West 45th Street
USA – New York, NY 10036